Enabling Community
Practice in Architecture
and Urban Planning

WeOwn
TheCity

Francesca Miazzo
Tris Kee
Editors

trancity*valiz

with CITIES and The
University of Hong Kong

We Own The City was born in 2011, when CITIES collaborated with ARCAM, the Amsterdam Center of Architecture, in order to show the results of a joint investigation into the development of bottom-up initiatives and their relationships with the history of the city. In 2012, Tris Kee from the Community Project Workshop (CPW) in the Faculty of Architecture of the University of Hong Kong brought the project to Hong Kong in order to raise awareness about the issue. CPW, together with other local partners, organized a symposium and exhibition, which included presentations by scholars and planning representatives as well as the Asian offices of Dutch architecture firms OMA, MVRDV and UN Studio. After the symposium, CPW and CITIES set a new ambition for We Own The City: to collaborate on a book examining how traditionally 'top-down' players are changing their working processes to adapt to the current system in which a more active urban population is setting new rules and standards.

From March 2013 till the following year, a global comparative design research platform and a consortium of partnered local organizations were created. This process has been supported by the University of Hong Kong, which is the co-editor in collaboration with CITIES Foundation. From October 2013 on, The Creative Industry Fund, based in Holland, made it possible to expand this research to a global scale. The Design Trust for Public Space from New York, the Strelka Institute from Moscow, and the Community Empowerment Center of Taipei got involved in contributing to a new network of local organizations supporting this research on bottom-up development. The result of this process is the book We Own The City – Enabling Community Practice in Architecture and Urban Planning, published in 2014.

Preface

This is an important book, but only partially for the reasons modestly claimed by its editors. It is a book about the practice of bottom-up urban planning, written by practitioners for practitioners. This is one of its claims for significance and I agree with that claim. Too many books about 'people's planning' have been written by people with too little planning experience. But the book's importance goes deeper than this.

Since the earliest settlements were built among the newly invented arable landscapes of what is now Eastern Turkey, there have been two alternative ways of ordering urban space, society and economy: by centralized corporate action and by decentralized individual action. Planned versus spontaneous order. Coordination by government or by bi-lateral exchange. Top-down versus bottom-up.

The medieval theologian-economists of the learned town of Salamanca near the Spanish-Portuguese border produced the first modern seeds of thought about the relationship between spontaneous and planned social order. Classical political-economists of the Scottish Enlightenment such as Adam Smith picked up the ideas and turned them into grand theories of society. Austrian economists of the late 19th to mid-20th century such as Friedrich von Hayek developed them into sophisticated behavioral treatises. Modern scholars from psychology, anthropology, physics, urban science and behavioral economics are developing and testing social theories of emergence (emergence of global order from local decisions). The new paradigm of complexity that dominates post-modern physical, and increasingly social, sciences is one that focuses on the power of local processes to produce complex system behavior.

Architects studying and designing at an urban scale; urban planners and designers; transport, housing, real-estate and other urban professionals; and other scholars such as geographers, economists, sociologists and political scientists concerned with understanding cities and designing ways of governing them more efficiently. They are all urbanists and everything they do is affected by the tension between spontaneous and planned order. Many of their theories are designed to understand the paradoxes created by this duality.

That is why Jane Jacobs, the great American essayist achieved guru status in these circles. She captured something that others, in their focus on planned intervention, dared not express or formalize. Or perhaps it was that she managed to hold the tension together in a particular way that celebrated the consensus goals of growing cities full of energy, economy, humanity and surprise without alienating those who were contributing to the non-achievement of those goals. Such is the art of the seer and visionary. We need more. In this book you find some of them.

The subjects presented as examples of bottom-up city-shaping are actually quite diverse. They include community gardens, a community-organized neighborhood bar, land designated by city planners for self-built housing, a neighborhood art network, community engagement by a national housing authority and by a municipal government, grassroots planning of an eco-village, activist-initiated city cycle maps, hybrid work-community space in a CBD, innovate collective-production space for designers, a university community project workshop, community-association organized architectural conservation and others.

One of the intriguing claims of the editors is that the bigger pool of initiatives that these examples are sampled from represents something of a paradigm change in how cities are becoming organized. This is a significant claim because it is made by practitioners who sense a sea change in the culture of urban governance. I would urge readers to take this as an hypothesis and to use the evidence in the book's compelling case studies, along with their own observations, to test it. I am inclined to share the editors' views, but maybe with some additional reasons not elaborated in the book but very relevant to its arguments and message.

Let me mention three such reasons for thinking that urban governance might be developing a stronger local dimension.

First, for a number of historic reasons, neighborhood government in the 20th-century western model of the municipal state has, in most countries, led to a wide institutional gap at the neighborhood scale. This gap has been waiting to be filled. The gap probably emerged because of the strong redistributive emphasis in the postwar municipal model (strong neighborhood governance can be expected to work against redistributive goals for obvious reasons).

Second, in most developed countries there is a general rolling back of the state, under the influence both of fiscal poverty and ideology.

Bottom-up planning and spontaneous urban order has always been de rigeur in contemporary developing countries, as it was of course, in western countries when they were at earlier stages of development. But the retrenchment of the state, whether purposeful or pragmatic, in the developed west has encouraged the kind of experiments documented in this book.

Third, the institutional infrastructure for bottom-up place-making is much more diverse than sixty years ago, when top-down multi-purpose municipal governance really took off. Condominium law was invented in France 200 years ago by Napoleon. It took off in the USA in the 1960s as an important institution for bottom-up neighborhood governance and it was not until 2004 that Britain enacted the first common-hold institution in its long history of land law. In just about every country in the world, including all those covered in this book, there have been rapid advances in the laws governing co-ownership and collective planning. For example, a sophisticated new land readjustment law is being drafted, as I write, by the Dutch Government with help from academics at Radboud and other universities. The law will enable the forced pooling of private property rights to allow regeneration under rationalized land allocation and then the return of private land to original owners pro rata, less any land needed to create the rationalized new layout. This is an example of a legal innovation that facilitates hybrid micro-level collective, bottom-up planning in tune with top-down urban plans. In the UK a profound experiment is underway to include community-initiated neighborhood plans as part of the national town planning system, while in Brasilia squatters are no longer only fighting for private property rights but are also asking for condominium rights so that they can get on and organize neighborhood public goods and services that the municipal state has failed to provide. Co-ownership laws are necessary for any sustained local-level initiative in place-making.

The editors and authors of We Own the City being practitioners, it is natural that this fabulous book focuses on evidence of the entrepreneurial energy driving these developments. I encourage readers to think about the broader drivers I have mentioned as they reflect on the stories and analysis. For between the two: individual entrepreneurs and the enabling framework of laws, there might just well be the beginnings of a virtuous cycle. Better legal frameworks for doing 'small things collectively' encourages more community entrepreneurs. And more of those, yields more examples for others to follow and a greater demand for small-scale urban innovations. As the dynamic proceeds, it might just be that we shall discover a new, more healthy, artistic, sustainable, rewarding and, dare I say, efficient and equitable, way of designing, planning, making and governing urban places.

Chris Webster
Dean, Faculty of Architecture
The University of Hong Kong

March 2014

Contents

Introduction

Theoretical Framework

❝ Larger strategic planning may be useful for establishing a framework within which more immediate tactical planning can function. Many planners already engage in 'tactical planning' as they often work on short-term projects that fit within larger strategic goals. Further, while a number of urbanists and academics (Jacobs 1961, Sennett 1970), have historically critiqued institutionalized planning and planners for operating in a rigid, top-down manner, many planners today are increasingly experimenting with collaborative models of planning to engage diverse stakeholders in the formulation and implementation of plans. ❞

— Richard Sennett, 2008.

Since the 1800s, cities in the Global North have become more and more organized. Careful planning, intervening and regulating are government duties when trying to provide basic necessities and amenities for their populations. Of course, carrying on these activities is of undeniable importance; however, over the years this process has resulted in an extensive, bulky system of city-making and city management (Haydn & Temel, 2006). In opposition to this complex, lumbering pattern, there has been a recent surge in small-scale initiatives that challenge the highly institutionalized processes of city making. What can be labeled as a process of self-organization, or citizens' participation, is increasingly visible in urban practice, social theory and political art (Stickells, 2011). But what is this process? Who are these citizens? How can we define this nouvelle vague? And where does it come from?

Diversity makes it quite difficult to capture these resistance practices in a few words. In general, it can be stated that we see an upsurge of urban development projects including end users as not only consumers but also as co-decision makers, co-creators, and/or co-managers before, during and/or after the construction/renovation phase.

This process can be labeled bottom-up development, and the citizen-subjects bottom-uppers. By contrast, top-down development processes create urban artifacts, infrastructure or space by following market rules, political ideologies and projections according to which the final user is usually consigned to the passive role of consumer, rather than that of a co-creator or decision maker. In this scenario, the institutional actors are called top-downers – most commonly real estate developers, public organizations, architects and housing associations. In this book, we dichotomize these two positions to help bring clarity to urban actors and processes, although in reality it is difficult to pinpoint a genuine bottom-up or top-down process. As we will see in the following chapters and case analyses, the two often occur together, and the time is ripe to learn how these forces can catalyze a new era of collaborative creativity.

In the second section of the book, we narrate examples of interactions between these two actors. While We Own The City focuses on the relationship between top-down and bottom-up approaches, the text will also seek to contribute to the many past attempts at creating a definitional framework around the bottom-up movement. Several neologisms are used to describe this discourse: tactical urbanism (Lydon et al., 2010; McFarlane, 2011), pop-up urbanism (Bishop & Williams, 2012), emergent or post-modern urbanism (Pinilla, 2007; Hélie, 2009), guerrilla urbanism (Hou, 2010), ephemeral or temporary urbanism (Schuster, 2001), emancipatory practices (Swyngedouw & Kaïka, 2003) and DIY urbanism (Iveson, 2013). These terms all refer to interventions in the urban realm that can be social, cultural, political, commercial, artistic and/ or communal. Most importantly, they are initiated by local individuals or grassroots groups; they are not sanctioned by any higher authority and sprout from the needs and ambitions of citizens or communities. Often, they are associated with urban informality, unintended uses of public space and the exploration of alternative modes of spatial production (Stickells, 2011).

In a wider theoretical framework, significant variation in the breadth and depth of participation exists according to the different historical, social, political and legal traditions of each country (Atkinson & Carmichael, 2007; Atkinson & Eckardt, 2004; Rowlands et al., 2009; Van Kempen et al., 2005). In this publication, we consider bottom-up development at every stage of citizens' participation. For instance, Blanc (1999) identifies 'action' as a type of participation, including resident participation in the social life of a neighborhood through, for example, cultural and leisure activities, but also collective efforts to improve the quality of life such as neighborhood management. 'Decision participation' (Kedadouche, 2003, 15) can be defined as 'the group of actions organized and financed with the goal of linking the persons most directly affected to the conception or realization of a complex project'. Similar to the creative city and the sustainable city, the bottom-up city is becoming a 'dominant interpretation frame' (Giddens, 1979): a discourse that becomes part of the dominant mode of thinking about the city.

Though spontaneous city making is the oldest form of urbanization, bottom-up urbanism appears to be underexposed in planning literature and practice, which primarily concerns itself with the organization of space and the ordering of resources. In city thinking, however, similar notions have been pitched before, such as 'everyday urbanism' (Chase, Crawford & Kaliski, 1999), which deals with the 'everyday space of public life' and sees the city as 'above all a social product, [as] the goal is to make a work of life' (Fraker, 2007, 62). Everyday urbanism is strongly related to the earlier ideas of Michel de Certeau (1984), Henri Lefebvre (2004) and Guy Debord (1994). Debord was a central figure in the Situationist movement, known for its work on radical planning and architecture. The Situationists called for new ways of experiencing the city, with a focus on spontaneity, flexibility and variability (Stevens, 2007, 16), and they even demanded mobile spaces and modifiable architecture that could evolve along with the preferences of their users (Ronneberger, 2006). The primary issue of everyday urbanism, on the other hand, is part of a long tradition of documenting the positive values of a street or a neighborhood in order to save them from demolition, otherwise known as renewal. The attitude sometimes referred to as 'parochialism' or 'insular reclusion' (Chase, Crawford & Kaliski, 1999, 95), is a narrowed mental approach towards the urban process, one that does not consider the wider context of political systems and social issues. On this account, we highlight the tension between resiliency and globalization in the conceptual framework of this book, a publication that tackles local issues on a global scale, while a more specific overview of the results is presented in the concluding remarks. This introductory section frames and defines the core theme of this book: the rise of bottom-up development and its potential to link with top-down players in an era of newly collaborative urban development. In the following sections, we illustrate our approach towards the subject, our research design, and our goals and ambitions.

We Own The City: approach and positioning – understanding the enabling mechanisms

In the previous section, we postulated the argument that demand for greater involvement in the planning and development of our built environment is rising from increasingly active local communities. We believe planning processes need help to accommodate the participation of community groups, professional institutions, district stakeholders and other representative organizations in discussions of future development issues. We support the idea that spontaneous/participatory projects are small-scale initiatives challenging the technocratic, hierarchic urban planning doctrine. The pivotal argument guiding this publication is that bottom-up initiatives are increasingly emerging in urban environments, while institutions, government offices and developers find themselves inadequately organized to enable or support these initiatives.

Many publications, events and projects have focused their attention on the growing role of civil society in city-making processes. These tend to list or catalog innovative experiences, skim the surface of project locations and architectural standards, or describe the process in brief phrases. This book attempts to bring analysis one step forward, digging deep into the process of innovative, small-scale city making in relation to institutional actors. Why? In the course of analyzing the rise of the bottom-up movement, we have realized that institutional organizations and governments are actively looking for patterns, similarities and differences in order to set new institutional standards that can accommodate this trend. This new openness on the part of traditional top-downers is a generational shift in the urban planning discipline. The research presented in this book focuses on how the top-downers are changing their approach to enable the bottom-up movement, and how both actors can better collaborate in the future. We position this publication as the inception of a movement of city makers that values the significance of working with the local community, deeply understanding its developing assets, while taking into consideration economic, political and social issues surrounding and affecting the neighborhood realm. We Own The City is a choice and a statement, which we hope to provoke through this book.

Research Design

The purpose of this book is to provide new recommendations to top-downers, based on the need to carefully (re)construct our cities through interactive processes that respond to community needs and people's aspirations, Within an international context, our research seeks to answer the question: How are traditional top-down players rethinking their implementation processes in order to enable more involvement from civil society or the local community? What innovative approaches are they using?

In answering this question, we will try to determine in which way, shape or manner something is occurring in a specific context, taking into consideration actions undertaken by different actors (Baxter & Jack, 2008). In order to give a better idea of our research rationale, we will now frame our analysis through description and contextualization (Huberman & Miles, 2002).

We focus on urban redevelopment projects in cities where top-down players traditionally perform prominent roles. Specifically, we analyze the implementation process of urban redevelopment projects where the local community represents the implementing actor, the decision maker, or the target of the project. The final scope of this research is to evaluate these interventions, defining the innovative strategies undertaken by top-down actors in order to offer insight and advice further enabling future bottom-up approaches.

We confined our research to five cities – Amsterdam, Hong Kong, Moscow, New York City and Taipei – because their histories display the typical patterns of top-down development. Other cities, such as São Paulo or Mexico City, have long histories of bottom-up/informal development and are, at the moment, working in the opposite direction: implementing more substantial planning regulation from the top down. By contrast, our focus cities are environments where traditional top-down urbanism has heavily affected development in the past. In the selected cities one can find networks of traditional top-down organizations and agents that are transitioning towards more bottom-up approaches – each in different ways and with different levels of involvement.

In Amsterdam, public/traditional top-down urbanism made the decisions shaping the entire country through a well-organized series of spatial policies, followed by detailed, functional organization of the urban landscape. Although this tradition started earlier, and peaked in the 1970s alongside the squatters' movement and the social housing development, more recently, and especially thanks to the economic crisis, citizens and professionals are re-thinking their power to affect the urban environment in a proactive, apolitical and quite practical way. In Hong Kong, a city famous for the successful implementation of real estate development projects in combination with top-down infrastructural planning, an increasingly vocal public has expressed a preference for redevelopments that address social and cultural needs. In New York, as in Hong Kong, the city experienced a Golden Age of top-down real estate development in commercial and residential areas. However, due to the financial crisis, citizen initiatives are revitalizing the urban landscape. Development in Moscow was strongly influenced by the soviet regime; however, thanks to the development of a more cosmopolitan social order, the city is currently witnessing the development of several initiatives that endow citizens with the power to be urban makers. In Taipei, bottom-up space-making started with social movements pushing for transformation into a democratic society starting in the late 1980s. Now, there is a growing evolution of bottom-up initiatives in urban space that parallel political developments. While all these cities shares in this global/local trend, they all differ in social, economic and urban development backgrounds, providing a wider spectrum of information, experience and knowledge.

Each city's analysis is based on a handful of specific case studies representing different forms of bottom-up development. The researcher serves as a narrator, telling stories to explain the implementation process of each case. Direct interviews with project leaders, co-producers and end users, together with desk, library and Internet research have been used to collect data. Local researchers approached citizens, organizations, foundations and private and public actors involved in the cases. We selected this research methodology in light of Baxter and Jack's (2008) logic: employing different data sources facilitates the researcher in the exploration of a phenomenon within a specific context.

Each case tackles the following:

Contextualize urban landscape and history in each particular city;

Describe motivations and driving factors leading to the project's initiation;

Explore specific factors of success, problem-solving actions and implementation challenges;

Elaborate findings by extrapolating specifics regarding the role of traditional top-down player(s).

Each case is presented through narratives of redevelopment projects in which traditional top-down players, such as real estate developers, governmental organizations, architects or urban planners and housing corporations, enabled, allowed, helped, motivated, oversaw, or supported the involvement of the community in the implementation of the project. In the end, the case studies reveal strategies used to enable more bottom-up integrated neighborhood redevelopment processes. The conclusions identify potential strategies for top-down players to further enable future bottom-up/top-down cooperation.

The following is an overview of each case:

Cascoland Kolenkitbuurt
Cascoland is an international network of artists specializing in urban interventions. The group was commissioned by the Dutch government to improve the livability of a troubled neighborhood in Amsterdam West, Kolenkitbuurt.

'I Can Change the World With My Two Hands'
'I Can Change the World With My Two Hands' is a neighbor-initiated community garden. Taking a broad approach to the idea of a community garden, it focuses on how it can contribute to the overall food cycle of the neighborhood. For example, tomatoes are grown for the nearby snack bar and compost is made from leftover food from a neighborhood restaurant.

NoorderparkBar
While enjoying the cultural program at the NoorderparkKamer, a socio-cultural community center in Noorderpark, a few residents independently decided to add a bar to the area. The director of NoorderparkKamer introduced the residents to each other, which led to NoorderparkBar's first design.

Vrijburcht
In IJburg, a recently built urban expansion project, planners reserved several plots for collective commissioning or self-built architectural projects. In these projects, a group of end users (e.g., residents or workers) cooperatively realize the construction of houses, generally assisted by partners such as architects, housing corporations or the municipality. These projects can be considered 'bottom-up' because end users have complete control over the design and construction of their future homes.

**Energizing Kowloon East Office (EKEO) –
Bridging the Urban Planning Gap**
The newly established Energizing Kowloon East
Office (EKEO) is a government entity that attempts to
inject new vibrancy to a changing neighborhood by
engaging the public in urban activities. In projects like
'Fly the Flyover', city ownership is realized through
active engagement with relevant stakeholders.

**Institutional Incubator for Community Outreach –
The Community Project Workshop at the
University of Hong Kong**
The Community Project Workshop engages the city
through community outreach. As the institutional
incubator for research and knowledge exchange
in Hong Kong University, the workshop aspires to
provide a cross-disciplinary consultancy utilizing
expertise from architecture, urban design, landscape,
and conservation. Through research for local districts,
the workshop generates discourses and debates on
pressing urban community issues.

**Building a Collaborative Effort – the Hong Kong
Housing Authority's Experience**
Harmony Homes & Upper Ngau Tau Kok Estate
illustrate how Hong Kong's Housing Authority
collaborates with residents and community groups
to identify potential ways of improving citizens'
living environments. Objectives are to articulate
better planning strategies related to housing issues,
including infrastructure facilities, public amenities
and green open spaces.

**Voices From the Vegetable Garden: Grassroots
Planning and the Design Of Choi Yuen Ecological
Village**
When Hong Kong's government decided to relocate
a village to make way for the construction of a high-
speed rail link, a protest movement was started.
The new village was designed by a small local
practice and it marks a turning point for formulating
alternative planning strategies, facilitating bottom-up
development and organic/sustainable agriculture.

Cyclification
Beginning in 2010, Moscow activists began creating the first city cycling map, highlighting pedal-friendly routes. Following the first attempt, more groups and websites emerged to address cycling issues, such as where to have bicycle racks and how to get them installed.

Delai Sam
Since 2010, a coalition of media and activists has been organizing a marathon event called Delai Sam, meaning 'do it yourself' (DIY) in Russian. Held every six months, the self-organized event's goal is to create a more livable and sustainable city. To establish themselves and their goals, the group created a citizen manifesto in 2010. Ever since, the biannual festival invites various experts from across Russia and the world to support realizing their vision.

Mitino
In 2012, the Strelka Institute and Partizaning (a participatory urban planning group) collaborated on a project called 'Cooperative Urbanism' as a meeting point for bottom-up planners, DIYers, architects, planners, creative interventionists, institutions and municipal authorities in Moscow. Looking beyond the center of the city, the goal was to activate people to transform their environment. The most interesting and lasting results came from the district of Mitino, where a local deputy invited letters from citizens in order to discuss and address local issues. As a result of innovative communication strategies and the deputy's support and attention, many simple infrastructural repairs were promptly made.

Nagatino
Nagatino, one of Moscow's southern districts, is opening a new co-working space located in one of the district's main business centers. Opened in January 2014, the space seeks to not only function as a business center, but also as a community and social space.

Garden of Eden

Garden of Eden community garden was implemented on the grounds of a New York City Housing Authority (NYCHA) project. As part of the NYCHA Garden and Greening Program (established 1962), the garden went through a process of beautification and environmental education that benefitted residents and the community.

BRIC Arts | Media + UrbanGlass

This case analyzes the partnership between two cultural nonprofit organizations: BRIC Arts | Media and UrbanGlass. Through these groups, free and low-cost programming and resources are offered to audiences, media makers, and artists of all ages and levels – from emerging to mid-career and to established professionals. Different types of residencies are offered, providing artists with space to work in multidisciplinary teams and a stage to share their creations with the public.

New Lots Triangle Plaza

New Lots Triangle Plaza is a community-requested public space implemented through the Department of Transportation's NYC Plaza Program to enhance neighborhood streets and local businesses. Conflicting and intimidating streams of traffic previously surrounded the 3,800-square-foot pedestrian triangle. The changes requested by the New Lots Avenue Triangle Merchants Association and supported by Brooklyn Community Board 5's transportation committee have calmed traffic, reduced pedestrian and vehicle conflicts, created a brighter, larger pedestrian-only public space, eased access to businesses and transit and laid the groundwork for a future capital project to make the plaza permanent.

Manufacture NY

Manufacture New York is a fashion incubator/factory hybrid dedicated to providing independent designers with the resources and skills to streamline their production process and transform local manufacturing into the most affordable, innovative option for all. The newly established headquarters are being built to include a fully-equipped sampling room, manufacturing facilities, classroom space (open to the public), private studios for rent and a state-of-the art computer lab complete with the industry's latest software for design and production.

Treasure Hill

Treasure Hill village is a 'favela-like' settlement sprawled on a hill bordering Taipei City and New Taipei City. When city government intended to demolish the settlement to make room for a new park, the Village's long process of protest and coordination saved the land and transformed it into hybrid use. Under an adaptive reuse project aiming to open the settlement to more people, some original residents were relocated to renovated houses, while the rest of the vacant buildings house the Taipei Artist Village. As the village contains features such as a cultural industry cluster, exhibition space, and youth hostel, Treasure Hill has become one of the most popular places in the city for young people to hang out.

Qing-Tien Community

Qing-Tien is a community located between National Taiwan University and National Taiwan Normal University. Scattered old Japanese-style wooden houses serve as teacher dormitories in the neighborhood, where these old houses and trees make up a green, low-density community. To save the old trees and houses from redevelopment construction, the local community association successfully made the city government change zoning and land use rules by engaging concepts of historic settlement. Through their action, they saved the green historical urban landscape from extensive damage and changes by real estate developers involved and interested in the area.

Huaguang Neighborhood

Next to the Chiang Kai-shek Memorial Hall in the center of Taipei City, at the former site of the Taipei Prison that marked the beginning of the Japanese colonial period, a new mixed-use commercial project is planned. So far, it has displaced more than 600 households, and as no adequate rehousing arrangement has been provided, a battle between squatters and the government continues. Displaced residents and concerned citizens have found an opportunity to challenge the project by engaging a historic preservation discourse. This case study explores how citizens can mobilize place memories to establish a space of insurgent planning.

Greenlife Roosevelt

The widespread, government-led Taipei Urban Regeneration Project rests on the theme of 'beautifying Taipei'. Through a range of government-provided zoning incentives, private investment was encouraged to redevelop the city to prepare for the International Flora Exposition in 2010. As some community improvements were only temporary, these actions evoked significant criticism. Moreover, a series of 'urban regeneration stations' were launched to mobilize cultural capital and the power of civil participation. As nothing substantial was achieved, civil groups continue to question the project's underlying agenda.

Architectural Practices

We address real estate developers, governmental organizations and housing corporations as the traditional top-downers. However, as a traditional part of strong urban planning disciplines, many architectural processes are also top-down players.

During the March 2013 We Own the City symposium held in Hong Kong, keynote speakers from OMA, MVRDV and UNStudio explained their views on how to give more power and authorship to the end users of their architectural designs. This generation of designers appears to be facing a turning point, implementing new methods and planning strategies in order to channel bottom-up energy in a productive way.

For example, OMA is developing a high-rise that integrates, rather than replaces, an existing fishing village; MVRDV promotes mixed land use and a free interpretation of a traditional masterplan. Can these examples represent inspirational moments for other traditional top-down players who are struggling to find a way to meet the needs of local communities?

This chapter presents insight into how architects and architectural firms are changing their working processes. The interviews cover the work of participants in the Hong Kong Symposium: OMA, MVRDV, UNStudio and a fourth practice, the younger but equally innovative and internationally oriented Next Architects.

Book Objective and Direction

This book analyzes the diverse dynamics and intensities of citizens working together to implement urban redevelopment projects in Amsterdam, Hong Kong, Moscow, New York and Taipei. Focusing on the processes in action, we take a closer look at the challenges facing protagonists of traditional top-down planning as they try to accommodate increasingly emergent and significant bottom-up initiatives. We seek these answers as local governments, housing associations, real estate developers, design offices and other traditional top-down players experience difficulty in accommodating bottom-up developments because their working processes are based on incompatible frameworks – rigid bureaucratic procedures aiming to provide high levels of control over processes. As a consequence, even when institutions understand and want to support bottom-up initiatives, spontaneity is at stake. We seek to understand and advance cutting-edge, auspicious urban development patterns by examining the processes of working together through case studies and in-depth analysis.

Made by professionals for professionals, this book is equally suited for experts, citizens and students involved in, or aspiring to become involved in, the act of creating new urban topographies. The role of the city maker in today's urbanity is under constant pressure, motivating the authors to explore the relationship between civil society and government. In conclusion, this exploration presents recommendations targeting public governments, housing authorities, architects, town planners and real estate developers in order to provide new foundations for legislation (or practices) in which inclusive urban development plans are no longer experimental, but set the standards for future evolution.

The book is organized in chapters, each focusing on a specific urban context. Before starting to 'dig deep' into the narratives describing the processes of bottom-up development, we present a graphic comparative data overview of the urban contexts under analysis. Since this book does not seek direct comparison of the cases under analysis, the issue of contextualization is quite critical in a publication of such a wide scope. As a consequence each chapter will include a map of the city, showing where the cases under analysis are located. While each city and case will be contextualized by a general introductory text, a small overview of the urban topography where the cases develop is also presented. Each chapter was written by a different team of local researchers, who have talked to a great variety of local actors. As a consequence, each chapter is unique. To bind the publication together, each chapter is concluded by a list of progressive cutting-edge urban development actions made by institutions to enable the narratives under analysis in each city. At the end, in the concluding remarks, we work towards a generalization of the findings, providing an overview of possible scenarios. By telling the story of the bottom-up, we hope to learn how to help top-down players to sanction this trend into a more established urban process.

Locating the Projects

USA

Government
Presidential system,
Consitutional republic

CO₂ emissions (tons)	18 (2008)
HDI	0.937 (2012)
GINI coefficient	45 (2007)

China

Government
Single-party state,
socialist state

CO₂ emissions (tons)	5.3 (2008)
HDI	0.699 (2012)
GINI coefficient	47.4 (2012)

Russia

Government
Semi-presidential system,
Consitutional republic

CO₂ emissions (tons)	12 (2008)
HDI	0.788 (2012)
GINI coefficient	41.7 (2011)

New York

Amsterdam

Taipei

Hong Kong

Moscow

Netherlands

Government
Monarchy

HDI   0.921 (2012)

GINI coefficient   30.9 (2007)

Taiwan

Government
Semi-presidential system,
Consitutional republic

CO$_2$ emissions (tons)   5.3 (2008)

GINI coefficient   34.2 (2011)

5 Cities, One Book:
Comparitive Data

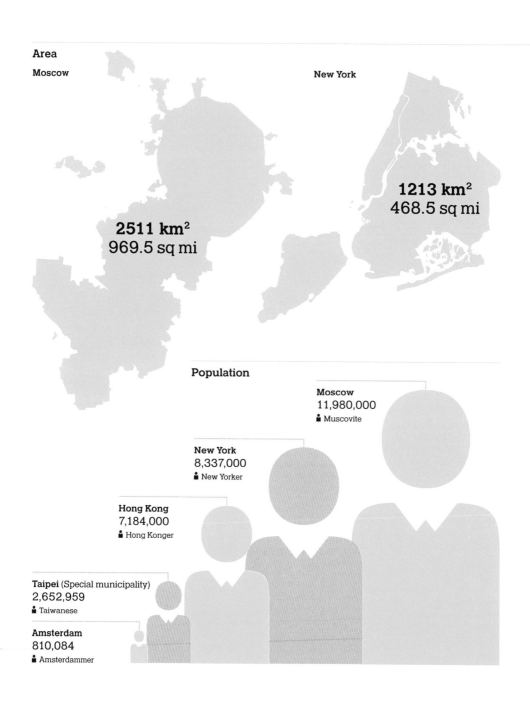

Area

Moscow

New York

1213 km²
468.5 sq mi

2511 km²
969.5 sq mi

Population

Moscow
11,980,000
👤 Muscovite

New York
8,337,000
👤 New Yorker

Hong Kong
7,184,000
👤 Hong Konger

Taipei (Special municipality)
2,652,959
👤 Taiwanese

Amsterdam
810,084
👤 Amsterdammer

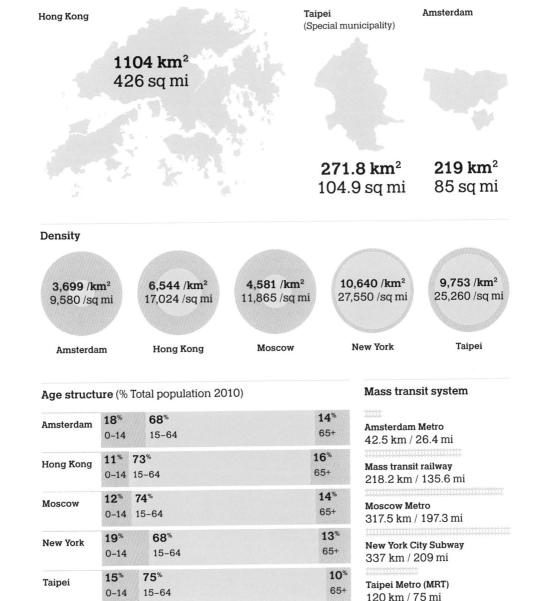

Hong Kong

1104 km²
426 sq mi

Taipei
(Special municipality)

Amsterdam

271.8 km²
104.9 sq mi

219 km²
85 sq mi

Density

3,699 /km²
9,580 /sq mi
Amsterdam

6,544 /km²
17,024 /sq mi
Hong Kong

4,581 /km²
11,865 /sq mi
Moscow

10,640 /km²
27,550 /sq mi
New York

9,753 /km²
25,260 /sq mi
Taipei

Age structure (% Total population 2010)

	0–14	15–64	65+
Amsterdam	18%	68%	14%
Hong Kong	11%	73%	16%
Moscow	12%	74%	14%
New York	19%	68%	13%
Taipei	15%	75%	10%

Mass transit system

Amsterdam Metro
42.5 km / 26.4 mi

Mass transit railway
218.2 km / 135.6 mi

Moscow Metro
317.5 km / 197.3 mi

New York City Subway
337 km / 209 mi

Taipei Metro (MRT)
120 km / 75 mi

Bibliography

Arlt, P. (2006) 'Urban Planning and Interim Use'. In: Haydn, F. & Temel, R. (eds.) Temporary Urban Spaces: Concepts for the Use of City Spaces. pp. 39-46. Basel: Birkhäuser.

Atkinson, R. & Carmichael, L. (2007) 'Neighbourhood as a New Focus for Action in the Urban Policies of West European States'. In: Smith, I., Lepine, E. & Taylor, M. (eds.) Disadvantaged by Where you Live? Neighbourhood Governance in Contemporary Urban Development Policy. Bristol: Policy Press.

Baxter, P. & Jack, S. (2008) 'Qualitative Case Study Methodology: Study Design and Implementation for Novice Researchers'. The Qualitative Report. 13 (4). pp. 544-559.

Bishop, P. & Williams, L. (2012) The Temporary City. London: Routledge.

Blanc, M. (1999) 'Participation des habitants et politique de la ville'. In: Blondiaux, L., Marcou, G. & Rangeon, F. (eds.) La démocratie locale, représentation, participation et espace publique. Paris: Presse Universitaire de France.

Certeau, M. de (1984) The Practice of Everyday Life. Berkeley: University of California Press.

Chase, J., Crawford, M. & Kaliski, J. (1999) Everyday Urbanism. Monacelli Press.

Debord, G. (1994) The Revolution of Everyday Life. London: Left Bank Books and Rebel Press.

Fraker, H. (2007) 'Where is the Design Discourse?'. Places. 19 (3). pp. 61-63.

Giddens, A. (1979) Central Problems in Social Theory. Houndmills: Macmillan Education.

Hélie, M. (2009) 'Conceptualizing the Principles of Emergent Urbanism'. Archnet IJAR. 3.

Hou, J. (ed.) (2010) Insurgent Public Space: Guerrilla Urbanism and the Remaking of Contemporary Cities. Routledge.

Huberman, A.M. & Miles, M.B. (2002) The Qualitative Researcher's Companion. Thousand Oaks: Sage.

Iveson, K. (2013) 'Cities within the City: DoItYourself Urbanism and the Right to the City'. International Journal of Urban and Regional Research. 37 (3). pp. 941-956.

Kedadouche, Z. (2003) Rapport sur la participation des habitants dans les opérations de renouvellement urbain. Paris: Inspection Générale des Affaires Sociales.

Kelbaugh, D. (2005) Michigan Debates on Urbanism (Vol. I-III). Ann Arbor: University of Michigan.

Lefebvre, H. (2004) Rhythmanalysis: Space, Time and Everyday Life. London: Continuum.

Lydon, M., Bartman, D., Woudstra, R. & Khawarzad, A. (2010) Tactical Urbanism (Vol. 1). Recuperado el, 15.

McFarlane, C. (2011) 'The City as a Machine for Learning'. Transactions of the Institute of British Geographers. 36 (3). pp. 360-376.

Pinilla, C. (2007) 'Emergent Urbanism'. Space Fighter. The Evolutionary City (Game), pp. 80-93. Barcelona: Actar-D.

Pogoreutz, M. (2006) 'Urban intelligence'. In: Haydn, F. & Temel, R. (eds.) Temporary Urban Spaces: Concepts for the Use of City Spaces. pp. 75-80. Basel: Birkhäuser.

Ronneberger, K (2006) 'From regulation to moderation', In: Haydn, F. & Temel, R. (eds.) Temporary Urban Spaces: Concepts for the Use of City Spaces. pp. 47-54. Basel: Birkhäuser.

Rowlands, R., Musterd, S. & Van Kempen, R. (2009) (eds.) Mass Housing in Europe: Multiple Faces of Development, Change and Response. Basingstoke: Palgrave Macmillan.

Schuster, M. (2001) 'Ephemera, Temporary Urbanism, and Imaging'. In: Imaging the City: Continuing Struggles and New Directions. pp. 361-96.

Sennett, R. (2008) 'The Open City'. In: Burdett R. & Sudjic, D. (eds.) The Endless City. pp. 290-297. London: Phaidon.

Stevens, Q. (2007) Ludic City: Exploring the Potential of Public Spaces. New York: Routledge.

Stickells, L. (2011) 'The Right To The City: Rethinking Architecture's Social Significance'. Architectural Theory Review. 16 (3). pp. 213-227.

Swyngedouw, E. & Kaïka, M. (2003) 'The Making of 'Glocal' Urban Modernities'. City, 7 (1). pp. 5-21.

Van Kempen, R. et al. (eds.) Restructuring Large Housing Estates in Europe. Bristol: Policy Press.

Yin, R.K. (2009) Case Study Research: Design and Methods (Vol. 5). Sage.

Case 3

Amsterdam

Case 4

Amsterdam:
Urban Development Context

Written by Bob Knoester,
Francesca Miazzo and Mark Minkjan

In order to better contextualize our case studies in a wider development framework, we will briefly introduce some elements of Dutch planning history and its guiding concepts. We will then focus on the city of Amsterdam and the spatial, social and market forces that affect the urban identity of the city. By introducing these aspects, we hope to facilitate the reader's understanding of the following sections of the book, which will specifically address the neighborhood level by describing four different bottom-up urban development processes in Amsterdam.

In order to introduce some elements of Dutch development, it is useful to shed light on the dominant role of spatial planning in the Netherlands, and then briefly explore the development of national spatial policies and some dominant urban development concepts. In general, it must be underlined that the spatial sector in the Netherlands is a complex, but fairly successful one, especially when compared to other countries in Europe and beyond (Van Oort, 2004).

Dutch cities have long been examples of egalitarian, accessible, safe and social cities, with low levels of crime and social unrest (Faludi & Van der Valk, 1994). This success is due to the pivotal role of planning and its link with the Dutch welfare system (Hoekstra, 2003), in combination with a consensus-based decision-making system. This combination has produced a society that has been labeled as egalitarian, regulated and tolerant (Deben et al., 2000). The highly centralized system is administrated through a decentralized unitary state that defines the framework for implementation of national planning policies. The system is highly centralized from a financial perspective as

well, as ninety percent of municipal income is allocated by the national government, but municipalities are self-governing and autonomous, especially when it comes to defining new trajectories and strategies for housing and urban planning (Deben, et al., 2000). Historically, postwar population growth and mobility first led to suburbanized areas and, during the 1970s, to New Towns, within nationally managed city-region frameworks. In the 1980s this approach had to give way to the famous 'compact cities' policy after the inner cities started to experience an outflow that led to impoverishment (Dieleman et al., 1999). Dutch cities have been built upon high concentrations of functions and facilities, the availability of public transportation, employment and recreational amenities. In addition, central areas are highly concentrated and functionally mixed, while some residential areas are characterized by socially diverse environments (Faludi & Van der Valk, 1994). These aspects have been influenced by the Dutch ABC classification of employment centers, where public transport accessibility requirements are taken into consideration to define the location of new urban development projects. In the last few decades, with the increasing internationalization of the market, those distinctive features have been challenged and local control over planning processes has been diminished. Besides market forces, social principles have also affected the Dutch approach to development and planning history, especially in the case of Amsterdam.

The city of Amsterdam has a rich history; what once was a small harbor town at the mouth of a river at one point became the world's most important city because of its position at the center of international trade. Today, Amsterdam is considered a small yet world-class city (Derudder et al., 2003). In the 17th century, during Holland's Golden Age, the canal ring of Amsterdam was built to welcome the goods and population that were flowing in from all over the world. The city was planned to house the prosperous segments of society in the city center, while the Jordaan area was built for the working class. At that time, and up until the 20th century, social issues were not a concern (Wagenaar, 1998). The city bore witness to another wave of expansion in the second half of the 19th century, when the first residential area outside of the canal ring was built in what is today the northern part of the De Pijp area (Feddes, 2012). The concentric expansion typical of the canal ring could not sustain the car-driven developments of the 20th century. As a consequence, in the 1930s, green areas were left open behind the canal ring and urban development was organized along radial corridors of transport following the Modernist movement (Deben et al., 2000: 63) and in accordance with CIAM ideas, which were a new set of rules for building the city associated ideologically with Ebenezer Howard and defined by the Congrès Internationaux d'Architecture Moderne (CIAM) between 1928 and 1959 (Domhardt, 2012). Halfway through the last century, the neighborhoods of Osdorp, Sloten, Bijlmermeer, Buitenveldert and Amsterdam-Noord were built to house the growing working class, following new international standards and opening up green spaces according to Howard's 'garden city' doctrine.

In order to understand the current status of the city, it must be underlined that not only spatial assets but social and market forces as well played a pivotal role. In the 1960s and 1970s, social unrest and student protests challenged the primacy of the central commercial core, which affected urban development patterns till the 1990s, when market forces and international competitiveness entered the game (Healey, 2007). In particular, some spatial characteristics of Amsterdam were defined in the 1960s and 1970s. Instead of demolishing the 19th-century areas of the city, urban renewal created mixed-used neighborhoods, control of historic fabric and road space and support for diversification (both social and spatial). Starting in the 1970s, the polycentric development of Amsterdam started (Faludi & Van der Valk, 1994) together with the abandonment of the port activities on the river IJ, due to deindustrialization and reallocation of port functions outside the urban core. In the 1980s, Amsterdam was resurrected as a major economic center, with culture and tourism as additional assets (Dahles, 1998). From the 1990s, more attention was paid to involving private actors in the urban planning game and new housing projects emerged in the city center.

In particular, the role of project developers became dominant although the city government continued to exercise control over the projects by means of building permits; these were intended to ensure that the plans of project developers fit within the structural plans of the municipality. In the 1990s, when the majority of urban renewal was relocated to the postwar neighborhoods, the redevelopment of the waterfront became a major focus area (Musterd et al., 2004), but because of access to transport, the southern axes and Schiphol Airport were preferred by project developers and thus emerged as new commercial centers. In the 2000s, Amsterdam became a champion of 'creative city' policies and continued its expansion towards the waterfront, the Noord and what is now called Nieuw West.

The waterfront is the focus of the new-millennium urban development scheme and since commercial players have traditionally preferred other, more accessible parts of the city, housing has become the major component of the IJ River bank, including between 30 and 40 percent of social housing (Marshall, 2002). The whole waterfront has been redeveloped together with private developers and new public buildings have been carefully spread around the central area, including a Science Museum, Architecture Center, Music Hall, Court of Justice and Film Museum.

Many contest Amsterdam's current urban development plans, especially as they relate to housing. Around 60 percent of the city's housing supply consists of social housing and there is a lack of lower-middle-class housing, which creates a gap between the affordable houses and the next step on the housing ladder. The status quo is further challenged by the current financial crisis (Engelen & Musterd, 2010) and new visions of active citizenship and community involvement are emerging. Due to the crisis, governments, housing corporations and welfare institutions have cut down their investment in neighborhoods, and instead are calling upon residents' own responsibility to improve their environments. This is kick-starting bottom-up initiatives in Amsterdam, and slowly the top-down institutions are acknowledging the need to incorporate these initiatives in their own policy and neighborhood agendas.

The following section will showcase several examples of community involvement in the current urban development of Amsterdam through bottom-up initiatives. They range from low-budget temporary functions to multimillion-dollar projects that are built to last fifty years, from semi-institutional or government-requested projects to projects with a loose and unstructured organization, and from highly conceptual to down-to-earth, pragmatic community contributions.

The Urban Development Protagonists:
The Oligopoly of Housing Corporations in Amsterdam

From the 20th century on, the role of housing corporations in Amsterdam became increasingly pivotal, leading to their current status as an oligopoly – a state of limited competition, in which a market is shared by a small number of sellers. As part of the social welfare system in the Netherlands, social housing is provided throughout cities for those families who are less well-off. This started just over a century ago, in 1901, when a few decades of rapid industrialization had left thousands of factory workers living in impoverished slums surrounding factories. These poor living conditions led to the spread of disease and crime, and the government began to demolish many of the slums.

At the same time they started to provide financial support to the existing nonprofit housing corporations that had been initiated by citizens. From this moment on, the number of government-supported housing corporations rose quickly, and between 1900 and 1940 around one million social houses were built. After the Second World War, the demand for houses was enormous and corporations built tens of thousands of them.

Until 1960, housing corporations were relatively small and focused on the social housing stock in one city or even just one part of one city. These small, public organizations, founded on religious or political ideologies, were responsible for their members, the renters, and overall social wellbeing.

The late 1980s brought a crucial moment in the urban development of Amsterdam: from 1988, the national government decided that privatized corporations would better serve the communities. From then on, corporations would be responsible for independently financing the construction of houses and taking the accompanying risks, stimulating them to be more efficient. A financial system was set up to make sure that the risks that corporations would take were acceptable, and governments would support this construction while the privatized corporations would still have some responsibility for the public interest: affordable housing and neighborhood investment. (Boelhouwer, 2002). From 1994, housing corporations became private entities, acting in the free market within the framework of the public interest given to them by the government.

They are required to provide quality low-rent housing for 90 percent of their stock, and are responsible for the livability of the neighborhood. Currently (2013 data), 2.4 million houses in the Netherlands (30 percent of the total housing stock) are owned by a decreasing number of housing corporations (Van Kempen & Priemus, 2002).

Case 1
Cascoland Kolenkitbuurt –
Building Bridges, with Institutions
as the Facilitators

❝ Growing dialogues across and between urban
and spatial theory, and artistic and cultural
practice, have considerable potential for
inspiring and developing critical approaches
to cities. ❞

> – Pinder, D. (2008)
> Urban Interventions:
> Art, Politics and Pedagogy.

Neighborhood
The Kolenkit is a neighborhood in western Amsterdam
with a bad reputation. It was built immediately after the
Second World War as part of a major urban expansion
plan, following the 'Garden City' principles outlined
by Ebenezer Howard. Today, the neighborhood is
characterized by a repetitive pattern of monotonous,
4-story tenement blocks. 95 percent of the mostly
small (smaller than 60m²) houses are in the social-

Cascoland Kolenkitbuurt

50m

rent sector, and they are occupied by some 7000 people, many of them from large immigrant families.

When it was built, the neighborhood wasn't given a name but a number and later residents began to call it by the same nickname as the church around which it is built: coal-scuttle, or 'Kolenkit'. Fifty years after it was built, the neighborhood had fallen into despair, and it was proclaimed the least popular neighborhood of Amsterdam in 2004, with all livability indicators in red: high unemployment rate, poverty, youth crime and a relatively high rate of high school drop-outs. According to a study undertaken by the University of Amsterdam (Boterman et al., 2010), the neighborhood was an accumulation of socioeconomic problems and a thorn in the eye of the responsible local government. In 2003, an urban renewal program was started, demolishing over a thousand houses and building back bigger houses to diversify the housing stock and attract more wealthy residents.

In 2007, when neighborhood livability and social security were made priorities on the national political agenda, the Kolenkit was listed as one of the 'worst neighborhoods' in the Netherlands

(Ministry of Housing and Integration, 2007). The forty neighborhoods on this list were targeted with an intensified program to prevent ghettoization and improve the physical, social and economic situation. These programs were to be carried out by coalitions of partners such as housing associations and municipalities.

Social investment

The need for a different approach to solving the problems of disadvantaged neighborhoods has been widely supported in theory and practice. Scholars argue that bottom-up urbanism can respond more quickly to societal needs compared to a top-down approach (Lydon et al., 2010). In particular, according to Schwarz (2009), because of its potential to change patterns of urban impoverishment, planners and politicians could benefit from encouraging more bottom-up developments in order to focus attention on specific areas of the city. The Kolenkit is an example of this strategy. For the Kolenkit improvement program, a budget was reserved by the Ministry of Education, Culture and Science, the government of the Amsterdam West district, housing corporation Rochdale and 'Koers Nieuw West' - a subsidized

Left
Out for a stroll

Previous spread (left)
Overview of
Cascoland Kolenkitbuurt

Previous spread (right)
Barbeque area

28 | 29

program to improve the socioeconomic position of residents in the troubled neighborhood. This budget was used for social investments, and for the physical urban renewal program that was already underway.

For the social part of the program, the district government adopted an unusual approach. A tender call was put out to garner ideas on improving the livability in the neighborhood. The eventual winner would be awarded the chance (and an operational budget) to execute this plan for a limited amount of time, during which it could prove its value in the neighborhood. Although it can be stated that these kinds of interventions might lead to an increasingly wide socio-spatial segregation in the neighborhood, (Uitermark, 2012), in the case of the Kolenkitbuurt results disprove this argument.

The tender call was won by Cascoland, a small organization of community artists. They had been working in the area during the three years prior to this tender call as part of a study by the University of Amsterdam into the role of cultural enterprises in disadvantaged neighborhoods. The fact that the representatives of Cascoland were known by the major stakeholders in the neighborhood and were residents themselves created the preconditions to define a higher degree of local embedment, which gave them an advantage over the other competitors. Their winning plan was characterized by an open and participatory process based on the activation and involvement of the local community. According to Graham (2012), one of the advantages of bottom-up urbanism is that it highlights creativity (in addition to encouraging entrepreneurship, providing incentives to property owners to maintain properties, and supporting environmentally sustainable development). On this account, Fiona Bell and Roel Schoenmakers, the founders of Cascoland, acted as cultural process managers for bottom-up initiatives and ideas. Due to the open character of their approach, no promises could be made about the outcome of this process, and this openness was the reason why policymakers were initially reluctant to unconditionally accept Cascoland's approach.

Cascoland
Cascoland (www.cascoland.com) is an international network of artists, architects and designers. The network was formed around the Dutch community artists Fiona and Roel. Each of their works requires different skill sets, so each involves a unique team built from members of Cascoland's network. In all of their work, Cascoland focuses on interdisciplinary interventions in public space that are shaped by a process of activation and participation within local communities. This means that the artists act as process managers who assist groups of residents in forming their own environment. In each case the outcome remains uncertain, as it depends entirely on the questions and solutions that residents themselves will come up with. Using these methods, Cascoland has guided participatory projects in South African slums, in Rio de Janeiro and in Durban, among other places. Cascoland provides an empty casco, or 'frame', of facilitation and artistic skills, which is eventually given meaning by local communities.

The research phase: understanding the neighborhood needs
After Cascoland was selected as the winner of the tender call for the Kolenkit neighborhood, the collective had the opportunity to run a pilot project for 8 months. For this pilot phase, from August 2010 to March 2011, Cascoland was provided with an operational budget allowing two or three artists to work in the neighborhood. In addition, the housing corporation involved made two small locations available for free. During the first months, Cascoland started by enquiring in the neighborhood about needs and ambitions using different methods. For instance, in order to develop a better knowledge of local residents and better understanding of what services or activities were lacking in the area, Cascoland organized weekly activities in one of the two locations. In particular, the first action was to organize an open neighborhood dinner where ideas were exchanged over an affordable meal. By hosting activities with a low barrier to entry, Roel and Fiona managed to gather many participants sharing information about what the community experienced as problematic, and what small additions would impact the quality of life in the neighborhood most efficiently. According to planners and policymakers, the Kolenkitbuurt was suffering from what can be defined as lack of livability (Wagner et al., 2012). However, the 'research phase' revealed that the issue of livability in itself was something that residents did not perceive as problematic. Thanks to the knowledge collected during the research phase, Cascoland developed small interventions, creating new meanings, experiences, understandings, relationships and situations.

Examples of Cascoland's interventions in the Kolenkitbuurt

Local families, many originating from rural areas of Morocco and Turkey, expressed a desire to keep small cattle as they had done in their home places. Also, many residents loved to leave the city in the summer to have barbeques and enjoy the outdoors.

The desires of the residents were translated into separate interventions that were developed by working groups of locals, with help from the artists of Cascoland. In practice, the residents themselves were helped in workshops with Cascoland to determine the outcome and organization of their projects. Following the definition of Wallerstein (1992), 'empowerment is a social-action process that promotes participation of people, organizations, and communities towards the goals of increased individual and community control, political efficacy, improved quality of community life, and social justice'. Henceforward, the process undertaken in the Kolenkitbuurt increased the residents' feeling of responsibility about the interventions and services developed in the neighborhood. Moreover, the empowerment process increased the residents' happiness with their living environments because they could replicate some habits and activities typical of life in their home countries. In the authors' opinion, the understanding of this vacuum in the community life represents a necessary step in the process of integration.

Henhouses

Initial research revealed that the residents felt the need for more meeting places in the area, such as parks. As a consequence, one of Cascoland's first interventions focused on a one-acre plot that had been vacant for years. The plot was derelict and surrounded by a fence, and as a result it was perceived as a source of discomfort. Still, this piece of land was considered valuable because of its central location and its proximity to shops and the main walking routes in the neighborhood. Cascoland started by organizing playful activities connected to the boundaries of the site, creating a labyrinth made from the fences so that people could interact with the fenced environment in a positive way.

Some residents had also expressed a desire to keep domestic fowls. For this reason, the initiators decided to develop four mobile henhouses for the site, which were designed and made in collaboration with residents. Several neighborhood families with children were selected to keep the chickens, under the condition that they would feed them and clean the henhouse, and eventually the location developed into a meeting place. The henhouses stimulated commitment from the neighbors and encouraged them to take responsibility for the management of their public space.

The government saw the success of this intervention and eventually removed the remaining fences, allowing the community to fully reappropriate the unused plot. The mobile henhouses were a great success: the number of neighbors who showed interest in keeping chickens was so great that the initiators could not meet the demand. Roel and Fiona from Cascoland saw this as an opportunity to implement another important aspect of their approach: empowerment. They helped the interested neighbors to apply for a permit at the district office, which enabled the community to independently realize the enlargement of the henhouse project.

Following the big success of the mobile henhouses, Cascoland started looking for a more permanent way for neighbors to keep chickens. After sessions with residents, they decided to cooperatively design and build a large chicken coop, surrounded by fruit trees in containers.

Barbeque, guesthouse and other interventions

Many residents in the Kolenkit neighborhood frequented barbeque places outside the city, and expressed their wish to have the same type of facility within their own neighborhood. As a result of the pilot phase of the Cascoland intervention in the neighborhood, the residents were involved in the 'HoutsKolenkit,' a publicly accessible area furnished with three barbeque grills and several picnic tables. At this time, other districts of Amsterdam were developing stricter regulations to prevent the development of barbeques in parks and on squares, but thanks to the moderation of Cascoland and the involvement of the local community, Kolenkitbuurt had a chance to implement this project nonetheless. The picnic area created a viable meeting place for residents, where they could cook dinner and eat together. Ultimately, this meeting place proved to be a valuable social asset to the neighborhood.

Cascoland's strategy is based on embedment and empowerment and therefore it goes further than to simply facilitate general requests from residents. Cascoland was also able to identify less visible and less specific problems around the neighborhood. For instance, it appeared that children at the neighborhood school were often tired in class. This problem was related to the fact that families were having visiting relatives sleep in the children's bedrooms, due to the lack of space in the households. As a consequence, the kids were forced to sleep on the couch and the following day they were tired. Cascoland, together with the residents, thought of a simple solution. One of the vacant apartments was turned into a neighborhood guestroom, maintained and managed by neighbors, that can be booked for a small amount.

The above examples are just a small sample of over twenty interventions that have been implemented since the beginning of the project in 2010. After a pilot phase of six months, Cascoland's contract was extended, allowing the team to continue to work in the neighborhood. Other interventions included the decoration of a formerly dark and dank tunnel by neighbors, the creation of an ice-skating rink, and a festive neighborhood breakfast. Each project has its own purpose, planning, management and financing process, and different combinations of artists and residents have been involved in each one.

A critical overview of bottom-up developments in Kolenkitbuurt and the role of institutions
As mentioned before, at the beginning of this process, policymakers were reluctant to agree to such an open-ended project. This aversion to risk-taking is a common problem with traditional top-down players. Accountability and management become more difficult for institutions, which have to audit, evaluate and base every decision upon actions and expenses. At the same time, long-term planning, with specific results and actions, can fail due to this limited understanding of continuously changing urban circumstances. The case of Cascoland is an inspirational example of a successful bottom-up process.

In Kolenkitbuurt, the Cascoland team negotiated several aspects of the project; one of them was the availability of land. The field where several of the interventions took place was owned by the district, and they were initially reluctant to make the land available. However, Cascoland argued that a condition of abandonment might prevent potential developers from buying the land, and its value would then decrease. By guaranteeing the temporary and mobile nature of the project, Cascoland managed to convince the district council to go along with their plan. Also, the land happened to be located right next to the district office, making it quite literally one of the most intensely supervised projects in Amsterdam.

Left
Taking the hens for a walk

Right
Outside seating area

Another condition negotiated by the team was the condition of temporary use, which allowed the development of a set of tailored, small-scale interventions that were very successful. Opening an ice skating ring on the field generated a lot of media exposure, and the henhouses, mobile gardens, barbecues and the guesthouse were all well used by locals, making the square a lively place in the neighborhood and a good example of how to empower people by giving meaning to their urban environments.

From the institutional perspective, Cascoland Kolenkit is a specific type of bottom-up project, where institutions allow the intervention of a mediator to work with and within the local community. Hiring external experts to bridge the gap with local communities is not always a recipe for success. In the authors' opinion, the choice of the mediator is of critical importance. The selection of a mediator with high social and geographical embedment in the neighborhood is important. The approach of Cascoland is focused on participation and activation, as the problems and needs of the community are served and citizens are strongly involved and empowered. This is all achieved in a relatively efficient way: the top-down institutions involved do not need to hire experts in community activation themselves, but 'outsource' this task to others. Bottom-up players were able to pay an operational budget to Cascoland from the community participation budget, which was reserved by the coalition of partners mentioned earlier.

The budgets used to finance the different interventions were set up separately for each single project, using sponsors from the neighborhood, grants from the central city or the district, or from foundations that aim to improve neighborhood social cohesion.

Case 2
I Can Change the World with My Two Hands
– A Neighborhood Miracle

**Placing 'I Can Change the World
with My Two Hands' in context**
Urban agriculture can be employed as an affordable
way to produce food within the urban edge; especially
when complemented with rural products, this practice
often provides healthier food and helps to offset
seasonal fluctuations in food supply (Mougeot, 2000;
Smit et al., 2001). In addition, urban agriculture,
and especially urban community gardens, can be
considered sustainable places for education and
recreation (Johnson & Lawson, 2009). According
to Schmelzkopf (1995), community gardens are a
common practice in the Global North, especially
in periods of crisis. Moreover, it seems that urban
agriculture can put to use waste products and idle
lands, transforming citizens from consumers to
creators of resource-conserving, health-improving,
sustainable products (Smit & Nasr, 1992). The case
of 'I Can Change the World with My Two Hands'
is an example of how all of the above have been

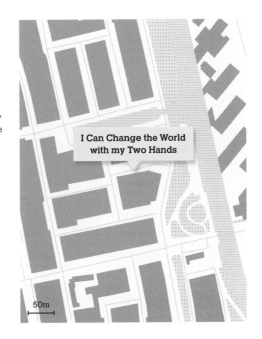

I Can Change the World
with my Two Hands

50m

implemented in the city of Amsterdam. In order to contextualize the case, it may be appropriate to frame the current situation of urban/allotment gardens in the city of Amsterdam, where there has always been a demand for farming land. Like other Dutch cities, Amsterdam has large fields along its edges, which are divided into dozens of small allotments. In the past, these allotments were used mainly by elderly and immigrant populations, but recently this has changed. Now younger people and people of all nationalities have begun to develop an interest in gardening, resulting in waiting lists for many allotments (De Vries & Schöne, 2004).

'I Can Change the World with My Two Hands' is a community garden in the Landlust neighborhood of Amsterdam West, which was built during the urban expansion projects of the 1930s. The neighborhood is characterized by long strips of tenement housing blocks four or five stories high. The tenement blocks consist of smaller houses (around 60 m²), of which more than half are social rent. The population of the neighborhood is relatively elderly and around 25 percent of the residents have a low income by Dutch standards. A recent spate of crimes in the

neighborhood's shops has led the municipality to install CCTV to improve security. Given the current high rate of youth unemployment, the future of the neighborhood doesn't look promising. In response, the district councils and housing corporations have started their investment program focusing on youth, the physical state of the houses, the local economy and family issues.

'I Can Change the World with My Two Hands' is located within a housing block, on a plot that formerly held a public swimming pool and playground. Due to failing management and public spending cuts, the site was closed several years ago. One of the local residents, Natascha Hagenbeek, saw that there was no plan for the 1200-square-meter area even two years after closure, and she decided to take the initiative to reappropriate the plot. Natascha works as an artist and had no experience whatsoever in running a garden of this size, but she saw this as an opportunity to start something communal that would improve the neighborhood. She was not alone: in fact this kind of move is becoming quite common in crisis-impacted cities of the Global North.

There are several elements that can help explain the momentum of the trend. First of all, the current precarious financial times have reduced the leverage of governments and developers to invest in the city. This has stalled construction projects, leaving voids in the urban fabric and in the urban plans for the future. Through the media, and also through everyday experiences, citizens come to recognize certain vacuums in their environments (Cumberlidge & Musgrave, 2007). Moreover, the welfare state in many western countries has been hollowed out to some degree, with services, amenities and safety nets being dismantled. As a result of this ideological shift, economic, spatial, political and financial resources increasingly favor economic growth over the wider societal good (Fainstein, 2010; Harvey, 1989). This affects nationwide structures, but also the production of cities and the reality of daily life on a neighborhood level (e.g., the closing of community facilities and meeting places and a decrease in maintenance and programming of public space).

The narrative, from pilot project to comprehensive urban food strategy
In 2009, Natascha contacted the local district to apply for permission to use the derelict plot, but at first her application failed. At that time it was not common for the local government to assign the management of public space to private citizens, and there were no procedures in place to undertake this task. After months of trying to reach and convince different officials within the municipality, Natascha finally succeeded in 2010. During a meeting for residents, she explained her needs and ambitions to the responsible policymakers and her fellow neighbors, and the idea began to attract political support and enthusiasm. From there, she managed to get permission to deploy a pilot project in the garden for one year without having to pay rent for the space. During the summer of 2011, Natascha organized a neighborhood gathering and the group cooperatively developed a concept. The 1200-square-meter space is divided into several shared and private gardens. At the edges are 17 'private' gardens for individual neighbors, so that they can grow crops for their own households. In the center of the plot, a large communal garden is managed by several volunteers. The harvested fruits, vegetables and herbs of this shared garden – including apples, parsnip, peas, tomatoes, elderflower and mint – are taken up into the neighborhood food cycle in ways that will be

detailed later. Parts of the garden are reserved for neighborhood kids so that they can learn about gardening and grow their first crops; in other areas are a greenhouse, a compost pile that can be used freely by all the gardeners, and a 2-meter-deep well. In total, around thirty-five neighbors are involved in the management of the garden, and over a hundred residents profit from the harvested products on a regular basis. This relatively large-scale and professionalized approach makes 'I Can Change the World with My Two Hands' stand out from many other community garden projects in Amsterdam, where they tend to appear in smaller bits of underutilized public space. Natascha's project is much bigger in scale, and uses the entire surface of the big plot for food production.

The proven benefits of urban agriculture are many. First, the community gardens can play a social role in a neighborhood, connecting neighbors and building community cohesion with all the related benefits. Second, vacant and derelict plots within residential neighborhoods generally have a negative effect on the perceived security and livability. The 'I can change the world with my two hands' garden provides a (temporary) function to such a plot and takes away this negative connotation. Third, 'I Can Change the World with My Two Hands' contributes in some small way to the economic resilience of the neighborhood because the harvest becomes part of the local food chain. In fact, production is the aspect that is considered most important by the team of 'I Can Change the World with My Two Hands' and the harvest of the shared garden is used for multiple purposes. In the harvest season vegetables are sold on Saturdays, under the name 'food from the hood'. In 2013, a small convenience store named 'access to tools' opened in the neighborhood, where the produce from the garden is sold alongside other products from the neighborhood, as well as books and other gardening-related products such as fertilizer and tools. The store is open three days a week and also functions as a project space to organize workshops for both children and adults on topics related to nutrition and gardening. In addition, some products from the garden are used and sold in businesses in the neighborhood, such as the tomatoes from the greenhouse that are served in the adjacent street at an organic snack bar. A group of residents, who cooperatively buy meat and vegetables from farmers in the outskirts of the city, also receives some of the harvest. This system creates

a virtuous cycle of food production and consumption, which is also accompanied by a smart up-cycling process of existing resources. Wherever possible, materials used in the garden are taken from the neighborhood. The wooden borders that separate the different plots, for example, are made from scrap wood found in the streets, and the bricks that surround the natural water well were left after the swimming pool on the plot was demolished. Fertilizer is partly made from food waste from one of the nearby restaurants, and even the supplies that simply could not be obtained from waste or reuse were purchased in shops in the neighborhood whenever possible. In this way, the project contributes to the environmental, social and economic resilience of the neighborhood.

Strategic thinking and visionary approach, conceptualization and replication

'I Can Change the World with My Two Hands' is a project initiated by an artist who decided to focus on concept rather than local circumstances. Both in choosing the name and in managing communication with stakeholders and the public, the project has been branded not only as a community garden but also as an innovative example to demonstrate how cities can improve sustainability and resilience in the future. Natascha's argument is that when applied on a larger scale, production-oriented community gardens have the potential to make neighborhoods less dependent on the 'import' of food, and to strengthen the viability of a closed-circuit neighborhood economy. The resilience of urban societies remains a popular theme,

especially in times of crisis, and in order to improve this resilience, 'I Can Change the World with My Two Hands' is constantly looking for opportunities to expand the concept. In the spring of 2013, the project managed to acquire a storefront in an empty house that was provided by the housing corporation. In the space, which she called 'A tribute to the whole earth,' Natascha set up a store to sell produce and organize activities. She also brought in the expertise of Cityplot, which organizes urban farming courses in Amsterdam, to help her expand the list of activities and educational programs that make use of a specially allocated plot of the garden.

Institutional approach, from rejection to support: the issue of trust

Allowing citizens to manage community gardens is a relatively inexpensive strategy to support occupancy of the public space and enhance social cohesion, which makes urban agriculture a popular (temporary) function in a city in crisis. On the other hand, trusting residents to manage public space independently is still relatively uncommon. In the case of 'I Can Change the World with My Two Hands' the local government allowed the group of residents to use the plot without paying rent for the first year, and this has since been extended. The necessary start-up costs were covered mostly from the 'neighborhood participation budget', a budget that is funded jointly by the municipality and housing corporations and is reserved for applications from the neighborhood to improve livability. Although

Previous spread
Overview of the garden

Left
Exterior of the greenhouse

Right
Inside the greenhouse

this procedure is transparent and openly accessible to any initiative, securing political willingness is helpful.

Most of the work on the garden was done on a voluntary basis by the neighbors owning and managing the plots, which would have been impossible if the plot was still managed by the municipality. Trusting the residents with the management of the plot has enabled this commitment. In 2013, the permit to use the garden was extended with another five years, further enabling the residents to invest in the garden and make long-term plans. Besides the granted application for the local participation budget, 'I Can Change the World with My Two Hands' has been rewarded with help from the local housing corporation that lowered the rent of the storefront to one third of the commercial price in order to encourage workshops for the neighborhood children. The district has allowed the team to use the plot too, without complex permit constructions.

In practice, 'I Can Change the World with My Two Hands' is an example of how institutional support does not always have to be in the form of economic resources. Especially in crisis-impacted cities such as Amsterdam, innovative institutional approaches can facilitate local bottom-up developments by loosening regulations regarding the rent and by bargaining spatial permission. The increasing popularity of urban farming has led the municipality to initiate a few guides. Online, they have published a map of Amsterdam with all the urban agriculture projects,

as well as information about how to start a farm, with do's and don'ts. Also, the city plans to open a small office where information and regulation about urban agriculture projects can be obtained.

A project such as 'I Can Change the World with My Two Hands' is a good example of a cost-efficient way of managing public space, organized from the bottom-up and with benefits that go beyond the financial aspect. Of course, the question remains whether the implementation of such projects on a more structural basis will actually lead to a more sustainable city, or if the externalities of these uncoordinated projects will ultimately stand in the way of their success. It is possible that the benefits of social cohesion may not be shared with the entire community but remain limited to a small number of residents (Arlt, 2006). In this case, even if urban agriculture were implemented on a larger scale, the effect of community gardens on complex social problems would remain relatively small (Uitermark, 2012). Large-scale industrialized food production in rural areas will remain cheaper and more productive, especially in a country like the Netherlands where the countryside is both productive and easily accessible. However, from the institutional, social and urban perspective, this project is a positive example of a temporary reuse of derelict urban areas.

Case 3
NoorderparkBar –
Doing More with Less

Contextualization of NoorderparkBar

The city of Amsterdam is situated along the shores of the river IJ, which has played an important role in the development of the city as the main transport route from the sea. In the spatial pattern of the city you can still see the channels on which storehouses were located in the 17th century. Without the river IJ, Amsterdam would have never reached such a high degree of international connectivity (Marshall, 2004).

But the river is also a barrier between the two parts of Amsterdam. The part on the southern shore offers the globally known facilities that attract millions of tourists each day; the northern part is where tourists rarely go. The 'Noord' neighborhood was built to house the people who worked in the shipyards, and when the North Sea Canal was completed in 1875, the IJ began to decline in importance (Marshall, 2004, 143). As a result the Noord became isolated because of its bad connectivity to the rest of the city. Moreover, low-

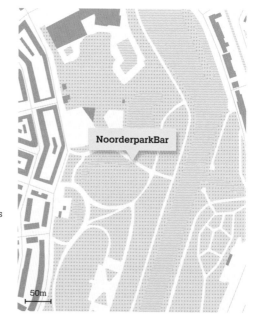

income communities were located here, transforming it into a socially segregated area with higher poverty and crime rates (Engbersen et al., 1998). People living on the other side of the river were reluctant to consider Noord as a part of Amsterdam until recently.

In the past decade or so, the perception of Noord has begun to change thanks to the redevelopment of the IJ riverbanks, which started in the 1980s; the improvements in public transport (a higher frequency of free ferries to the center and a metro line that will be in use from 2017); and a new locus for creative industries in the former shipyards. Some have referred to this urban process as 'The Noord District's Hip Rebirth' (The Wall Street Journal, Europe Edition, July 2011). Amsterdam Noord is still an underexplored portion of the city, with immense potential for urban integration and regeneration, especially when compared to the intense densification of the historic center (Suchar, 1993), and the gentrification of its surrounding working-class neighborhoods (which have been populated by the post-industrial workforce, fighting its way against millions of tourists daily). Amsterdam's core is characterized by a sense of 'busyness' that is still difficult to perceive in Noord.

Van der Pek is the neighborhood immediately surrounding the Noord's ferry station, a location with great potential that was identified around two decades ago by the housing corporations (which own around 95 percent of the houses in the area). Recently the EYE Film Museum was also located here, providing a

futuristic type of landmark across the IJ. The Van der Pek neighborhood was built in the 1920s as a lower-class garden city of small, three-story houses and tiny gardens offering an alternative to the impoverished lower-class neighborhoods in the city center. With working classes and industry on the same river bank, there was no need to invest in costly infrastructure or public transport at that time. This is beginning to change as the area's potential is becoming clearer.

NoorderparkBar in a wider theoretical framework
It seems that in Western Europe, a new orthodoxy of resident participation is rising (Atkinson & Eckardt, 2004). This new type of citizens' involvement can help guide the future direction of a site, for example by suggesting new uses (Cumberlidge & Musgrave, 2007). Following this trend, the NoorderparkBar is a project initiated and developed by three neighbors who felt the lack of facilities in the area where they live. Centrally located in this area lies the Noorderpark, a park which extends for thirty acres along the Buiksloterweg, the canal that connects the river IJ with the agricultural land in Noord.

In 2007, local resident and cultural professional Floor Ziegler was disappointed with the lack of cultural activities in the park and so she opened the NoorderparkKamer ('kamer' is the Dutch word for 'room'); it was intended as a 'cultural living room' in the park, in and around which theater, music and children's activities could be programmed by cultural professionals from Amsterdam Noord. Floor's initiative

Previous spread (left)
NoorderparkBar in context

Previous spread (right)
NoorderparkBar

Left
NoorderparkBar

Centre
Patio

Right
Window Wall

was welcomed by both the municipality and an important local housing corporation, both of which helped her to realize her plan. Over the past few years, the 'room' has developed into a popular meeting place for neighbors and has become so popular that extra space was needed. Three regular visitors of the 'room' approached Floor separately with their own plans to add an extra pavilion, with a hospitality function, to be able to enjoy a drink in the park. Joining forces, they developed the first plan for the NoorderparkBar. Just before the economic crisis struck, the housing corporation that owns the largest share of social housing in the area was contacted in order to ask for financial support. The corporation reacted enthusiastically and the plan grew to include a wide variety of programmatic uses in dozens of containers. Unfortunately, in 2008, economic support for the project was withdrawn. The initiators abandoned the idea, but two years later the corporation approached them again to reconsider making the bar more modest, smaller and cheaper. With only around a tenth of the original budget, the initiators had to be inventive in the construction process and in the acquisition of funds. In 2012 the bar opened its doors and has since been a busy center for the neighborhood.

Adapting bottom-up development ambitions to the current local conditions
As in other bottom-up projects in Amsterdam, the initiators made use of the neighborhood participation budget to start up the project. However, additional resources were needed and they were found through crowdfunding. Crowdfunding describes a collective operation supported by people who network and pool their money and other resources together, usually via the Internet, to support efforts initiated by other people or organizations (Roebuck, 2011). In terms of material resources, the initiators started collecting the necessary bits and pieces from an auction website: frames, wood, windows, tiles, lights, paint, glass. Everything was brought back to Amsterdam in a van, while the construction process began in another neighbor's barn. Considering the tight budget, the initiators had no choice but to do almost all of the construction themselves, on a voluntary basis. A year later they had finished the bar, brought it to the park and served the first couple of beers. The bar became popular quickly and now it attracts visitors from the neighborhood and beyond. What makes this project unique is that the bar does not have a contractor, a formal owner or a business model. Nobody owns it and as such everybody does. The adjacent NoorderparkKamer uses the bar's profits to invest in cultural programs.

**The institutional approach –
top-downers as final users**
The role that top-down organizations played in the development of this project should not be underestimated. It started with the appreciation of the area and the park as places with potential. The location in an underutilized neighborhood in Amsterdam, and the recent focus on revitalizing this part of the city, shaped the perfect context for

active citizenship. The first stage, when the plans were expanded out of the corporation's enthusiasm and then later cancelled, shows that such bottom-up initiatives still depend to a large extent on the involvement and capabilities of larger institutions, both financially and legally (as in the case of permits). The second stage is a great example of how bottom-up and top-down meet: the top-downers asked the bottom-uppers to reconsider their plan in a more modest version, and no irregular forms of financing were used, only the budget that had already been reserved for citizens' ideas and initiatives. With similar budget arrangements, larger institutions enable citizens to influence the development of their area. Participation budgets, or citizens' budgets, have been criticized and could probably be improved, but the potential they have to enable citizens to participate in spatial policy in a more serious way is undeniable.

At Noorderpark the institutions have applied an innovative approach by allowing the initiators a certain degree of independence. This kind of independence, however, relies on a trusting relationship between institutions and initiators. In this case the initiators succeeded in earning this trust because of the conceptual value of the project and the way they had created support within and outside of the neighborhood. Top-downers could learn from this experience: there are many benefits of creating closer ties with initiators. Successfully communicating with the community leaders (or professionals) and being more open in outsourcing the management and provision of amenities to engaged citizens are both good strategies. Bottom-uppers should learn from this as well: investing in relationships with top-downers increases the chance of success (in this case, the district's executive councilor frequently enjoys the terrace of the bar). In building NoorderparkBar, the trust the initiators gained gave them the freedom to deviate from regular forms of organization and application and still secure the required permits.

A critical analysis of bottom-up development
Since the bar was built using only second-hand materials, the project has been nominated for several awards, which is quite unusual for bottom-up initiatives; they are not generally known for their aesthetic qualities. However, since the three initiators of NoorderparkBar have backgrounds in architecture and design, the bar is a beautiful object of high-quality design. Three units were made from the stripped frames of construction trailers, and walls were made from second-hand window frames and other wooden boards. Every single piece of material has a history: personal stories from many of the sellers were collected and put on a blog together with their pictures. This meticulous attention to the 'story' behind the construction enhances that sense of belonging and uniqueness that is so difficult to find in contemporary standardized urban landscapes (Harvey, 1989).

Process-wise, the NoorderparkBar is also a unique case. The project was granted construction permits and licenses for serving alcoholic beverages despite its clear noncompliance with the normal requirements. For example, a permanent building permit was granted although the project has no formal ownership. The preservation committee, a committee consisting of architects who judge building plans on their aesthetic qualities, approved the construction without being informed about how the bar was going to look (at the time even the initiators didn't know, as the finished appearance was entirely dependent on the materials that could be found).

From the financial perspective, the project was partly paid for by using an innovative funding strategy. Instead of looking for a few big investors such as banks that are willing to provide large sums, a large number of small investors was sought through crowdfunding, an alternative funding strategy that fits perfectly within the current zeitgeist of budget cuts at traditional institutions. The strengths of crowdfunding are many: a chance to test marketability, the accessibility of capital, benefits for communities, rights to make company's decisions stay in the hands of entrepreneurs (Valanciene & Jegeleviciute, 2013).

Projects of social relevance, with the right message, will be able to create support from communities with the possible financial benefits that come with that. Some might label this process bottom-up financing (Annis, 1987).

Together with the crowdfunded budget, and the money provided through the neighborhood participation budget, the economic conditions to implement the project were met. However, meeting budget needs is not always enough to bring a bottom-up initiative to completion. According to a study on twenty-five initiatives in the Global North carried out by Anne-Marie Conway and Liam Murphy, the operationalization of the project idea is the most critical phase for success. Operationalization of a project is about carrying out strategy, actions and tactics during the implementation process (Pinto & Slevin, 1988).

We can conclude that since both the idea and the realization of the NoorderparkBar were carried out by the residents of the Van der Pek neighborhood, this project is an example of successful bottom-up development. Its success is also linked to the fact that the NoorderparkBar provides an urban amenity that was needed in the community. The fact that there is no formal ownership and the artifact literally belongs to the community is another unique factor, which could equally have become a reason for failure. Sometimes, after an enthusiastic startup, the lack of a charismatic figure bringing its goals alive can undermine the long-term success of a bottom-up project. In the case of the NoorderparkBar, however, the adjacent organization/location NoorderparkKamer was engaged in the management of the Bar and connected its program with the whole of the park and its cultural activities.

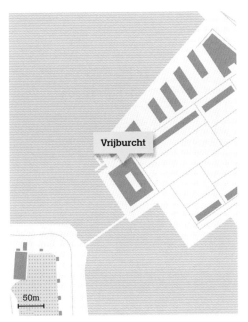

Vrijburcht

50m

Case 4
Vrijburcht – Self-made Diversity

❝ By collectively assuming the role of client,
inhabitants can create more functions in
their living environment. This has a positive
effect on the time management of inhabitants,
social infrastructure and livability of the
neighborhood. ❞

– De Haan, H. & Tummers, L.

Urban contextualization of the case

According to the results of an investigation
undertaken by CITIES Foundation in collaboration
with the Amsterdam Center for Architecture, many
bottom-up initiatives in Amsterdam are located
in impoverished areas where urban regeneration
plans have not yet been implemented. The case of
Vrijburcht is different. Vrijburcht is a building complex
combining housing, office and leisure located in
a recent urban expansion site, just east of the city
center. Over the last few decades, Amsterdam has
been increasing the density of its built environment

and the potential of artificial islands in the water has become a focus of interest. Since the 1990s, instead of building on the outskirts of the city, the city government has chosen to reclaim land along the IJ River, in locations near the city center (Salet et al., 2003). Recent projects include KNSM Island and Java Island, in the former harbor area, and IJburg, just outside the city.

Of these projects, IJburg is the largest. In 1996, the decision to build this project was taken, consisting of three separate islands that would provide 18,000 homes, housing 45,000 inhabitants. The project was also planned to accommodate economic activity and offer 12,000 jobs. The construction of IJburg fits within the Dutch Vinex policy, which aims to concentrate the growth of cities in nationally designated areas (Snellen & Hilbers, 2007). Unfortunately, after the first island was completed, the housing market collapsed (Snellen & Hilbers, 2007) and the development of the other islands was stopped. By 2013, five islands were created, while another four remain in the planning stage.

In developing the residential parts of IJburg the planners went beyond traditional construction plans and strategies. Besides working with housing corporations and project developers that built houses on a large scale, space was also reserved for private commissioning and collective commissioning, a form of urban development that first appeared in Holland in the 1980s (De Haan & Tummers, 2007). Individual

commissioning (which also includes collective commissioning) is an emerging and 'alternative' trend in the Dutch landscape, and the government started encouraging this practice in the 1990s. According to the Netherlands Institute for Spatial Research, which published a book about this issue in 2007, support for private home ownership has been growing since the failure of the Dutch mass housing policy. A clarifying definition is provided by the same institution:

❝ Individual commissioning (particulier opdrachtgeverschap in Dutch) involves one or more private individuals acquiring land and deciding themselves which parties to commission for the design and construction of homes for their own use. It distinguishes itself from the mass build market (projectmatige bouw in Dutch) by 'reversing' the construction process: the prospective resident does not appear at the end of the line as a customer, but at the beginning as the commissioning party. ❞

– Netherlands Institute
for Spatial Research

In practice, what is more formally called CCH/CCA or Collectively Commissioned Housing/Architecture works as follows: individuals buy a piece of land and build a home themselves or commission its design and construction. This controlling role of the residents is relatively uncommon in the Netherlands, where

real estate developers and housing corporations tend to manage the majority of private and public housing development. However, in the planning phase of the western part of IJburg, several plots were reserved for collective commissioning projects. Groups of citizens were invited to take the initiative and buy plots all over the island to realize their dreams; of these, Vrijburcht is the most notable project.

Vrijburcht
Vrijburcht is the result of a collaboration between a group of neighbors from Nieuwmarkt, a historic neighborhood in the center of Amsterdam. The idealistic architect and former squatter Hein de Haan had previously worked on several Collective Commissionership (CC) projects for clients, and when the plot on IJburg was made available he saw a chance to take on this challenge, this time in the role of commissioner rather than as a facilitating architect. Together with about twenty of his neighbors he developed a plan for a sustainable affordable housing complex that also included workplaces, catering services and other functions. The governing municipal body accepted their plan, and the group was able to buy the land in 2004 (the project was completed in 2007).

In this part of IJburg, several adjacent plots were reserved, and next to the group of neighbors from Nieuwmarkt were three other groups with CC aspirations. However, these other projects struggled with finding consensus during their early meetings and eventually dropped their ideas, which meant that the plots they had claimed became available again. After a while, Hein de Haan and his neighbors were asked by the municipality if they were interested in taking over the development rights to these additional plots and making a plan for the whole block. In this manner, they were able to develop Vrijburcht, a unique complex realized from the bottom up, with a variety of programmatic functions including more than fifty homes and workplaces.

Interpreting Vrijburcht
In 1979, Giddens defined the concept of the 'dominant interpretation frame,' which is 'a discourse that becomes part of the principal regime of thinking and focus on the city'. In the last decades, we have seen the development of several shared nomenclatures to define the development of our built environments. After the 'creative city' (Bianchini & Landry, 1994), came the 'sustainable city' (Gangloff, 1995) and in recent years, the 'bottom-up city' discourse is becoming increasingly central, at least in the Global North. Though spontaneous city making is the oldest form of urbanization, this form of urbanism appears to be underexposed in planning literature and planning practice, which is primarily concerned with the organization of urban spaces and the ordering of urban resources. In city thinking, however, similar notions have been pitched before, such as 'everyday urbanism' (Fraker, 2007). In the case of Vrijburcht, we see the pivotal role of the end users, the juxtaposition of different functions and a greater

attention to sustainable issues, which together create a comprehensive exemplar of bottom-up urban development representing every aspect of the most dominant contemporary urban interpretation frames.

The combination of functions is also the main feature that makes Vrijburcht a notable case compared to other collective commissioning projects. The complex offers 52 residences, including social housing (owned by a housing corporation), 16 companies in spaces that perfectly fit the needs of their owners, a daycare center, a special area where disabled people live under supervision of professionals, and a small theater with sixty seats that is run by volunteering neighbors who program cinema, theater, and kids' theater and musical performances. The complex also has a bar/restaurant open six nights a week, affordable guestrooms for visitors of the residents, and a small harbor and sailing school for neighborhood kids. The above-mentioned public facilities were realized by the residents themselves, and are managed on a not-for-profit basis.

The narrative of a bottom-up / demand-oriented development

Due to its demand-oriented development, this building perfectly fits the needs of the residents. Tailored housing, business areas and services meant lower construction costs and, in the end, lower rents. Given the tight housing market in Amsterdam, the opportunity to develop affordable housing was a key feature of the project for the aspiring co-developers. After Vrijburcht grew to include the adjacent plots, one of the challenges was to attract new members that would commit to the project and invest in the development of the complex. To accomplish this, the organization of the process was of the utmost importance. The fact that every single member of the group of prospective residents and users had a vote in every decision about how to design the building, what materials would be used, which energy supplier would be contracted, etcetera, made it a very complex process. To ensure that the group of involved residents would arrive at an efficient process of collaborative decision-making, a minimal number of external professionals were hired at various stages of the process. From the preparation phase until the moment that the residents moved in, the group was legally organized as a foundation with a board that took care of daily management, such as financial management, acquiring and introducing

new 'members' to the foundation, and communication. Aspiring buyers would transfer money to the account of the foundation, which then purchased the plots and paid for other services (i.e. applying for permits). Besides great attention towards the needs of the residents, which developed into an appropriately managed juxtaposition of functions, sustainability also became a key goal.

Sustainable materials were preferred during the construction process, with a focus on insulation, energy supply, and a community garden in the complex. Moreover, the fact that working and living spaces were combined can be considered a sustainability improvement. When compared to monofunctional neighborhoods, mixing functions decreases travel time and transport waste, and creates a socially vibrant place (Jacobs, 1970). Demand-oriented urban development together with a focus on sustainability might seem quite costly as a strategy. However, thanks to the collective character of the project, finances were administrated in a collaborative manner that decreased costs compared to other privately owned properties.

Of course, compared to large housing corporations and project developers, small groups of residents are less able to carry the financial risk of an enormous project such as Vrijburcht, worth over 12 million Euros. To manage this investment risk, a backup contract with housing corporation De Key was signed as a kind of insurance policy. If it happened that the properties could not be sold, the housing corporation agreed to purchase the remaining houses. At the same time, the housing corporation developed some services in the complex, such as the spaces for the disabled, the daycare center and the restaurant. Since full occupancy was reached well before the time the project was finished, the back-up contract was never implemented. However, without the contract it would have been much more difficult to realize the project. Most private commissioning projects remain limited to (a small number of) single houses, and Vrijburcht is quite unusual in its size and complexity. Cooperatively hiring one architect and one builder created an economically sustainable situation, which provided the group with return to scale profits. Aside from the more tangible benefits, the intensity of the project also resulted in a group of committed neighbors who know that they can rely on each other.

In conclusion, taking the Vrijburcht case into consideration, it can be stated that, provided there is a professional organizational structure and a serious level of commitment, citizens are able to create affordable, vibrant and sustainable developments without any outside investment from any government, corporation or project developer (and only a backup contract in case of vacancy). Collectively commissioned projects build their successes from an existing demand and an active community, decreasing the accompanying risks of real estate sales and spreading them over the participating residents. Stimulating private organizations (for instance, through fiscal measures) to support these projects with backup contracts to decrease the risk for participants would lower the threshold even more for interested people, and would potentially increase the impact of this community-oriented urban development method.

Where the role of institutions seems absent: an overview of top-down players in Vrijburcht
Although it seems that top-down players are absent in this case, it must be underlined that in Amsterdam an increasing amount of land is reserved for private or collective commissioning projects. This process allows traditional developers to shift the construction risks to the end users. This practice grew out of Amsterdam's specific economic and social circumstances. During the last century, the role of project developers and other institutions slowly headed towards mass-produced supply-driven urban development, without proper insight into the demand. During the crisis, however, top-down organizations found themselves less equipped to build complete residential neighborhoods and to take the risks involved in these projects, and so other methods had to be found. The role of the municipality in this project was relatively small, but necessary. The piece of land was reserved and a competition was organized. The winning group was awarded the opportunity to purchase the land from the municipality. After the purchase of the land, the municipality was only involved during the enforcement of the normal planning permits concerning, for example, the environmental impact and the construction quality. Currently, the government is stimulating Collectively Commissioned projects (three houses or more), subsidizing professionals that take the role of process managers in the initial phase of a project, as well as providing an affordable loan for the plan development. Also, online information about regulation, finances, and project management for residents, professionals and government officials is provided. Recently the government has launched the 'self-building' team, a team of public officers responsible for selecting plots, providing information and supporting (aspiring) private or collective commissioning projects (http://www.amsterdam.nl/wonen-leefomgeving/bouwen-verbouwen/zelfbouw/).

Another top-down institution that played a pivotal role was the housing corporation, which provided some basic and special social services in the complex, such as the daycare center and the social housing. Moreover, they agreed upon the backup contract with the group of residents, in which they committed to buy remaining houses if full occupancy would not be reached. In this way they took over some of the risk that the residents as individuals couldn't take. According to Mr. de Haan, the initiator of Vrijburcht, 'housing corporations taking part in projects like this one is a practice that belongs to the period before the crisis [2008]'. Currently De Haan is exploring other methods to complete the financial picture and decrease the residents' risk for yet another collective commissioning project in Amsterdam.

By analyzing the case of Vrijburcht, we conclude that offering an equal chance for everyone to take part in shaping his or her community seems not only advisable, but commendable. However, some risks have already been identified. Vrijburcht's bottom-up development might seem the ultimate urban dream for what has been defined as collective individualism (Perry, 1949, 97). But critics say that bottom-up developments can become a smokescreen for privatization (Maskell, 2010) and that the process might have negative effects on 'the poor, the frail, the old, the sick and the dependent' (Coote, 2010). The case of Vrijburcht offers a counterexample to this argument. Thanks to the involvement of a housing association, basic services for disadvantaged citizens have been provided, opening up the community to a wide array of people. In conclusion, it might seem significant to underline that the involvement of a traditional top-down player (the housing association) created, to a certain extent, a collective urban development that might look less elitist than others.

Conclusions
Embedding Fluid Solutions

Written by Francesca Miazzo

National, provincial, local and sub-local levels of government all play a role in urban development, alongside housing corporations and project developers. However, since 2008, Amsterdam and other western cities have been seriously impacted by the financial crisis. Currently, the imploding housing market and decreasing land values are causing those institutions to implement austerity and cut down their budgets for (re)construction and demolition plans or community projects. The urban development motor that had seemed unstoppable is now entering a different era (Engelen & Musterd, 2010). This situation is illustrated by numerous vacant lots where projects have been put on hold, residential neighborhoods where physical investments have been delayed, and vacant office buildings with no alternative uses (Nieuwe Generatie, 2012).

Although we have analyzed just a few examples here, it is clear that citizens and communities are increasingly assessing their position in today's city by assuming more central and more empowered roles. We do not know what paradigm will come next, but thanks to the knowledge collected here, we can definitively try to understand how institutions are modifying their procedural routines, and we can try to foresee some possibilities for the future. We dedicate this chapter to traditional institutions, or 'top-downers', that are exploring the best ways to facilitate urban dwellers who wish to organize bottom-up initiatives. Whether they are seeking to improve or manage public space, or organize smaller activities with social, environmental and economic benefits, these project initiators are providing a valuable service to their cities. Community

gardens, temporary office spaces in vacant buildings and collectively commissioned architecture projects are populating Amsterdam's landscape, and urban dwellers, formerly only the 'clients' of urban development, are taking ownership of their urban surroundings.

The research journey brought us from the smallest community gardens to projects aiming to transform complete neighborhoods. Below is a short overview:

Cascoland Kolenkitbuurt is a project initiated by an international network of community artists, some of whom are also residents of the neighborhood. These artists specialize in urban interventions in public space galvanized through community participation and activation. The local government and the housing corporation organized a contest in the area of Amsterdam West, where the project is located. Cascoland's proposal was to act as an artistic process manager, aiming to gain an understanding of the needs and problems in the community, and to translate these, together with citizens, into interventions. The openness of the project, which did not include a precise set of outcomes but rather a working method, can be considered its strength. Openness was, however, the most difficult point for the sponsoring institutions to accept, because of their budget constraints and bureaucratic procedures. The project also offers other lessons. Besides facilitating the needs of the community, the initiators focused on empowering the community to keep the project going in the long term. In time, this approach will help the residents to initiate and manage their own projects without help. This makes the projects resilient and

Cascoland in itself redundant, so that they can move on and focus on new initiatives. Of course it remains questionable whether this aim is realistic, and whether future citizen's projects will in fact get initiated, communicated, and realized.

The project 'I Can Change the World with My Two Hands' is illustrative of another barrier that the institutional environment might erect, the one of distance between the living, breathing world of citizens and the systematized world of large institutions such as governments and corporations. Current urban development methods do not invite citizens to participate in structural, active roles. The language of policy and licensing is not very accessible to the average citizen. A common complaint from active residents is that their initiatives often meet with negative responses from large institutions, rather than a welcoming and inviting response that would result in a constructive collaboration. In the project 'I Can Change the World with My Two Hands' it was difficult for the initiator to convince the responsible stakeholders in the neighborhood of the value of the idea. However, as with other projects we analyzed, the initiator is an inhabitant of the neighborhood and aware of the needs and the deficiencies of the area. This aspect of embedment is, in the authors' opinion, key for the success of a bottom-up initiative. The focus on communication and the professional approach of the initiator may also have contributed to creating support among residents and possibly the institutions.

In the case of NoorderparkBar, the initiators spent hundreds of hours working on a voluntary basis to construct a bar for their local park. This labor structure of voluntarism appears in all the projects analyzed here. In the NoorderparkBar project, we also see the ability of a group of residents to understand the needs of the whole community, and the possibilities of representing those needs using different means. Local architects or artists, professionals who often work with people from different backgrounds, are more likely to work as initiators, to 'build a bridge' by speaking both languages: the one of the community and the one of institutions. The issue of language is relevant in the communication of this project, as a blog and other methods of online connectivity allowed team members to collect personal stories and provide unofficial ownership for its supporters.

In the collective commissioning project 'Vrijburcht,' a group of neighbors developed a housing complex with over 50 housing units, workspaces, a theatre and bar, and a small harbor with a sailing school for neighborhood kids. The initiative was proposed and realized by the neighbors themselves, with help from a few selected specialists that they hired. While in progress, this project took advantage of changing circumstances to expand its scope. From Vrijburcht we can learn that bottom-up projects do not have to limit themselves to the small-scale or temporary realm; instead, a wider and more comprehensive vision about development is often important to address wider socio-spatial and economic aspects. The issue of magnification of the process is what we consider a cornerstone in the institutional approach towards the bottom-up movement. In fact, the number of collective commissioning projects, in which constructions are realized with minimal investment from traditional institutions, is increasing.

In this research, we have deeply analyzed the process of creation and management for four different bottom-up initiatives over a time span of two to five years. Although there are some obvious points of success related to the motivation and background of the initiators, we also defined some other elements that we consider pivotal to the shifting perspective of the bottom-up actors. It seems that while institutions may be willing to work more with bottom-up players, they nonetheless have difficulties in understanding which programmatic actions to undertake. By pinpointing some specific issues, we seek to develop a set of strategies or recommendations. In the cases analyzed here, there are recognizable factors for success:

Embedment of the initiators in the local context

Openness about the final results

Voluntarism

Empowerment of the citizens to carry on projects in the long term

Language and communication of the project with the outside world and with institutions

Magnification to expand the impact of the initiative

Traditional top-downers are still looking for the best way to make use of these motivated communities. How can they share responsibility with active citizens, and how should this cooperation be structured?

In these final paragraphs, we will try to share the knowledge we collected and set forth some ideas.

Working with local communities is a difficult process. Through this small but in-depth analysis, we learned that citizens that are embedded in the local contexts tend to have a better understanding of the problems and needs of the whole community, compared to people who are not from the area (**Embedment**). We also saw that the community, together with the environment where it stands, is sometimes affected by small problematic issues (social, environmental, infrastructural etc.) that are not easy to recognize. In order to understand what a community needs and consequently to pinpoint the final solutions, the institutions should provide support (in kind, time, or resources) for open-ended and nonspecific processes (**Openness**). Another aspect is the incredible amount of voluntary work needed to implement bottom-up initiatives. Due to a general lack of funding, and a consequent lack of public services, in these cases citizens decided to overtake the role of the urban agent (**Voluntarism**). Citizens' initiatives can ultimately provide public services if they have a collective of individuals who will work for free. Institutions should define a set of circumstances to support and reward the work of these new urban agents whether they are of a social, environmental or practical nature. It is up to the institutions to bargain with the whole community to figure out how to support the start-up phase. According to our analysis, we discovered that no result should represent the final stage of the process. When institutions support the start-up phase of a bottom-up initiative, they should also define the conditions to transmit the management of the process to the citizens themselves (**Empowerment**). The long-term success of a bottom-up initiative is strongly related to this set of decisions: local residents that already have experience in working with people from different backgrounds, together with some practical knowledge in understanding the language of the institutions, are definitively the preferred individuals (or groups) to carry on communication and management activities (**Language**). Together with other local residents, these individuals understand the needs of the neighborhood and can define some programmatic actions to overcome and meet the requirements. If this first phase is successful, institutions can help to support, expand, or replicate the project (**Magnification**). Magnification of a bottom-up project might even create employment opportunities. By taking into consideration the above-mentioned aspects, traditional top-downers can start stimulating bottom-up initiatives, unveiling their urban, economic and social potential.

Together with local businesses and organizations, institutions are urged to recognize the potential of bottom-up developments, and support their proliferation through campaigns and programs. Institutions have the power and the authority to involve the whole community in the process of bottom-up development. What is important is sharing a common goal with a wider set of local actors and addressing every pivotal issue of bottom-up development (Embedment, Openness, Voluntarism, Empowerment, Language, and Magnification).

Bibliography

Annis, S. (1987) 'The Next World Bank? Financing Development from the Bottom Up'. Grassroots development, 11.

Arlt, P (2006) 'Urban Planning and Interim Use'. In: Haydn, F. & Temel, R. (eds.) Temporary Urban Spaces: Concepts for the Use of City Spaces. pp. 39-46. Basel: Birkhäuser.

Atkinson, R. & Eckardt, F. (2004) 'Urban policies in Europe: the Development of a New Conventional Wisdom'. In: Eckardt, F. & Kreisl, P. (eds.) City Images and Urban Regeneration. Frankfurt: Peter Lang.

Bianchini, V.F. & Landry, C. (1994) The Creative City.

Boelhouwer, P. (2002) 'Trends in Dutch Housing Policy and the Shifting Position of the Social Rented Sector'. Urban Studies. 39 (2). pp. 219-235.

Borowski, G. (1005) 'De geschiedenis van Amsterdam-Noord in vogelvlucht'. Studiekring 'De Meeuw'.

Boterman, W.R., Karsten, L. & Musterd, S. (2010) 'Gentrifiers Settling Down? Patterns and Trends of Residential Location of Middle-class Families in Amsterdam'. Housing Studies. 25 (5). pp. 693-714.

Campbell, K. (2011) 'Smart Urbanism: Making Massive Small Change'. Journal of Urban Regeneration and Renewal. 4 (4). pp. 304-311.

Conway, A-M. & Murphy L. (2013) Compendium for the Civic Economy: What Our Cities, Towns and Neighborhoods Can Learn from 25 Trailblazers. Amsterdam: Valiz/Trancity.

Coote, A. (2010) Cutting It: The 'Big Society' and the New Austerity. The new economics foundation.

Critchley, A.D.W., Bouma, S.A.D.J. & de Lange, S.P. (2011) Urban Agriculture in Amsterdam.

Cumberlidge, C. & Musgrave, L. (2007) Design and Landscape for People: New Approaches to Renewal. London: Thames & Hudson.

Dahles, H. (1998) 'Redefining Amsterdam as a tourist destination'. Annals of Tourism Research. 25 (1). pp. 55-69.

Deben, L., Heinemeyer, W.F. & Van Der Vaart, D. (eds.) (2000) Understanding Amsterdam: Essays on Economic Vitality, City Life and Urban Form. Het Spinhuis.

Derudder, Witlox & Catalano. (2003) 'Hierarchical Tendencies and Regional Patterns in the World City Network: a Global Urban Analysis of 234 Cities,' in: Regional Studies, 3.

Dieleman, F.M., Dijst, M.J. & Spit, T. (1999) 'Planning the Compact City: the Randstad Holland experience,' in: European Planning Studies, 7(5), pp. 605-621.

Domhardt, K.S. (2012). 'The Garden City Idea in The CIAM Discourse on Urbanism: A Path to Comprehensive Planning,' in Planning Perspectives, 27(2), pp. 173-197.

Engbersen, G., Snel, E. & Ypeij, A. (1998) 'De andere kant van het armoedebeleid. Beleid en realiteit in Amsterdam-Noord,' in: Effecten van Armoede.

Engelen, E. & Musterd, S. (2010) 'Amsterdam in Crisis: How the (Local) State Buffers and Suffers,' in: International Journal of Urban and Regional Research, 34(3), pp. 701-708.

Fainstein, S. (2010) The Just City. Cornell University Press.

Faludi, A. & Van der Valk, A. (1994) Rule and Order: Dutch Planning Doctrine in the Twentieth Century (Vol. 28). Springer.

Fraker, H. (2007) 'Where is the design discourse?' in: Places. 19(3), pp 61-63.

Feddes, F. (2012) A Millennium of Amsterdam - Spatial History of a Marvellous City. Bussum: Thoth,.

Gangloff, D. (1995) 'The Sustainable City,' in: American Forests 101 (5-6).

Graham, S. (2012) Temporary Uses as Tools for Urban Development. (Master's Thesis.) University of Manitoba

Haan, H. de & Tummers, L. (2007) 'Over(al)tijd: de achtergronden'. TU Delft, Department of Urbanism, Sept. 2007

Harvey, D. (1989) The Condition of Postmodernity (Vol. 14). Oxford: Blackwell.

Healey, P. (2007) Urban Complexity and Spatial Strategies: Towards a Relational Planning for Our Times. Taylor & Francis.

Hoekstra, J. (2003) 'Housing and the welfare state in the Netherlands: an application of Esping-Andersen's typology'. Housing, Theory and Society. 20 (2). pp. 58-71.

Hou, J., Johnson, J. & Lawson, L.J. (2009) Greening Cities, Growing Communities: Learning From Seattle's Urban Community Gardens. Landscape Architecture Foundation.

Howard, E. (1965) Garden Cities of To-morrow (Vol. 23). MIT Press.

Jacobs, J. (1970) The Economy of Cities.

Kempen, R. van & Priemus, H. (2002) 'Revolution in Social Housing in the Netherlands: Possible Effects of New Housing Policies'. Urban Studies. 39 (2). pp. 237-253.

Lydon, M. et al. (2010) Tactical Urbanism. (Vol. 1). Retrieved from http://streetplans.org/research_and_writing.php.

Marshall, R. (2004) '9 Waterfronts, Development and World Heritage Cities'. Waterfronts in Post-Industrial Cities. p. 137.

Musterd, S., Bontje, M. & Ostendorf, W. (2004) The Changing Role of Old and New Urban Centers.

Netherlands Institute for Spatial Research (2007) Particulier opdrachtgeverschap in de woningbouw [Private Initiatives in Housing Development], Den Haag/Rotterdam: NISR / NAi Publisher.

Oort, F.G. van (2004) Urban Growth and Innovation: Spatially Bounded Externalities in the Netherlands. Ashgate Publishing.

Perry, R.P. (1949) Characteristically American. New York: Alfred A. Kopf,.

Pinder, D. (2008) 'Urban Interventions: Art, Politics and Pedagogy'. International Journal of Urban and Regional Research. 32 (3). pp. 730-736.

Pinto, J.K. & Slevin, D.P. (1988) 'Critical factors in successful project implementation'. Engineering Management, IEEE Transactions. (1). pp. 22-27.

Poindexter, G.C. (1997) 'Collective Individualism: Deconstructing the Legal City'. University of Pennsylvania Law Review. 145 (3). pp. 607-664.

Priemus, H. (1997) 'Marketoriented Housing Policy: a Contradiction in Terms. Recent Dutch experiences'. International Journal of Urban and Regional Research. 21 (1). pp. 133-142.

Roebuck, K. (2011) Crowdfunding: High-Impact Strategies - What You Need to Know: Definitions, Adoptions, Impact, Benefits, Maturity, Vendors. Emereo Publishing Limited.

Salet, W.G., Thornley, A. & Kreukels, A. (eds.) (2003) Metropolitan Governance and Spatial Planning: Comparative Case Studies of European City-Regions. Taylor & Francis.

Schmelzkopf, K. (1995) 'Urban community gardens as contested space'. Geographical Review. pp. 364-381.

Schwarz, T. (2009) 'Ad hoc urbanism'. In: T. Schwarz & S. Rugare, Pop up city: Urban Infill Vol. 2 (pp. 49-60). Cleveland, OH: Cleveland Urban Design Collaborative.

Seelos, C. et al. (2011) 'The Embeddedness of Social Entrepreneurship: understanding variation across local communities'. Research in the Sociology of Organizations. 33. pp. 333-363.

Smit, J. & Nasr, J. (1992) 'Urban Agriculture for Sustainable Cities: Using Wastes and Idle Land and Water Bodies as Resources'. Environment and Urbanization. 4 (2). pp. 141-152.

Snellen, D.M. & Hilbers, H.D. (2007) 'Mobility and Congestion Impacts of Dutch VINEX Policy'. Tijdschrift voor economische en sociale geografie. 98 (3). pp. 398-406.

Suchar, C. (1993) 'The Jordaan: Community change and gentrification in Amsterdam'. Visual Sociology. 8 (1), pp. 41-51).

Uitermark, J. (2012) 'De Zelforganiserende Stad'. In: Essays Toekomst van de Stad. Den Haag: Raad voor de Leefomgeving en Infrastructuur.

Valanciene, L. & Jegeleviciute, S. (2013) 'Valuation of Crowdfunding: Benefits and Drawbacks'. Economics and Management. 18 (1). pp. 39-48.

Vries, S. de & Schöne, M.B. (2004) Volkstuinen in Amsterdam; de sociaal-culturele dimensie. Wageningen: Alterra, Research Instituut voor de Groene Ruimte

Wagenaar, M. (1998) Stedebouw en Burgerlijke Vrijheid. Bussum: Thoth.

Wagner, F. & Caves, R.W. (eds.) (2012) Community Livability: Issues and Approaches to Sustaining the Well-being of People and Communities. Routledge.

Wallerstein, N. (1992) 'Powerlessness, Empowerment and Health: Implications for Health Promotion Programs'. American Journal of Health Promotion. 6 (3). pp. 197-205.

Weickgenant, J. (2011) 'The Noord District's Hip Rebirth,' in: The Wall Street Journal, Europe Edition. Retrieved from http://online.wsj.com/article/SB10001424052702 30456950457640569006773 0056.html

http://www.ijburg.nl/

http://www.west.amsterdam.nl/diversen/nieuws/buurtnieuws-bos/algemeen-bos-lommer/staat-agenda-bos/

9789079203017 – draft translation: http://docs.china-europa forum.net/a_089collectively_commissioned_housing.pdf

http://www.denieuwegeneratie.nu/bankruptcity/

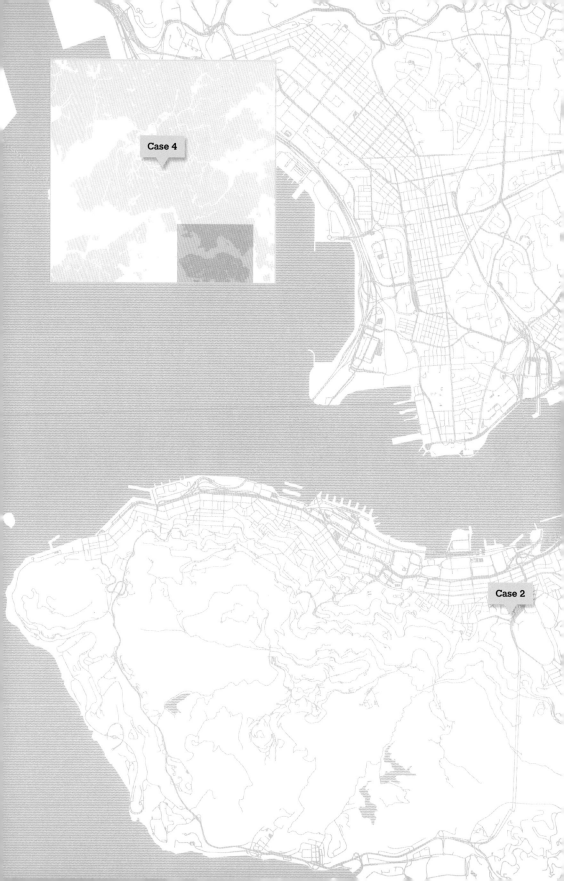

Case 3

Case 1 Case 2

Case 3

Hong Kong

Urban Renewal and Regeneration:
Connecting with the Community in Hong Kong

Written by Peter Cookson Smith

Every city is unique in some way, but Hong Kong is truly a special case with regard to its stage of urban development. The people of Hong Kong have never controlled its lands; it began its urban life as a colony of the British Empire, and when the British ceded their possession in 1997 it was with a promise of eventual Chinese rule. In the meantime, Government holds the land in trust, leasing parcels out for maximum profit with minimal regard for the delicate machinery of community building or sustainable practices such as historic preservation.

The beginnings of a civil society in this city must also be sensitive to its long-term relationship with the Mainland. As one graduate student wrote after a semester-long study of community planning, 'there are intrinsic uncertainties originating from the 'One Country, Two Systems' political arrangement after 1997 whereby the development of Hong Kong into a democratic society cannot necessarily be assured, [therefore we can only recommend guiding principles] and the actual success of the planning system to a great extent depends on the future development of Mainland China.' (Chan, 1990, 74).

Current developments in Hong Kong are encouraging, in that public administrators have begun to listen to their seven million constituents more and more. However, while Government does increasingly recognize the need for community engagement, the process is moving slowly and is still in its early stages. Government agencies are only just learning that they must reflect public opinions, reconciling them and taking them into account when making planning decisions. This will help citizens to shed past frustration with the process and become more truly engaged. In this way citizen participation can offer a platform for simple and open communication, rather than the more dramatic but arguably less effective modes of conflict and protest.

Hong Kong is not, after all, defined only by its political system and its particular place in a historical continuum. It is also unique in its form: an astonishing vertical topography of buildings and mountains, bounded by the ocean and navigated through a highly developed overlay of interwoven pedestrian walkways that have led some to call it 'a city without ground'. In a sense this city, like all cities, exists in four dimensions: the three spatial directions, plus the fourth element of time. Hong Kong's rich and storied history, and its past and future links to widely disparate cultures, all inform the daily experiences of its residents. When thinking about any city we must remember the importance of the city's identity, variety and texture that participatory planning aims to engender and preserve.

Current challenges
Contemporary urban issues in Hong Kong are multi-facetted, and most urban development initiatives have an almost immediate impact on large numbers of people. For the past twenty-five years, both the new towns and comprehensive redevelopment programs have been responsible for major shifts in population involving different degrees of dislocation. As priorities change and the emphasis shifts to the physical and economic regeneration of the city, particularly its public realm, it becomes increasingly clear that planning

and large-scale urban renewal initiatives should no longer be applied through top-down processes, but need to be carefully constructed through an interactive process that is more responsive to community needs and aspirations. This should enable those who might be potentially affected by development to contribute to the process in some way. It also needs to be acknowledged that in every community there exists a wealth of knowledge, energy and creativity that can be tapped into. It is of fundamental importance for the future of Hong Kong that the community becomes more effectively involved in urban regeneration, as an equal partner. This is central to matters of urban policy and procedures wherever planning is carried out. The first step might be to give more credence to the social workings of the city and put the process of regeneration on a par with the product.

'Owning the City' is a bold and rather optimistic term – a hopeful idea. In fact, if we actually owned the city, in Hong Kong this might be translated into a very necessary reason for community responsibility. Realistically in Hong Kong however we don't own the city. Government owns all the land and it is a valuable commodity. It has historically sold it at colossal prices on leases that last until 2047, which is the projected end date of the current interim 'One Country, Two Systems' policy. This essentially means a unique constitutional principle whereby Hong Kong can still continue to have its own political, legal, economic and financial systems, including external relations with foreign countries, while remaining under the sovereignty of the People's Republic of China. In the urban area, which is where we have our older well-established communities,

our mixed-use environments, and where we used to have a great many heritage buildings, all land is zoned, and every site technically has a development value set out in the Buildings Ordinance based on plot ratio and site coverage. Over the years, these things combined have actively incentivized redevelopment rather than regeneration, essentially skewing our planning, urban renewal and urban design processes towards financial objectives and land management, and of course it has led to, some might say necessitated, a generally top-down approach to planning which still remains in place. This is a shaky basis for community practice, and implies that environmental betterment is based almost solely on development i.e. monetary value, rather than community value.

We have to be honest with ourselves on the subject, and admit at the outset that, as yet, we don't have a fully developed culture of community planning in Hong Kong. There are several challenges specific to this city that have prevented easy realization of the many opportunities inherent in shaping a comprehensive approach to urban regeneration. First, our political system has had to evolve over the last fifteen years since the handover that ended British colonial rule. Under the current system, Government has to arm itself with a measure of community support to get proposals through the system. However the consultation process remains ill-defined and time-consuming, and can generate an overwhelming amount of information. In the end, in several high-profile cases, decisions have been seen to be predetermined, leading to frustration among the citizens who participated in the process and offered feedback.

We have, as a result of 150 years of top-down or 'bureaucratic' thinking, ended up with a highly expedient and engineered city, where even our historical street matrices lying within older inner districts – the foci of community and visitor attraction precisely because of their flexibility, vitality, mixed use and relatively cheap accommodation – can be bulldozed to exploit their redevelopment potential taking away valuable areas of contrast and heritage, but sweeping away the sense of community as well.

All too often, redevelopment is mistaken for regeneration, as it clearly is when the main underlying purpose is to maximize an area's development potential through our prevailing institutional mechanisms. However, there are signs that we are starting to acknowledge this. For example, it is perhaps no coincidence that the 'We Own the City' symposium was hosted by the Energizing Kowloon East Office, which has been set up to oversee the largest-ever regeneration area in the city.

Looking forward, we must acknowledge that the political will for genuine community involvement doesn't come about easily. Some would say that it is not in the cultural DNA of our community, given its past as a colonial outpost and its indeterminate future as a Special Administrative Region of the Mainland. We all need to help Hong Kong to progress towards a more mature system of government that might encourage and activate civil society. Mechanisms for genuine public involvement in Hong Kong's planning will only emerge slowly, but when they do they can gather momentum very quickly. People generally know what is best for their community and they will oppose

what is not. Studies in the USA and Europe clearly indicate that local communities, whatever their size, can ably identify opportunities through community based planning initiatives. This entails networks of bodies – public, private, voluntary, that share some common concern and can work together on common initiatives for the good of the city.

The case for community planning
Currently in Hong Kong there is a growing demand for greater citizen involvement in the planning and development of the city. This is at least partly the result of public antipathy towards what is increasingly perceived as overly expedient development processes dictated primarily by the priorities and values associated with engineering infrastructure and highways and, in terms of urban renewal, by the private development sector. The planning process itself clearly needs to provide more opportunities for community groups, professional bodies and other representative organizations to be given an early opportunity to contribute ideas on ways in which the city should be developed. This should prove no impediment, either to government or the Town Planning Board, in pursuing the plan preparation process.

Urban design is essentially an interdisciplinary activity and, even within an extremely high-density city with enormously high land values, there is a need to reflect increasing levels of planning concern through working forums where specialists and key stakeholders, and the priorities and insights these represent, can be introduced into mainstream planning. In this process, Urban Design Assistance Teams (UDATs) may have a significant role to play in teasing out issues and using design devices to stimulate vision, stitching together three-dimensional aspects of the built environment and courses of action as they emerge from various process planning sessions, action planning events, interactive exhibitions and formal consultations. A fundamental objective of this process is to ensure an increase in the sense of community belonging, responsibility and civic pride as part of a 'Better City' program directed towards improving the overall quality of life. Whilst the accepted urban design process can come up with a wealth of ideas, the challenge is to transfer the techniques to the mainstream planning process as a result of interdisciplinary and community liaison.

The broad objective is to achieve a vision for the city and its various parts based on public awareness that cannot be obtained in any other way. This would provide a mechanism to identify complex development issues and goals, foster a consensus among different interest groups and act as a catalyst for action. Innovations to the planning process would need to be introduced carefully, and there are signs that Government's own process is becoming more responsive to the need to consult with the public, together with various professional and interest groups and Legislative Council members, so as to build up a consensus before actually submitting firm plans to the spectrum of bodies charged with their approval. What is now needed are means to make the process less abstract and distant in the minds of the community, and instead to place their concerns firmly on the main agenda.

The Urban Task Force that reported on urban regeneration in the UK concluded that it was essential to promote 'neighborhood management which gives local people a stake in the decision-making process'. In this sense 'change management' is needed in Hong Kong to incorporate environmental and social factors into the decision-making process in terms of policies, plans, indicators, programs and institutions within an identified and agreed vision. This implies a strengthening of the existing institutional framework with respect to administrative procedures, and a complementary participation and communication program. It also requires a necessary change in the role of professionals working in the city-building process from 'management' to 'facilitation'.

In terms of community planning it is likely that the benefits are commensurate with the inputs. The fostering of community participation and representation will help to improve the renewal process itself and enable better facilitation by authorities and professional representatives, i.e. those who experience change and those who help to bring it about. The approach should be to ensure maximum involvement by the key players according to clearly stated aims. Sufficient resources need to be allocated and specialists should assist in facilitating community involvement and training. This is particularly important as there needs to be a careful 'balancing' role to reconcile the views of different stakeholders, geared to assisting the renewal program to improve the living standards and quality of life for the community.

Defining community
Defining what we mean by 'community' can be a problem in Hong Kong because of its massive density and lack of urban

differentiation. How do we define ourselves in terms of a network of bodies who share common concerns and who can work together on common initiatives? The UK Department of the Environment, Transport and Regions (DETR) criteria for community definition are based on a number of characteristics – beliefs, skills, economic position, personal attributes, relationship of local services and identification with place. Community identity will therefore vary in relation to the composition of key characteristics. In forming a basis for regeneration partnerships there need to be factors within the community that act to bind people together with a combined sense of belonging and supportive relationships. This is likely to be most successful if local communities are prepared, in advance of regeneration initiatives, through participation and action group programs related to planning. Whilst the specific nature and context is different from that of the UK, the basic issues still aim to bring about environmental improvement, to extend social and economic opportunities, to gain access to better housing, and to avoid discrimination against particular deprived groups.

The definition of 'community' in a workable sense must be recognizable and accepted by the people who live in the area in question. One can conveniently define a 'target area' population for example, but a community would be unlikely to fit such a concise spatial definition, which is only a physical abstraction unrelated to urban life. In this sense the term 'community' must reflect a number of different factors, not all of which are necessarily related. These include relationships to 'place', provision of local services, economic position,

skills and capabilities, beliefs in terms of political, cultural or religious background, and personal characteristics. Community involvement in planning projects can take any of five specific roles. Community members can be the beneficiaries and users of services; they can be long-term partners in the regeneration process; they can be a source of community activity; representatives of local opinion; or they can help in delivering parts of a program.

Uncertainty as to the way forward
In Hong Kong today there is much hesitation and confusion as to how to involve the local community in any planning situation. The Land Development Corporation holds public meetings, although these are mainly geared to meeting the concerns of affected residents and demands for compensation. Government presents planning proposals to District Boards, but these are not genuine public forums nor are members able to realistically participate in major planning decisions. Fundamental to future improvements must be the notion that neither planning nor urban design are ends in themselves, but frameworks and stimuli for a range of uses and mix of functions. Economic conditions and priorities should not be so enshrined within large-scale development proposals that they are frozen at one point in time. Conditions for change, variation and diversity need to be encouraged and this implies a more incremental process of development and renewal. This in turn can assist and possibly instigate local rejuvenation and revitalization with a sense of purpose. There is therefore a need for some practical guidance on the means to improve both the quantity and quality of public involvement, and the need to incorporate

a common 'language' relating to different aspects of participation. We hope that the following case studies can provide a baseline for future work.

Hong Kong case studies

This chapter will focus on case studies from Hong Kong with a particular emphasis on how they fit into the city's political and institutional systems, in recognition of the fact that Hong Kong's context is quite specific. It reflects the fact that DIY urbanism in Hong Kong tends to take the form of larger-scale conceptual studies or, at the other end of the scale, very small interventions. In many cases projects or studies have been commissioned by Government or a Government–related institution, which brings into question the relationship between the commissioning body itself, the stakeholders, and the planners or designers as mediators. Hong Kong's Government is clearly trying to better address the need for public forums, while on the flip side members of the public – including several of the groups profiled in the case studies – are demanding more opportunities for real inclusion.

Though diverse in scale and form, these projects demonstrate a unified sense of optimism. Through examination of this work it becomes clear that all residents, whether they are Government representatives, designers, academics or citizens, want the best for their city. Each of the following case studies seeks to illustrate how traditionally bureaucratic, 'top-down' organizations – like architecture firms or Government agencies – are recognizing the benefits of grassroots urbanism, and how others can learn from their methodologies.

Energizing Kowloon East Office (EKEO) is a multidisciplinary office under the Development Bureau of Hong Kong's Government. It is a multidisciplinary office that seeks to engage public support for evolving district-planning schemes. Their 'Fly the Flyover Operation' is just one example of many programs aimed at creating new interactions between local citizens and their urban environments.

The University of Hong Kong's Community Project Workshop steps outside the circumscribed bounds of the teaching curriculum to foster intergenerational and interdisciplinary ways of working.

Hong Kong's Housing Authority's new initiatives reflect the way in which public sector clients are becoming more responsive to their constituents, and evolving new initiatives to further this goal at each stage of design and implementation.

Choi Yuen Village illustrates how a simple participatory approach can foster a stronger sense of residential community.

Case 1
Energizing Kowloon East Office (EKEO):
Bridging the Urban Planning Gap

Text courtesy of the
Energizing Kowloon East Office

Introduction
For many years, the visitors' introduction to Hong
Kong was a vertiginous drop over a jumbled urban
landscape to a runway jutting out into open water;
this was the (in)famous approach to the former Kai
Tak airport. Since the airport moved to a new location
in 1998, this part of the city has been under intense
review as its future is discussed.

Kowloon East (KE) is an area comprising the former
airport as well as Kwun Tong and Kowloon Bay
Business Areas. The airport is not the only part
of the neighborhood that has changed: this area
witnessed the rapid growth of an important industrial
base in the heyday of Hong Kong's manufacturing
industry, creating hundreds of thousands of jobs and

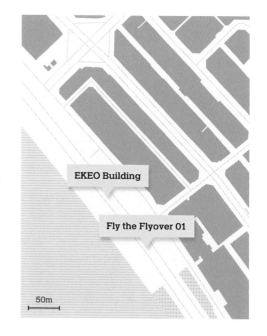

EKEO Building

Fly the Flyover 01

50m

Top
Percussion performance at
the opening ceremony of
Fly the Flyover 01

Bottom
Fly the Flyover 01's location
before development

Next spread
Fly the Flyover 01's location
after development

propelling Hong Kong's prosperity in the decades after the 1950s. However, following the relocation of the airport and the overall loss of manufacturing jobs to the Mainland in the 1990s, Kowloon East has lost some of its past vibrancy, leaving an established, dense population and a huge stock of underutilized industrial buildings. Recent proposals for the district's public areas include a new Cruise Terminal and transport hubs, canal-side pedestrian walkways along the Kwun Tong Promenade, waterfront parks, and retail centers.

Policy background: creating a new central business district for Hong Kong

While many industrial activities have moved away from Kowloon East to Mainland China, Hong Kong's economy has remained strong. The city's central location and established industries continue to attract large numbers of financial and service sector jobs, and many multi-national companies still locate here. However the traditional Central Business District (CBD) on Hong Kong Island – long the center for the banking industry – has become too cramped and can no longer meet the demand for quality office spaces. Private developers have begun to relocate their head offices away from Central to Kowloon East in a search for alternative high-grade office buildings and retail centers.

The Hong Kong 2030: Planning Vision and Strategy (The HK2030 Study), which was completed by the Government in October 2007, provides a long-term planning strategy for Hong Kong's future development and the necessary provision of strategic infrastructure. One of the main emphases in the HK2030 Study was the importance of maintaining a steady and adequate

supply of prime office spaces. As recommended in the Study, the Government will continue to consolidate and enhance the existing CBD, while exploring new quality office nodes in other parts of the city.

In the meantime, China's legislature, the National People's Congress, endorsed the country's 12th Five-Year Plan on 14 March 2011, giving support to Hong Kong's position as a financial and international asset management center on a global scale. Echoing China's top legislature on national economic and social development, the local government also announced an integrated approach in its 2011-12 Policy Address to expedite the transformation of KE into an attractive alternative CBD.

Energizing Kowloon East Office (EKEO)

Since the Policy Address announcement in 2011, there has been overwhelming support

from almost all quarters in society to execute the Government's blueprint with determination, speed and extensive public engagement to improve KE's urban development and connectivity as CBD2. To capitalize upon the opportunity to kick start transformation of KE in light of the general support of the community, a team was set up in the Development Bureau to prepare for the establishment of an Energizing Kowloon East Office (EKEO), intended to implement the Government's initiatives and embark on the immediate tasks pertaining to the urban transformation of KE. This multi-disciplinary office was inaugurated on 7 June 2012 to steer, supervise, oversee and monitor the development of the district with a view to facilitating its transformation into another premier CBD of Hong Kong. EKEO is a pioneer in applying the 'place-making' approach, which is an integrated strategy for planning, design,

implementation, management and community engagement with the end goal of creating quality public spaces for the enjoyment of the public and improvement of the pedestrian environment. With the clear vision to convert KE into another premier CBD, EKEO's main duties are to:

Explore options for strategic refinement of the existing Outline Zoning Plans which are the statutory framework governing the urban planning structure of Hong Kong.

Engage community stakeholders and the public to promote KE to local and overseas users and developers.

Provide support to land development proposals that are conducive to private sector development for transforming KE.

Coordinate Government's efforts and resources for area improvement works.

The setting up of the EKEO is worth studying, especially in the context of literary review and debates on institutional versus community planning theory and practice. For instance, Niraj Verma's Institutions and Planning (2007) outlines that there has been an ongoing dichotomy at work in various institutional planning models. The 'nonpartisan' model described by Michael B. Teitz in the chapter 'Planning and the New Institutionalisms' (Teitz, 2007) questions how to regulate development to support larger community interests while also examining how the placement of the planning function within local government structure shapes our city. While analyzing different approaches in planning theory, Teitz argued that most of the legal framework with regards to zoning and sub-division control has been largely affected by the legal and institutional structure that defines its social role and power. Planning, like other forms of governmental activities in a capitalist society, simply reflected the interest of the dominant class and its institutional structures were inherently oppressive (Verma, 2007).

These kinds of readings were useful when studying how a new office like EKEO could mediate between its dual responsibilities: performing the tasks set by the formal institutional framework, while also maintaining

responsiveness to public interest. EKEO seeks to implement district policy comprehensively while reflecting community stakeholders' choices and decisions.

**Community approach of EKEO:
public engagement**
EKEO's team aspires to exercise participatory urban planning by proactively carrying out community engagement sessions, urban improvement workshops, and place-making projects. The goal is to establish an administrative relationship with the public to facilitate implementation of both private and public sector projects in accord with the overall official planning and political strategy under the Development Bureau. By meeting district stakeholders on a regular basis, EKEO is able to consult various community groups, professional institutions, and District Councils to understand public interests through an 'appreciative planning approach' – an approach in urban planning which is based on 'mutual respect, trust, and care-based action' (Bushe and Pitman, 1991). At its best, appreciative planning can be a multi-faceted process that unites social interaction and social learning to enable cities and professionals to share the work of problem solving and decision making – for the benefit of their community. Although the cultural and ethnic mix of the district of Kwun Tong is rather homogeneous, comprising mostly 96.7% Chinese versus 3.3% non-ethnic Chinese population (Census and Statistics Department, 2011), the population still needs to implement a pluralistic view on multiple issues related to city planning. When confronting real conflicting issues, an appreciative planning approach avoids the one-way, 'scientific' problem solving process common to top-down bureaucracies (Ameyaw & Fred, 1999). Instead, the engagement happens through networking, communication, and dialogue with community groups.

In the process of place-making since 2012, EKEO has been in active dialogue with the community and operators to identify and implement measures on traffic improvement, pedestrian linkage provision, and street vibrancy enhancement. On-going activities have sought to build a pedestrian-friendly environment with attractive streetscape and urban greening. Physical environments where people work, do business, walk, stay and play have become the palette where EKEO injects new elements to achieve a community character. As Kendig and Keast

explained in <u>Community Character</u> (2001), the design of a community has positive effects on the social, economic, environmental, cultural and other physical elements that create the character of a neighborhood. EKEO's overall community approach of place-making can promote quality urban design and innovative architecture, create vibrant public space, bring people to the waterfront, and invite arts and culture to city life.

Fly the Flyover Operation
One of the most remarkable community events organized by EKEO has been the Fly the Flyover Operation. In Hong Kong's high-density urban environment, roads are among the most heavily used in the world, with over 640,000 vehicles on 2,090 kilometers, together with 1,321 flyovers and 1,182 footbridges and subways (source: Hong Kong Highways Department, 2012). While heavy traffic zooms at high speed on the interlinking concrete flyover structures, most of the spaces below the flyovers are left idle, without any human activities. There are strict rules against occupation by the homeless, illegal graffiti or any form of public utilization below these bridges. EKEO was inspired by ideas from community workshop participants that suggested possible uses for the fenced-off land underneath the Kwun Tong Bypass. In the summer of 2012, a brainstorming session was organized by EKEO together with local art and cultural groups to formulate ideas on how to utilize spaces under the flyover. Some art groups suggested the site be a place for 'art-jamming', public displays, exhibitions and

so on. Others called for more access and a place for public forums and debates. EKEO embraced these ideas and put them into action in 2013, in the form of a project entitled 'Fly the Flyover Operation 01'. Both Kwun Tong District Council and the Harbourfront Commission supported this idea and permitted early implementation as a pilot project for other flyovers in Hong Kong. Since 2013, 'Fly the Flyover 01' has kicked off a series of projects for future 'Fly the Flyover Operations' with the aim to open up the fenced-off lands underneath the Kwun Tong Bypass for public enjoyment. 'Fly the Flyover 01' became a new informal art and cultural venue built for music, art and cultural events or exhibitions. For the future, a number of place-making events have been arranged by the local youth organizations, professional institutions, cultural groups, rock music bands and skateboard groups. The feedback from the public has been positive, with activity participants leaving comments such as,

66 Please let me thank EKEO for putting all the people who care about Kowloon East together for such a vivid, inspiring yet mutually inspiring discussion this evening … Looking forward to seeing more small but beautiful events from EKEO in the near future. **99**

Others used social media to express their reactions:

Left
Dancers at the opening
ceremony of Fly the Flyover 01

Right
Playful Thursday@Tsun Yip Street
– Veggie | Arts Jamboree

❝ Being a resident of Kwun Tong, I am very
pleased to see the EKEO seems to be taking
a progressive approach to the district's
revitalization. I am passionate about public
space, and have cofounded a group, The
Pocket Parks Collective, to engage the
community through fun events which make
creative use of public space, and social
furniture. ❞

(source: The Pocket
Parks Collective @
www.facebook.com/
ThePocketParksCollective
(downloaded December 2012)

**Lessons learned: an urban incubator for
community activities**
A strong community network has always been in
existence in Kwun Tong, though it went under-
recognized. The EKEO, with the resources of a
government office, has been able to tap into this
network and formalize its wish lists by meshing them
with overall planning goals. 'Fly the Flyover Operation'
was one example of an urban activity that injected
vibrancy into Kwun Tong's vacant plots of land for
uses beneficial to the community; at the same time it
supported Government goals of branding KE
as a place of diversity and opportunities.

The case study showcases the innovative idea of
putting EKEO into place as an urban incubator within
a district planned for further development. Neighbors
who have interacted with EKEO have offered great
advice to EKEO such as:

❝ As a concerned citizen, born and raised
in Kowloon East – the zone with highest
population density in Hong Kong – I see
stories and endless cultures that lie within
people's day-to-day lives. I sincerely hope
EKEO is willing to find, to listen and to be
really open to the emotional content, not
anger, from the people we met today. The
panel discussion today shall be a start of this
long and winding road. ❞

The ownership of the city, though it may not be
physically realized through possession or financial
gain, can yet be realized through active engagement.
Here in Kowloon East, stakeholders have helped to
create an organic urban transformation as it moves
from its old industrial legacy to its new role as an
energetic and vibrant business district. As it develops,
the district will be enriched by public programs co-
organized by EKEO and local groups. Because its
team understands the sense of this place and has
discovered the potential of hidden public spaces in
the district, EKEO is a good example of the value of
communal place-making and the benefit of bringing
diversity and vitality to foster cooperation
of stakeholders in the community.

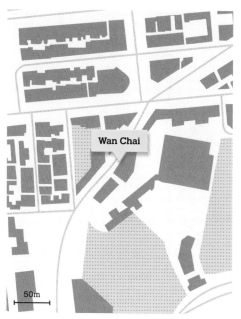

Wan Chai

50m

Kwun Tong

50m

Case 2
Institutional Incubator for Community
Outreach – The Community Project
Workshop at the University of Hong Kong

Written by Tris Kee

As Niraj Verma wrote in his book Institutions and Planning (2007), prevailing city planning theory that comes under the relationship of planning and institutions has long been characterized by debates and dichotomies. The vast literature on the inquiry of new institutionalism in planning is bursting into economics, political sciences and other disciplines (Verma, 2007). The traditional view is that within its top-heavy structures, planning brings together such diverse topics as efficient administration, social reform, and civic design. 'Institutions such as government or market provide the framework within which planning operates' (Verma, 2007). The demands of this knowledge base produced the professionalized planning practices common today (Alexander, 1992). Meanwhile, academic institutions such as universities are playing a more significant

role in exercising professional expertise in the practice. More and more universities have begun curriculum reforms that promote more interaction with the community. Research is no longer confined into library-based pure research; there is a wider audience among the general public that can benefit from scholarly output.

At the University of Hong Kong, there has long been a strong commitment to knowledge exchange. The University sees community engagement as a two-way process through which academic research can contribute to regional and global development. Seeing the added values both in terms of social impact and from the wider application of academic expertise, knowledge exchange has become the third 'core pillar' in the core missions of the University, alongside teaching and research. Prior to establishing any formal knowledge exchange unit in the University of Hong Kong, colleagues from the Faculty of Architecture had already been active in public life through exhibitions, lectures, charity work and other activities. In 2009, the Faculty set up the Community Project Workshop, dedicated to involving academic staff and students in community outreach. Acting as

Top and bottom
The urban setting of Kwun Tong Harbourfront is a study area for community planning research propositions by CPW

the institutional incubator for research and knowledge exchange, the workshop aspires to provide cross-disciplinary consultancy utilizing expertise from the fields of Architecture, Urban Planning, Urban Design, Landscape, Conservation, Real Estate and Construction. This chapter looks at how research and projects from the Community Project Workshop are formulated and how they have benefitted various sectors of the city using urban planning strategies with an emphasis on bottom-up participatory design.

Kwun Tong District Aspiration Study

The district of Kowloon East is currently being reimagined, as the enormous site of the former Kai Tak airport is being repurposed and its adjacent neighborhoods are transitioning from light industrial areas to residential and business districts. The opening up of such a large site in a central location presents a tremendous opportunity, and Government officials have already issued a Kai Tak redevelopment plan and founded the interdisciplinary Energizing Kowloon East Office (EKEO) to work with the public on achieving these goals.

Of necessity, the district of Kwun Tong – immediately to the east of the former airport – is rapidly evolving. The Community Project Workshop was invited to conduct an Urban Renewal District Aspirations Study to investigate potential impacts and solutions for Kwun Tong's issues: a lack of open space, traffic congestion, and the changes wrought by gentrification. The official Kai Tak Redevelopment Plan has produced proposals for the former airport's runway, in which its long stretches of waterfront will be turned into a cruise terminal with hotels and retail. Local Kwun Tong residents may feel some trepidation in the face of these massive changes, but ideally they will see the benefits of the linkages that will be created by new cruise terminal services, bridges over the Kwun Tong Typhoon Shelter, and improved pedestrian pathways.

In order to evaluate the impact of the proposed changes to this district, the research team explored four major strategies related to urban renewal: redevelopment, rehabilitation, preservation, and revitalization. The study undertaken by the Community Project Workshop was intended to illuminate the special characteristics of the district and its various community assets – material and cultural – and to provide a conceptual framework for a focused

strategy that will improve the environment and quality of living in the district.

To get started, team members assessed the district's existing conditions by making site visits, interviewing stakeholders, studying economic and demographic data as well as land use guidelines, and examining the fabric of the built environment including historic buildings, infrastructure and transport networks. They found that Kwun Tong was facing a unique set of circumstances. As one of the first satellite towns in Hong Kong, Kwun Tong was a thousand-acre development intended to ease crowded living conditions. After the Second World War it became a site for industry along with workers' public housing estates, but today, due to a decrease in local manufacturing, many of Kwun Tong's industrial buildings are vacant or have been converted into other uses. Over the past decade the Town Planning Committee has begun to revise zoning to enable a gradual focus on business activities for urban renewal. The Kwun Tong City Centre Redevelopment Project is the largest such project in the history of Hong Kong, converting the Harbourfront industrial area into a commercial zone and a number of old factory buildings into office buildings, shopping arcades and hotels.

Armed with the knowledge of existing conditions and changes in urban morphology already in place, the team's next step was to identify local residents' development needs and goals by gathering information through a survey questionnaire and simultaneously doing original analysis. A number of public community workshops were held as the culmination of this stage, the first of several formalized opportunities for citizen engagement. In the end, all the information and proposals were integrated into a development concept plan with design recommendations, which was unveiled at a second-stage community participatory design workshop where feedback was again solicited and incorporated.

With a clear vision of working for the community and with the community, the design ideas were a result of multiple public activities, surveys, and design workshops with professional team members' input on architectural and planning perspectives. Many local residents shared their concerns about accessibility and connectivity in the neighborhood, and so the proposals included linking the district's

Left
Community planning can raise
awareness and support the
formulation of common objectives
and values that might differ from
current public policy

Eastern and Western cores; creating a longitudinal park network with trails, playgrounds, and waterfront access along the entire promenade in order to link a few districts; rebranding formerly desolate canals as market areas and possibly even providing aquatic recreation opportunities; and rethinking industrial buildings as residential 'loft' spaces. Area residents and government officials responded positively to these proposals, and change has already begun to reshape Kwun Tong: the Public Cargo Working Area was closed in the end of 2011 to make way for Kwun Tong Waterfront Promenade Phase II, which is in progress, along with the redevelopment of Kwun Tong's town center. For the foreseeable future, this will be the most rapidly evolving neighborhood in Hong Kong.

Wan Chai Park Study
Hong Kong is an incredibly dense city, and yet because of its topography – particularly on Hong Kong Island – glimpses of nature are woven into the urban fabric. The forested slopes of Victoria Peak loom over the towers of the Central Business District, but even in the flatter reclaimed districts, green spaces offer breathing space to residents whose apartments are small, cluttered, and usually shared with other family members.

In 2010, the District Council of Wan Chai, a dense and evolving neighborhood on the north side of the island, commissioned the Community Project Workshop to research and analyze the existing park and open space system of the area. Though the district has 74 parks, they vary widely in terms of location, size, facilities, and patterns of use. Some are very popular, while some are rarely visited or even unknown to the public. As Jane Jacobs wrote, 'conventionally, neighborhood parks or parklike open spaces are considered boons conferred on the deprived populations of cities. Let us turn this thought around, and consider city parks deprived places that need the boon of life and appreciation conferred on them. This is more nearly in accord with reality, for people do confer use on parks and make them successes – or else withhold use and doom parks to rejection and failure.' (Jacobs, [1961] 1993, 116). Students and professionals from Hong Kong University's Community Project Workshop spent hours at all times of day surveying park users in representative locations in order to determine how these spaces could be improved.

Those surveyed came from all walks of life – from neighborhood housewives to immigrant workers and office staff – and each had a unique story to tell about how these places could and should be used. The public questionnaire method was chosen as a two-way mode of communication: while it facilitated the gathering of information for the project team, it also signified to park users that the District Council had an interest in citizens' opinions and desires. Moreover, filling out the questionnaire functioned as a spark to inspiration, giving people the opportunity to think deeply about their own living environments and public spaces.

After studying the results of the questionnaires and mapping and analyzing the existing park system in detail, the CPW project team collaborated to come up with several proposals that would serve the needs of Wan Chai's changing demographics on the macro scale, as well as the stated desires of the individuals interviewed. Necessary improvements included providing better facilities for specific user groups such as children, older people, and dog owners, while also enriching the environment to attract more people. CPW came up with four typological recommendations aimed at creating a better balance of provisions to match the needs of the population in the district as it has evolved up to now: a park for elderly users, a low-carbon park, a pets' park and a sensory park that would include various materials for physical engagement.

The projects' benefit to the community was broad. The survey raised awareness in the district, and data collected will be used in the future to provide direction for improvements. The design proposals appeared in a report that was made available to the public along with the results of the survey, with the hope of inspiring knowledge about the potential of Wan Chai's – and Hong Kong's – public spaces. Follow-up on the project has been productive. The local district council has hired an architect and design team, and commissioned the building of several pilot parks in the district.

Fostering multi-disciplinary collaboration with the community
As befits its place within the larger university, CPW is also engaged in an educational role. In 2012-2013, the team collaborated with teachers and specialists across the region to produce a teaching

kit for secondary-school students. Funded by the Government, the teaching kits were intended to introduce design topics within curricula across all topics, from science to arts to liberal studies. Clearly, the Government thinks it worthwhile to train a new generation to become better consumers of architecture and urban spaces. CPW has also undertaken several studies of architectural education methods, participatory planning as a teaching tool, and the impacts of volunteering in urban community-service projects similar to Habitat for Humanity – a nonprofit organization building simple and affordable housing in partnership with people in need. The Workshop has engaged district youth representatives in design charrettes, worked with underprivileged youth groups to create sustainability design proposals, and has repeatedly brought together groups of all ages to participate in its public events.

Though few of these initiatives have risen directly out of a demand from the community, the Workshop itself is a kind of mediator between the institutions of Government and higher learning, and the residents, students, and small local business owners. The successful implementation of the Wan Chai park concepts illustrates how a professional organizational structure can work to create affordable, vibrant, socially cohesive and sustainable urban projects. Future CPW projects will continue to foster multi-disciplinary collaboration with the community and impact the evolution of the city: currently the team is undertaking a study on how participatory planning can play a role in the development of public transport systems. However, the path from research to practice in Hong Kong can be long and complicated. The mechanisms controlling building and urban development are rather stringent and hierarchical as a result of the Government's social, political and

organizational structure, which does not always integrate or respond to proposals from members of the public.

Hong Kong is still struggling to adopt a mindset in which community participatory design could result in concrete change. Unfortunately, proposals often remain at the concept stage without ever being implemented, and this has been the case with many of CPW's studies. For now, organizations like this can best serve by acting as mediators, with the goal of opening up discussion and getting the public used to engaging with these issues. CPW continues to be inspired by examples where citizens achieve social cohesion and create a better living environment by means of small-scale architectural initiatives that nonetheless respected the city's planning framework. Despite heavy administrative duties and bureaucratic procedures, there are many positives to CPW's peculiar position as mediator. With administrative and financial support from the university, as well as repeat contract research projects from satisfied Government departments, CPW is able to operate more stably than a volunteer-only group would be able to do, and without the pressures of construction schedules the group is free to engage in creative urban research. It is a mutually beneficial relationship, as through the CPW team's studies and publications the university enhances its standing in the community and becomes a powerful force to advocate for participatory design.

❝ The designer's problem is not to create facades or architectural mass but to create an all-encompassing experience, to engender involvement. The city is a people's art, a shared experience. ❞

– Edmund Bacon

Case 3
Building a Collaborative Effort. The Hong Kong Housing Authority's Experience

Text courtesy of the
Hong Kong Housing Authority

Introduction:
informing, consulting, involving the community
It has been arguetd in some Western literature that resident participation constitutes something of a 'new orthodoxy' across Western Europe (Atkinson & Eckardt, 2004), but in Hong Kong the idea is still emergent. Hong Kong's Housing Authority (HA) may seem to be a definitional 'top-down' player in the development market, but it has recently begun to see the value in community planning and has implemented this approach in two landmark projects.

For many years, Hong Kong has experienced housing shortages as a result of extremely high land values, lengthy construction times and soaring housing prices. A huge number of Hong Kong citizens find

it difficult to make a down payment on a property loan. In this context, HA plays a critical role in society, similar to the Dutch 'housing association': to provide affordable public rental housing. Established in 1973 as a statutory body, HA is responsible for planning, designing, and building Hong Kong's new public housing and also managing and maintaining existing affordable housing complexes for those who cannot afford private housing.

Despite its powerful position as a public sector procuring entity, HA was inspired to adopt a people-centric approach from the inspiration of a case where HA – as a result of massive media coverage – was heavily criticized for neglecting the needs of the community. The incident occurred in 2006 at Lei Muk Shu Estate, where several 1.2-meter-diameter granite spheres had been installed as a landscape feature. Residents' children had predictably tried to play and climb on the structures, which aroused concern about their safety. This served as a catalyst to awaken HA's determination to close the gap between designers' intent and users' needs. HA saw the need to change its mode of operation by listening more to the views of the citizens and by communicating more with the

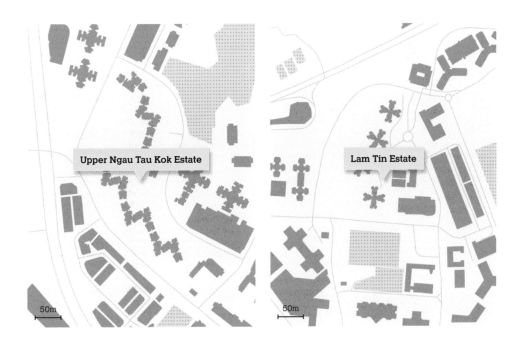

Upper Ngau Tau Kok Estate

50m

Lam Tin Estate

50m

community during the planning and design process in its housing projects. HA subsequently organized facilitated community engagement workshops with tenants and local communities in order to secure the understanding and acceptance of the existence of landscape features such as the granite spheres. The anecdote illustrates the importance of community engagement and effective communication to enable mutual understanding of estate design. In the past decade, despite changes in Government rhetoric, many Hong Kong citizens continue to perceive a lack of genuine grassroots involvement in regeneration decision-making processes. HA attempts to address this 'participation deficit' (Hall & Hickman, 2011) and to put core community values into practice to inform, consult, and involve the community.

This change in HA's mode of operation made a huge impact on the process of thinking, designing and implementing public housing projects. By initiating public engagement exercises for both planning and design stages of large-scale housing developments, HA introduced the 'deciding together' factor that is illustrated in the following two case studies.

Lam Tin: engaging the community to create harmony homes

Lam Tin can be translated as 'blue field', a Chinese phrase that reflects the site's long history: before Hong Kong expanded, it had been a salt field since 1163, under the Song Dynasty. Located in southeastern Kowloon, Old Lam Tin Estate was built in 1966 and comprised twenty-three resettlement blocks. To improve environmental and social living conditions, HA initiated a Comprehensive Redevelopment Programme (CRP) in old Lam Tin Estate in 1988. The CRP was carried out in multiple phases over a period of twenty years. While the original site area was about 4.2 hectares, 1.5 hectares was assigned for development of a new school, a multi-purpose municipal services building and for road improvement under the CRP. The remaining 2.7 hectares was allocated for construction of four 40-storey residential buildings providing 3,036 domestic units with retail commercial facilities development concentrated at ground level – a typical housing typology in Hong Kong to accommodate its high-density urbanism.

Since the program was an old-to-new estate resettlement scheme, there already was a close-knit community with strong aspirations about their

neighborhood. Consisting mainly of local shop owners, residents and retirees, this group had a relatively strong view on the development direction of their housing estate. HA engaged this community in the design process, beginning in 2004. One of the major community desires was to have more public open spaces. In response, HA invited the local community to prepare a master layout plan, comprising not only external garden areas around the domestic buildings, but also a covered multi-purpose communal space on the first level of the domestic buildings, integrating with the surrounding garden areas. Over the years, through a series of engagement activities that were organized for universal participation, a stronger sense of belonging and ownership was created. The end result was that residents and other stakeholders felt that they had created their own communal living areas out of this form of social interaction: a communal garden and a two-level pedestrian precinct which became the 'living areas' for all the residents.

The design outcome, which incorporated plenty of input from the community, became the pride and joy of the residents. Evidence of this people-oriented approach became a design inspiration for wall murals, walking trails, outdoor sculptures, and a community heritage display at the estate. This sense of ownership of the community was a direct result of working collectively. At Lam Tin, a generic housing regeneration project was made dynamic by injecting valuable community input. As a case study it showcases how an active participatory approach can result in very successful planning and architectural strategies.

Lessons from Lam Tin: institutional collaborative approach

The case study in Lam Tin exemplifies how top-down bureaucracy can meet bottom-up initiatives successfully. It can be observed that intervention from any housing corporation / housing authority / housing bureau is most effective when there is a strong commitment to resident participation (Hall & Hickman, 2011). An interface between government and urban stakeholders where bureaucracy operates not as a blocker but as a facilitator can offer a democratic platform for local participants to become key players in design decisions that will affect them.

Since the process of implementing a public housing project is often lengthy, in these cases it is especially important that public engagement sessions are planned well in advance and are organized to fit into the construction sequence. Community briefing sessions are recommended at the early planning and design stages, so that stakeholders such as District Council Members and residents can react to the overall redevelopment parameters and strategy. For instance, throughout the design and construction stages in Lam Tin, multiple design workshops allowed residents to share visions and work out the garden design with the architects, including the creation of a sculpture for display as a community art. HA also hosted a number of sessions at local schools for residents to design their installation utilizing renewable energy systems in order to encourage more environmental awareness in the Estate. Its holistic collaborative approach reached beyond workshops to include documentation of the oral history of the neighborhood as well as an essay-writing competition in local schools. As Patsy Healey explained in the chapter 'An Institutional Approach' in Collaborative Planning – Shaping Places in Fragmented Societies (1997), 'it helps to build up, across the diversity of ways of living and ways of thinking, an institutional capacity to collaborate and co-ordinate'. Healey also argued that 'collaborative process may have the potential to be transformative, to change the practices, cultures and outcomes of "place governance", and, in particular, to explore how, through attention to process design, such processes could be made more socially just, and in the context of the multiplicity of urban social world, more socially inclusive' (Healey, 1997).

The outcome of HA's new institutional approach was to generate productive results addressing shared concerns. The residents' participation in designing their urban living habitat was a mechanism to establish common targets, common interests and common goals for both the institution and the community. The 'Action Seedling' workshop, energy-saving system design and oral history became the vehicles through which the institution and the community groups addressed and achieved common targets – reducing the potential conflict that can arise under a typical top-down bureaucratic structure. Perhaps unsurprisingly, the Lam Tin project has achieved high post-occupation satisfaction, measured at over 96%.

Upper Ngau Tau Kok Estate: phase two

Even before the case of Lam Tin, HA was determined to integrate the mission of community participation into other housing projects and plans for redevelopment projects. Like the previous scenario, Ngau Tau Kok Estate was a resettlement process covered by the Comprehensive Redevelopment Programme. The original Lower Ngau Tau Kok Estate (LNTK) was built in the 1960s, and most of the residents had lived there for four to five decades (21% were over age 65). When the housing facilities were deemed obsolete, rehousing seemed a desirable solution, but initially many of the existing 12,200 residents rejected the offer. However, when the government announced that the estate would be cleared and residents would be moved to more remote locations, some residents felt pessimistic and decided that they had a right to express their preferences about their living environment, according to a research study by Professor Bernard Lim and his research team on the study of participatory projects in Hong Kong (Lim et al., 2005). Naturally there were multiple points of view with regard to how to move, when to move, who to move and where to move, causing several disagreements and delays.

Since HA was tasked with the process of moving these existing tenants to new flats, HA wished to establish a long term, positive relationship with local communities and relevant stakeholders throughout the planning, design, construction, occupation and post-occupation stages. As at Lam Tin, HA decided to exercise a collaborative approach, and this participatory process was planned at the beginning of Upper Ngau Tau Kok Estate Phase 2. Indeed, the evolution of the project developed incrementally in association with participatory activities initiated by community concern groups in earlier days, and then the institutional framework kicked in very quickly after the early design stage for this phase of the redevelopment.

The residents were assisted by local non-profit organizations, church organizations, and a community development center (namely the Hong Kong Sheng Kung Hui Ngau Tau Kok Community Development Centre) to conduct surveys and to solicit local residents' ideas regarding the resettlement arrangement (Lim et al, 2005). All stakeholders, including residents, non-governmental organizations, district councilors, government officials, multi-disciplinary professionals and academics, were invited to contribute. HA facilitated the environment by providing practical techniques, collaborative institutional experience and human resources in conducting community planning workshops. As Nick Wates explained in his Community Planning Event Manual, the underlying philosophy of community planning is interdisciplinary, collaborative and community-based, enabling all those affected (known as 'stakeholders') to participate in the planning process. The premise is that better environments can be created if local communities are involved from an early stage, working closely and directly with a wide range of specialists (Wates, 2008).

With this in mind, since 2002 HA has organized multi-disciplinary events including a Heritage Exhibition at the design inception stage, intended to boost community spirit and interest in the engagement exercise; a Workshop with Designers on developing individual domestic flat layouts; as well as a Planting event at the late construction stage to encourage future tenants' enjoyment and preservation of their new green landscape. These activities were structured with HA's active contribution in over fifty workshops from 2002 until 2009, in partnership with the local concern groups that motivated local residents to identify potential opportunities and room for improvement in their new homes, which were successfully relocated within the nearby neighborhood.

Through this process the participants began to understand the abstract spatial relationship between their private living environments and public communal space. More complex design issues related to the built environment were explained by HA so residents could attain the basic skills to understand and participate in the three-dimensional building design process. By enabling a proactive, developmental response to the conditions and relations of their own urban context, the community in effect built its own institutional capacity. Within culturally and socially bound dimensions, citizens' concerns about their local environment were brought to the discussion table. Planning issues related to infrastructure facilities, public amenities, programs, and moving schedules were discussed, as well as how to articulate strategies to address them. The idea of understanding and participating in the urban planning process helped to frame the way tenants

establish and develop a stronger sense of ownership to their neighborhood.

Lessons from Upper Ngau Tau Kok Estate: self-initiated community approach framing the governance

From the initial government announcement of the demolition of the old estate to the resettlement of the same group of tenants in the new estate, 15 years passed in which HA learned how to negotiate and resolve the continual, often conflicting, requests of this apparently homogeneous group of residents. The mission to foster a stronger sense of ownership in these new homes has yielded multiple results. HA has empowered local residents to take ownership of the project, evolved its own mentality and institutional approach, and conveyed community needs, preferences and messages to all authorities concerned, resulting in a satisfactory and cohesive outcome from this mostly self-organized community initiative. By allowing local residents to take part in the planning process, HA was able to generate a physical solution that implements residents' desires as well as HA's requirements. This attention to detail reached beyond the construction of the physical environment to impact people as well as buildings. In addition to inviting the usual relevant authorities, architects and planners to work on Upper Ngau Tau Kok Estate Phase 2, HA also involved social workers and councilors, and appointed 'ambassadors' to facilitate tenants' moving into the new homes. Upon completion of the project, HA even organized Estate Warming Ceremonies.

HA's experience at Ngau Tau Kok emphasizes that we live in 'pluralist' societies, which tend to generate multi-sided interest group conflicts (Brindley et al., 1989; Grant, 1989, Healey et al., 1988). Through a learning process of many years, HA managed to convert the initial confrontations between residents into a celebration of diversity. Attempting to sort out the dilemmas that inevitably arise when different people coexist in shared spaces, HA helped local community groups to devise key action policy plans. Since completion, Ngau Tau Kok Estate Phase 2 project has been studied by many scholars internationally as a successful case under urban regeneration policy. The HA's pragmatic approach has provided a way of realizing how a community-initiated advocacy can be framed into institutional governance, grounded in a thorough empathetic understanding of the community needs.

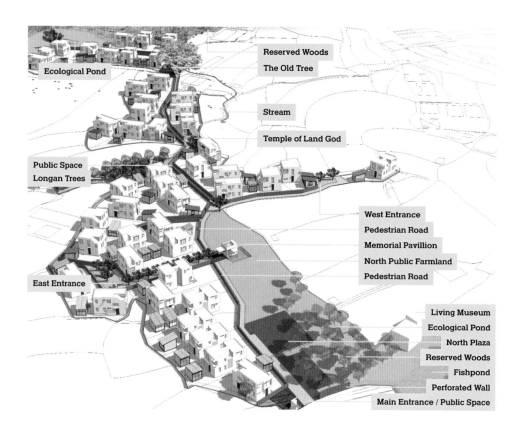

Ecological Pond

Reserved Woods
The Old Tree

Stream

Temple of Land God

Public Space
Longan Trees

West Entrance
Pedestrian Road
Memorial Pavillion
North Public Farmland
Pedestrian Road

East Entrance

Living Museum
Ecological Pond
North Plaza
Reserved Woods
Fishpond
Perforated Wall
Main Entrance / Public Space

Case 4
Voices from the Vegetable Garden –
Grassroots Planning and the Design
of Choi Yuen Ecological Village

Written by Wang Weijen Architecture

Choi Yuen Ecological Village is a physical design
and also a conceptual design for citizens claiming
their rights as participants in the planning process.
Physically, it is a community re-habitation project in
the New Territory of Hong Kong Special Administrative
Region. Conceptually, it is a movement that started as
a protest against village relocation to make way for the
construction of a High-Speed Rail Link. As such Choi
Yuen marks a turning point for formulating alternative
planning strategies to enable bottom-up development
and organic agriculture. Moreover, it is a case study
in green architecture and grassroots participation
in rural as well as urban Hong Kong.

The project comprised a set of designs for fifty low-cost
'eco-village' houses along with the village's public
facilities. Each element of the project demonstrates

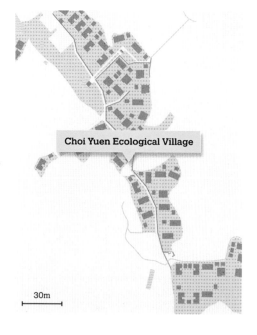

Choi Yuen Ecological Village

30m

sustainable design concepts: conservation of the existing ecosystems of fishponds and orchards, allocation of communal land for organic farming, provisions for a vehicular-free pedestrian system, and development of public spaces and infrastructures with rain water collection and waste water recycling. By formulating a typology-based participation mechanism, as well as a set of architectural measures for facilitating natural ventilation and lighting (rainwater collection and green roofs), the project opens up new opportunities for community architecture in contrast with the mainstream mode of housing development in Hong Kong.

From protecting their homeland to a grassroots civic movement
In December 2009, on a cold winter's night, farmers from rural Hong Kong, as well as social activists and supporters, gathered to demand their right to stay on the land they had settled for over fifty years. Two hundred villagers and thousands of supporters gathered at the Government Headquarters in Central to protest a relocation order that would take their farmland to make space for the construction of a High-Speed Rail linking Hong Kong to Beijing. The villagers

came from a small village near Yun Gang in Hong Kong's northwest New Territory, five kilometers away from the border with China. For the first time in Hong Kong's history, these rural citizens had the strength to reject the Government's plan to resettle them into high-rise public housing, insisting that they should continue their long relationship with the land.

Hong Kong is a city in which economic growth and development have always been prioritized, but the Christmas protest of Choi Yuen Village drew unprecedented public attention to several issues. Under what circumstances should the right of habitation be pushed aside in favor of development concerns? How can metropolitan Hong Kong maintain a system of sustainable agriculture and a symbiotic relationship with its own rural areas? In the context of increasing civic concerns with community and heritage conservation after the 1997 handover, the Choi Yuen villagers' message of protecting their homeland immediately gained support from the media and the general public. In particular, several progressive civic groups, academics and professionals came to the villagers' aid.

'Choi Yuen' translates as 'Vegetable Garden', an appropriate name for this rural village. It became a symbol for a new kind of grassroots civic movement that linked rural people from the vegetable farms to the green movements of the urban middle classes. Led by social activist YC Chan, Dick Chu and other volunteers, the loosely formed Choi Yuen Village Concern Group started to work alongside villagers on the village site in the New Territory. A community center was set up there to host workshops, while the original vegetable loading station was converted into an outdoor assembly hall for villagers' meetings.

Continuing protests and confrontations at the frontline were not successful, and the group began to painfully realize that they needed to make a long-term plan for village relocation. Aiding the core group of a dozen villagers, this multi-disciplinary team included academics and social workers, architects and planners, engineers and surveyors, lawyers and advocates for organic farming. The team came together to advise on various projects, from purchasing new land to acquiring permits all the way to the planning and design of a new village that will finally be built on a nearby site.

Two types of works were identified for dealing with the intermediate and long-term issues. The former were mostly social and political, with the primary goal of negotiating with the Transportation Department and Kowloon-Canton Railway Corporation to get an extension on the existing village's demolition date. This would enable villagers to better prepare temporary shelters and infrastructures before the new village could be settled. Intermediate measures also included protest logistics such as organizing a community patrol team, and preventing 'ambush' bulldozing and demolition attacks carried out by the police and the railway contractor.

When it came to the long-term planning of the new village, even the land negotiation for the new site was not easy. Local politicians and developers were concerned that if these Choi Yuen farmers moved in, their presence would change the dynamics of regional politics. After much struggle, a new site was finally secured: a long strip of land sitting along the foothill of Dalan Mountain. A small clearwater creek ran down the hill, passing through woods and orchards before pouring into a fishpond at the front of the village. Judging by any standards, this irregular and narrow piece of land was by no means the perfect site for a new village layout, but in the eyes of the villagers and their supporters, this was utopia: a new paradigm for self-organized planning and architectural design with a strong social and environmental emphasis.

Planning an ecological village: a collective democratic process
Wang Weijen Architecture was invited by the Choi Yuen Village Concern Group to join the design team and eventually take charge of organizing the physical layout of the village plan as well as the architectural design of the fifty village houses. Villagers of the Vegetable Garden had all agreed to build their new village in an ecologically sustainable manner, for several reasons: the farmers' innate respect for the land combined with the vision and idealism of their progressive urban supporters. Through a process of advocacy campaigns and debates, negotiations and workshops studying sustainable best practices, a consensus was reached among the villagers. The following principles were set as guidelines for laying out the plan:

Car-free village: Unlike a typical suburb dominated by car parks and vehicular access roads, the village will only have car park spaces arranged at the village's edge. Each dwelling unit will be accessed via a pedestrian road of one and half meters wide, like the old village had.

Communal farm land: With much less land area of land allocated to cars, more land is opened up to agriculture. The villagers agreed that 40% of the land should be designated for public use, including a large piece of communal land for farming. It will be, symbolically and functionally, the collective organic farm for the Vegetable Garden Village.

Fishpond and orchard: The idea of keeping the original (agri)cultural landscape and existing land features was put up for debate and finally agreed upon. Beyond the ideological implication of respect for history, it is also the best choice environmentally. The orchard at the village center and the fishpond at the lowest part of the site together work to collect and filter grey water before recycling.

Village road: The 300m-long road connecting the village from its north to its south end is the infrastructural spine of the village that also outlines a path for the main sewage, power and cable lines. A half-meter-wide rainwater ditch runs parallel to the one-and-a-half-meter wide pedestrian road, and it is filled with pebbles and water plants for filtering the grey water.

Water recycling: Along this roadside ditch, rainwater and grey water are gathered and gradually filtered by pebbles and plants into clean water while traveling down to the fishpond for collecting and irrigation recycling. Black water is collected separately at a large sewage tank specially treated by an organic filtering mechanism that uses oyster shell.

Infrastructural public spaces: The village is organized into north, central and south sections, each with their own commons. At every scale, the goal is to create public spaces through small neighborhood infrastructure nodes: light posts and trees landmark road junctions, patios create semi-public spaces, and water meter boxes serve as community benches.

The laying out of the village masterplan was developed in parallel with the establishment of the above principles. The design calls for fifty family units, each sitting on a 1600-square-foot plot located along the north-south main access road. Each home's land price is set slightly differently, based on each plot's nearness to the village's entrance. Through a process of open discussions and negotiations, three smaller sub-communities were formed to make up the north, central and south sections. Houses at the North Section will face either the large communal farmland or an adjacent green space that connects them to a park and the secondary village entrance with a bus stop. Houses in the Central Section will have a botanical focus: they will share an orchard of Longan trees, and a large old Banyan tree alongside their section of the main road. Houses in the South Section will nestle against the foothill of the nearby mountain, surrounded by woods and running water.

The main pedestrian road has been carefully programmed to be full of life, from the village entrance all the way to the mountain at the back. Starting from the parking lot, the road springs from the entrance patio (where mailboxes will be positioned) and the nearby village grocery shop, then leads to the communal farmland with a village pavilion in its center. Passing the 'orchard' junction, which will be marked by large trees, benches and patios, the road leads to the southern woods and the foothills of the mountain. The village is also planned to have good feng shui, with its comforting wind and water: it will be ventilated by the prevailing southwesterly summer breeze, which slides down from the mountain and brings fresh moisture along with it.

Designing a design process: prototypes and variations

When Wang Weijen Architecture began the design work on the village houses, there were major challenges in store. The budget was low, the schedule was tight, and another important question loomed: How can we develop a design process that will lead to building up village consensus and neighborhood harmony, rather than divisively amplifying the differences between people? How can this process sustain the original vernacular quality of Choi Yuen Village despite the fact that the new buildings will be designed by architects and built by contractors working in the contemporary mode of design practice? Three sets of dialectical relationships were identified, each with potential dilemmas to be resolved in an integrated way during the design process.

Modern design and vernacular process: Working in the mode of a modern architectural practice, how can an architect design fifty village houses within three months' time and still somehow give them the organic qualities of vernacular houses, which are normally developed over a long period of time? How can we transform the model of 'Prototype + Modification' in the theory of vernacular architecture into a design model that is applicable to modern housing design?

Collective form and individual space needs:
Within the mode of a contemporary construction
process, how can an architect meet the differing
needs of each individual household while
still developing a set of manageable working
drawings to facilitate a manageable tendering
process? Clearly the answer is not to produce
fifty unique units. How can we develop a design
system that allows flexibility while still making
the job easier and more cost-effective for the
contractor?

**Interactive bottom-up and effective
top-down:** Working within the model of
contemporary decision-making processes in
design, how can we moderate a participatory
process that can accommodate a variety
of inputs from different houses? It remains
important to use the professional's knowledge
effectively to coordinate the design as a whole.
If we choose not to adopt the usual participatory
design tactics (like user-design workshops
for making dollhouse-like models, or group
discussions with roundtable conclusions), what
other innovative ways can we develop to create
and manage an interactive design process that
produces sufficient feedback?

After mapping different patterns of existing village
houses, and surveying the functional expectations
of each household, the architects formulated two key
measures for designing the design process: 'Prototype
+ Variation' and a method for arranging design
clinics. These two measures proved critical to address
the dilemma of collective versus individual rights
and desires, as well as top-down versus bottom-up
implementation. The final house designs find
resolution in ecologically friendly moves: most houses
will be easily equipped with rainwater collection ponds,
and side windows facilitate cross-ventilation that will
also be encouraged by green roofs.

Prototype and variation
The first key measure was the establishment of three
basic house prototypes, each tailored to different site
dimensions, orientation and layout expectations: A),
the symmetrical three modular-bay horizontal block
developed from the basic unit of Chinese traditional
dwellings, with a public hall in the central bay and
kitchen in the side bay; B), the rectangular atrium

block developed from the prototype of Chinese
traditional shop-houses, with a public hall in the front
and kitchen /dining at the back; and C), the square
block popular among village houses developed in
Hong Kong's New Territory after the 1970s.

With the fixed structural dimensions set for all exterior
forms, stairway and service locations, each prototype
could be mirrored in plan to produce another twin
type, and each type could also be further developed
into more sub-types through partitioning (for different
numbers of bedrooms or living rooms, for example).
After selecting their preferred prototype from the
three basic A, B and C types, each household was
invited to participate in a workshop to refine their
partition preferences. This conversation led to the
final adjustments on that family's door style, window
patterns, colors and material options. At the end,
through the model of 'Prototype + Variation', the A, B
and C prototypes transformed into nearly fifty different
variations that nonetheless retain similar house forms.

Different tactics were developed to facilitate the
identification of villagers' preferred types and
the follow-up designing process. Three types of
color pamphlets were printed to look like upscale
developer's sale booklets, with the intent to make
villagers feel like their opinions were respected and
valued. Each pamphlet also included layouts with
plans, axiomatic renderings, and model images, with
tick boxes for villagers to mark their choices. Although
the final design decisions were made in the workshop
sessions, the pamphlets and the images contained
within prepared the villagers for design decision-
making and helped them to imagine their potential
spaces.

Design clinic
Before the final production of tender drawings, three
intensive weekend workshops were arranged for
design consultation. For each one-and-a-half hour
consultation session, four neighboring households
were invited to come together to take part. Sitting
around the large table with the large-scale site model
of the village and everyone's houses in front of them,
the villagers watched the architects demonstrate the
possible building layouts within each house lot, while
their future neighbors all sat around offering friendly
suggestions and making subtle negotiations on
matters such as potential blocking of views or winds.
Conflicting issues were usually resolved and public
interest was preserved through open consultation.

This page
Massing study models
of Choi Yuen Village

Top
Study models

Bottom
Wang Weijen Architecture
conducted a community meeting
engaging local residents

Next spread
Wang Weijen Architecture
constructed a pavilion at the
Hong Kong Biennale 2012
showcasing the design concept
of the new Choi Yuen Village

The architects found that the villagers would usually arrive early or stay behind to sit in on other sessions' discussions; they wanted to know more about the big picture. Over several weekends, twenty-four household design consultations were completed per day. It was an exhausting and intense time, but the end result was a design for a village that respects its predecessor while meeting the contemporary needs of its inhabitants.

Based on the agreed layout plans and the selected house types, one set of working drawings able to accommodate fifty unit variations was developed for the tendering process. Parallel to the architectural design, with help from expert team members, Choi Yuen Village Concern Group and villagers were holding meetings nearly once a week to resolve issues related to site formation, drainage and infrastructure including water and power supplies, waste, sewage and water recycling systems. Throughout, it was a challenging but optimistic and rewarding process for the team, who were all very aware of building the first bottom-up ecological village in Hong Kong. The real challenge for the villagers to overcome in the next two years was the village relocation and the accompanying frustration of waiting for construction to finish while living in temporary shelters.

Shelter and pavilion building as village process
After dealing with nearly one year of Choi Yuen's residents' struggles through demonstration and protest, with support from press reporting and TV documentation, the Government finally decided to take action and remove the village by the end of 2010, before the new village site was ready to be inhabited. Not only did the design have to consider the location and layout for the new temporary shelters, but before construction could be started, other issues had to be resolved. The logistics of moving the construction and demolition materials was important, and the layout plan strategically allowed for the reuse of the infrastructure and the materials of the temporary shelters.

In January 2011, villagers finally all moved into temporary shelters on their new site; for many, it was their first time spending the important Chinese New Year holiday away from the old homes where they grew up. So as to not affect the future construction, the shelters were built in planned open spaces in the north and south sections of the site. Common spaces

were also arranged for the temporary shelters, with one courtyard used for vegetable gardens and the other used for public gatherings, meetings, communal lunches and village banquet parties.

During the two years of village construction, this open courtyard was also used as a classroom for facilitating Hong Kong's community movements in general, hosting events like a weekend guided tour for rural engagement, a workshop on organic farming, and a session of experience sharing for sustainable planning strategy. These temporary shelters hosted visitors from different districts of Hong Kong as well as scholars and progressive community groups from Taiwan, China, and other places in Asia. In the end these humble structures provided the platform for a shared approach to alternative living.

The village construction did not get underway until April of 2013, due to difficult negotiations over the village access road, sewage disposal, and construction costs and terms. To boost village spirit during this slow waiting process, the architects and inhabitants designed a pavilion in Kowloon Park for the 2012 Hong Kong Biennale. In order to promote the idea of sustainability, the pavilion's materials were recycled back into the village after the exhibition closed. The pavilion's components were mostly made of recycling wastes or renewable materials: plastic bottles and recycled cement, recycled wood panels and steel construction, and a shading fabric more commonly used for rural agriculture. It also demonstrated experimental approaches in its solar panel and rainwater-collection systems. Through the public event of the Biennale, it was hoped that the ecological pavilion could take a role as the first construction project of the village's new incarnation.

The pavilion building was also intended to become a public platform shared by the villagers, providing space for groups to meet and discuss organic farming, self-organized bottom-up projects, and sustainable design/construction processes for rural Hong Kong. Through the action of dismantling, relocating and assembling the pavilion, the architects aimed to resolve differences and build consensus around the idea of sustaining the environment and protecting Hong Kong's history.

The voices that emerged out of this vegetable garden of Choi Yuen village have changed the discourse in

Hong Kong in surprising ways. This was one of the first cases when protesters were able to be heard and raise so much support from other interested people in the city. It was especially notable in this case as the villagers were rural people from Hong Kong's New Territories, not mainstream urbanites. Although the protest movement did not succeed in preventing the destruction of the old village, it did succeed in the larger sense of mobilizing large segments of the community and joining them together in a common purpose that will hopefully have an impact on future city decisions.

Besides looking at the Government's role, it is also instructive to look at the role of academics and professionals in this case. After the protests began to raise awareness of the villagers' plight, people from all walks of life joined together to work on this

issue. Professionals, including the architects from Wang Weijen Architecture, saw this as an engaging problem, one that had implications larger than this specific design. Nonetheless this design process, with its elements of community discussion and political engagement as well as environmental sustainability, can be seen as a model.

Village construction finally started one year after the Biennale exhibition and is scheduled to be finished in the spring of 2014. The building of this new Choi Yuen Village is a story of a specific struggle but also a larger tale about collective opposition to the usual procedures and rationales in Hong Kong's developmental decision-making. It is hoped that this village will kick off a new interest in alternative design and planning – a democratic and bottom-up process for shaping our city.

Conclusions
What Comes Next?

Written by Tris Kee and
Jessica Niles DeHoff

Participatory planning needs to be a key part of Hong Kong's future development. What we need now is for Government and other institutions to offer their support to self-help initiatives; to interact with the organizers of those initiatives in a reciprocal way; and to form relationships with community members that can last into the future.

Obviously, the best solution would be to put into place legislation to secure the role of citizen participation in development decisions and the entire planning process. Though it may be true that a 'democratic political structure can assist the process, whereby citizen participation can be effective and meaningful' (Chan, 1990, 78), perhaps a new sense of Hong Kong's evolving political structure can emerge out of citizens taking small but important roles to impact their city's future.

As we have seen, in most cases everyone benefits from participatory planning: developers and Government as well as residents. All need to be well-informed in order to recognize these advantages. An educated citizenry will be better able to judge architectural and planning decisions, and speak meaningfully at public engagement sessions and so on. This would enable institutions, planners and architects to work with the community rather than operate on its behalf. To this end, the Community Planning Workshop along with the Government has already created a series of teaching kits on design topics to be implemented at the secondary-school level.

Public-private partnerships are another way forward if legislation is not a possibility. In this scenario the funding and management

skills of the private sector could be brought to bear on the political process, on behalf of the public. This could offer a flexible system for resolving conflict and coming up with new solutions as the city evolves and changes. One local scholar recommends 'the approach of "3Ps", i.e. politician and public sector administrative reform, public participation and partnerships, as the means to promote a more sustainable development' (Kwan, 2004, 11). Partnerships could offer the best of both worlds as the 'management skills and financial acumen of the business community will create better value for money for taxpayers. It will contribute to institutions and practices that are flexible and networked, permitting the community to be more creatively responsive to change and conflict' (Kwan, 2004, 54).

These interventions can serve to strengthen civil society and a stronger sense of community linking the city's varied districts. At the very least, it will inspire better buildings and communities; at most it could change the future. As John Friedmann wrote in his essay 'World City Futures: The Role of Urban and Regional Policies in the Asia-Pacific Region': 'The state can move to suppress civil society, keeping it under a tight lid. It can misinterpret simple claims for accountability as undermining the state's authority and move to repress all criticism. It can even resort to terror. But, the long-term future of world cities cannot be imagined without a gradual process of democratization. Civil society will not be excluded from world city formation' (Friedmann, 1998, 48).

Lessons learned: magnifying the effects of local case studies
This chapter has focused on selected case

studies illustrating different methods for integrating the members of the community into the design and decision-making process. It can be demonstrated that such integration offers numerous advantages. A more inclusive process gives professionals access to the intimate knowledge of place that local people possess, and allows them to tap into their desires and needs for the future. All of this information can help 'top-downers' to break out of established modes of practice and create innovation in architectural form or simply in terms of design development processes. It may be as simple as investing in design education at all stages of the public schooling system, in order to create new citizens who are engaged and informed.

Urban evolution may require a certain willingness to experiment on the part of policymakers and private investors, and as Friedmann states 'To a large extent, the future of world cities will be determined by the vision, entrepreneurial daring and skill of their political elites who will need to break loose from traditional habits and patterns of thought so that the brave new world may come into existence' (Friedmann, 1998, 51).

In terms of the urban context beyond Hong Kong, what larger lessons can be gleaned from these case studies, and how can they be applied to magnify the impacts? In a sense, Hong Kong serves as a window into the future of its region, which may be particularly relevant at this time when so many Asian cities are in transition from a 'developing' to a 'developed' context. Projects in Hong Kong tend to be collaborative efforts in which a traditionally 'top-down' player invites the participation of community members. This demonstrates that the message is

spreading: even the 'powers that be' are coming around to the idea that participatory design processes have many advantages despite the possibility of added time or even added budget, and members of the public are beginning to believe it's possible for them to be agents for urban change.

Though some of these Hong Kong case studies are examples of huge, built projects – like the Housing Authorities' estates – others represent unrealized or partially realized plans, or simply studies of how things can be improved – like the CPW studies of Wan Chai parks. Despite this, they are still valuable. In the case of research studies, 'even if no direct links are established between research and policy, one should not underestimate the imperceptible influence such project findings might have on policy-makers, especially when the results are disseminated through policy seminars, easy-to-read publications and other vehicles. At the very least, policy-makers have been made aware of problems, and goodwill has been established between researchers and policy-makers' (Yeung, 1998, 207). This has certainly proved to be the case with the Community Project Workshop: the team's research recommendations are kept on file by clients for future reference, and many of these clients tend to build a relationship with CPW and solicit advice repeatedly. In this sense, local top-downers have shown that even institutional players can retain a sense of openness by remaining flexible in terms of final results.

While members of the Hong Kong community are generally happy to pitch in to better their communities, realistically speaking it is Government funding that makes many projects possible and makes wish lists come true. Institutions have power, authority, and money; they have administrative structures in place that can help to support grassroots initiatives. EKEO uses Government funds to sponsor local projects like 'Fly the Flyover' so they don't need to be profitable; the Housing Authority brings its considerable resources to bear on the problem of providing the best possible residences for the general public; and even CPW is supported by the institution of Hong Kong University and hired by the Government (or local Government representatives) to embark on its studies.

Based on these case studies, we can summarize a list of recommendations for supporting and enabling Hong Kong's DIY urbanism processes. Government agencies, developers or other traditionally powerful bodies should:

Invite participation from stakeholders. All of the Hong Kong case studies demonstrate the innovative ideas that stakeholders can bring to the table.

Allow for the possibility of unforeseen or even unrealized outcomes, as they will still generate ideas and possibilities. The CPW has found that studies can provide a platform for exploration even when they remain unbuilt.

Keep records of past brainstorms that might impact future policies – studies may become the projects of the future.

Whenever possible, provide funding and administrative support to enable programs, groups, events, or ongoing educational initiatives. Sometimes just having a venue or a photocopier available can simplify the process enough to make it viable.

Make institutional resources and intelligence available to the public so that nobody has to 'reinvent the wheel'. In the case of Hong Kong, EKEO has made a particular effort to put Government resources to work for the community. Beyond the funding and administrative support mentioned above, this has more to do with staff, research materials, and deep knowledge of the professions involved (urban planning, traffic planning, etc.).

All of these lessons indicate that we may have arrived at a moment where both sides want to work together, and participatory planning has become mainstream. '[Citizen participation in the planning process] can be conceived not as alternative to the conventional decision-making process pursued by the public planning agencies but as a decision-making partnership with the institutionalized framework of modern government' (Chan, 1990, 9).

Communication and participation is likely to motivate local stakeholders to conserve and develop their community and its projects. These case studies show different ways to bridge the gap between Government and real estate developers, on the one hand, and on the other hand the citizens who want to engage in city making.

Bibliography

Alexander, E.R. (1992) Approaches to Planning: Introducing Current Planning Theories, Concepts, and Issues. Gorden and Breach Publisher.

Ameyaw, S. & Abloh, F. (1999) 'A Historical Perspective on Community Development'. In: Campfens. H. (ed.) Community Development Around The World: Practice, Theory, Research, Training. Toronto: University of Toronto. pp. 279-327.

Atkinson, R. & Eckardt, F. (2004) 'Urban policies in Europe: the Development of a New Conventional Wisdom?' In: Eckardt, F. and Kreisl, P. (eds.) (2004) City Images and Urban Regeneration (Volume) pp. 33-65. Frankfurt/New York: Peter Lang.

Bacon, E. (1976) Design of Cities, New York City: Penguin.

Brindley, T., Rydin, Y. & Stoker, G. (1989) Remaking Planning: The Politics of Urban Change in the Thatcher Years. London: Unwin Hyman.

Bushe, G.R. & Pitman, T. (1991) 'Appreciative process: A Method for Transformational Change'. Organization Development Practitioner. 23 (3). pp. 1-4.

Census and Statistics Department (2011) 2011 Population Census - Fact Sheet for Kwun Tong District Council District, source: http://www.census2011.gov.hk/en/district-profiles/kwun-tong.html (Retrieved on October, 20th, 2013).

Chan, Pui-Shan (Esther) et al. (1990) Democracy, Planning and Citizen Participation: a Case Study of Hong Kong. (Unpublished dissertation). Hong Kong University Department of Urban Planning, Hong Kong.

Community Involvement in Urban Regeneration, European Union-Regional Policy and Cohesion, Community Development Foundation with support from the European Commission, 1997.

Department of the Environment, Transport and the Regions (DETR), Involving Communities in Urban and Rural Regeneration: A Guide for Practitioners. DETR, London, 1997.

Friedmann, J. (1998) 'World City Futures: The Role of Urban and Regional Policies in the Asia-Pacific Region'. In: Yeung, Y.M. (ed.) Urban Development in Asia: Retrospect and Prospect. Hong Kong: Hong Kong Institute of Asia-Pacific Studies, Chinese University of Hong Kong.

Grant, W. (1989) Pressure Groups, Politics and Democracy in Britain. Hemel Hempstead: Philip Allan.

Hall, S. & Hickman, P. (2011) Resident Participation in Housing.

Healey, P. (1997) Collaborative Planning: Shaping Places in Fragmented Societies. Vancouver: UBC Press; Basingstoke, Hampshire: Macmillan Press.

Healey, P. et al. (1988) Land Use Planning and the Mediation of Urban Change. Cambridge: Cambridge University Press.

Jacobs, B. & Dutton, C. (1999) 'Social and Community issues'. In: Roberts, P. & Sykes, H. (eds.) Urban Regeneration. London: Sage.

Jacobs, J. (1961) The Death and Life of Great American Cities. New York: Random House (1993).

Solomon, J., Wong, C. & Frampton, A. (2012). Cities without Ground: a Hong Kong Guidebook. San Francisco: ORO editions.

Kendig, L.H. & Keast, B.C. (2010) Community Character: Principles for Design and Planning. Washington, D.C.: Island Press.

Kwan, Wing-yee (2004). Heritage Conservation and Urban Regeneration: Promoting Sustainable Tourism and Sustainable Community in Hong Kong. (Electronic dissertation). Hong Kong University Department of Urban Planning.

Lim, W.F.B., Kan, K. & Wong, A. (2005) Practitioners' Guide to Design and Implementation of Participatory Project. The Chinese University of Hong Kong.

Regeneration in France, Housing Studies. 26 (60. pp. 827-843.

Teitz, M.B. (2007) 'Planning and the New Institutionalisms'. Institutions and Planning, pp. 17-35. Amsterdam: Elsevier.

Urban Task Force (1999) Towards an Urban Renaissance, London E&FN Spon

Verma, N. (2007) Institutions and Planning. Amsterdam: Elsevier.

Wates, N. (2000) The Community Planning Handbook: How People Can Shape their Cities, Towns and Villages in any part of the World. London: Earthscan Publications Limited.

Wates, N. (2008) The Community Planning Event Manual: How to Use Collaborative Planning and Urban Design Events to Improve your Environment. London: Earthscan Publications Limited.

Yeung, Y.M. (1998) 'Urban Research in Asia: Problems, Priorities, and Prospects'. In: Yeung, Y.M. (ed.) Urban Development in Asia: Retrospect and Prospect. Hong Kong Institute of Asia-Pacific Studies, Chinese University of Hong Kong.

Moscow

Introduction

Written by Shriya Malhotra
and Mehdi Comeau

❝ The situation around Moscow registers a fatal realism of modernity. Not being able to follow one clear plan of development over the last 20 years, the region has developed a unique urban framework answering the temporary needs of every owner... actors who truly denied any traces of collectivity in their near past produced this realistic tension of collective utopia. **❞**

– Ivanov

Introduction

This chapter touches on the past and explores the future of changing urban planning ideologies in Moscow. The featured case studies detail a selection of bottom-up urbanism projects emerging during this historic transition away from institutional, top-down centrality. As this previous model shifts to include rising citizen-initiated, bottom-up practices, new light is cast on the dynamic relationships between these actors as they envision and materialize the new urban landscape. The chapter's concluding insights offer future alternatives to traditional urban development, redefining how actors 'own the city' while resonating with both post-Communist urbanism and contemporary globalization.

In the past, Moscow's urbanization was led centralized Socialist planning in that the state and its institutions directed all urban planning decisions. The traditional planning guidelines initially established in Moscow under the Soviet Union were replicated in other Communist-bloc countries, as the Soviet Union's social, economic and political plans were achieved through state-led urbanization from the 1940s through the 1980s (Buernika, 2011; Coulibaly, 2012). As a result, similar planning approaches can be found in post-communist cities, while transitions toward more urbanized, neo-liberal or democratic states challenge shared Communist and Socialist legacies.

To better understand Moscow's context, brief historical notes situate an expanding 'global city' with strong traditional roots in the modern arena of citizen-driven urban development. The idea of the 'global city', which was introduced by Saskia Sassen (2005), marks cities prominently networked in the global economy and developing in line with contemporary globalization. Russia's capital fits the description, as Moscow's built, social and economic landscape appears to share more and more characteristics with comparable 'global cities'. At the same time, historic roots and urban legacies persist. This historic and modern, traditional and globalized interrelationship creates a unique urban development context as centralized plans to double the city's size are being charted to accommodate a growing population. As these state-led plans clash with the changing desires of the population, alternative narratives are emerging.

The text will begin by expanding on Moscow's past and present before examining four case studies: the city's cyclification (or bicycle-friendly movements and improvements), Cooperative Urbanism Mitino, Delai Sam and Co-working Nagatino. In the concluding section, the case studies are summarized and combined with insights for both bottom-up and top-down urban development actors.

Urban planning in Russia: revolutionary, utopian and socialist traditions

Historically, urban planning has been used as a tool of economic and political control in Russia, as is reflected in several ambitious restructurings of Moscow (Buernika et al., 2011; Gustov, 1968; Menu, 2013). As change continues, we see the effects of traditional top-down, centralized planning and Socialist principles influenced by the rise of market forces, all blending with an increasingly prominent resistance to such development. Today, a highly educated population is increasingly active, emerging in the form of bottom-up initiatives and grass-roots urbanism.

With a history of state planning and dynamic forms of resistance, an argument stands that Moscow is a traditional site for utopian visioning, often disconnected from reality (Ivanov, 2013; Menu, 2013; Moscow City Government, 2013). Evidence lies in the monumental scale of buildings, including housing and metro stations, and the correlating rigor in top-down planning. While the city currently tries to focus on the most pressing needs, the search continues for a middle way between idealism and practicality. In 1961, Moscow faced major restructuring with the addition of the MKAD, a four-lane ring road encircling Moscow. Spanning 109 km, the MKAD was imposed by city planners to redirect heavy traffic that used to pas through the city. Also in 2004, construction of the Third Ring imposed large-scale top-down restructuring to the capital city (Menu, 2013), leading to questions concerning the infrastructure priorities of the Greater Moscow project. Looking back, Moscow's urban development in the past 150 years does not follow a consistent trajectory (Menu, 2013), but is characterized by frequent and incremental spatial growth paralleled by a dynamic population growth (Loffe & Nefedova, 1999).

In 1918, Professor Boris Sakulin envisioned Moscow's distinct ring-shaped design. According to his plan, three initial rings were built around the city's economic center. Before Professor Sakulin's plan for Moscow, big cities had not experienced a comprehensive planning approach. Greater Moscow is comprised of the first two rings, and the Moscow Kremlin, an elaborate and large complex resting at the city center. The word kremlin translates to 'fortress', to give you an idea of this complex. Kremlin is also used to refer to the government, and the Russian President's website is Kremlin.ru. Today, one can note Moscow's expansion at different stages by the construction of additional rings, marking growth rates relative to the rising population in recent decades, with an estimated 11.98 million inhabitants in 2013 and no signs of slowing down. To deal with such growth, exceptional public transport systems and a complex road infrastructure facilitate mobility, while sizable forest parks and green spaces offer an outlet into more natural surroundings. Through such developments, including Tsarist legacies and the planning visions of dictators, expressed by monumental buildings, Moscow exemplifies how the ambitions of a few leaders, elites and experts have forged the spatial configuration of the city. In recent times, we have seen dramatic growth in low-density suburban sprawl, created by a heavy demand for single-family dwellings, as opposed to often congested inner-city apartments. More recently, the greenbelt surrounding the city, located between the rings, has become fragmented as smaller cities form along Moscow's periphery. Expansion of the greenbelt has significantly affected Moscow's spatial development, while the resulting proliferation of automobiles has induced heavy road congestion.

Moscow's urban planning context can be understood as a result of three succeeding major phases and their accompanying political and leadership influences: post-World War I, post-World War II, and post-Soviet following the Cold War. After World War I, Moscow was shaped by Communist ideology, while classical architecture, which had dominated urban planning until the Russian Revolution of 1917, experienced change through the rise of avant-garde architecture in the 1920s. The Bolshevik seizure of power marked the beginning of a new period in Moscow's development, when 'the new leadership of the city and the country supported new and innovative development plans for Moscow as the capital of the world's first communist state' (Moscow City Government, 2013).

In 1918, the same year the city's ring design was first envisioned, the right to private property was abolished in accordance with the principles of Communism, turning space into publicly property. In the 1920s, debates further concerned urbanization in regards to planning the ideal Socialist city supporting a Socialist society (Menu, 2013). Two main planning schools of thought dominated at this time. There were 'urbanists', who sought to make the city revolve around micro nodes and districts, and the opposing 'dis-urbanists', who sought to integrate with natural, rural environments (Glazichev, 2008). While no single school of thought prevailed, what remains is an underlying philosophical struggle between ecological and industrial oriented urbanism.

Benefits to Socialist planning and policies include subbotniks and subsidized social services (Malhotra, 2012). Initiated by Lenin, subbotniks were a form of voluntary work for general welfare. Primarily, the work focused on the maintenance of public spaces, such as courtyards and parks. In the past, there was a prominent negative association with subbotniks because the program forced volunteer work. Today, however, participation in similar volunteer work is experiencing a rebranding, increasingly understood in a positive light thanks to the association with social and communal values. In the past, plans for a Communist city prioritized equal mobility through public transport and walking access to parks and health/education facilities (Gutnov, 1968; Myers, 2008). When the USSR dissolved, Russia was left in a political and economic crisis, catalyzing a move away from Socialist principles of equality. Arguably, what followed were the first steps down an unsustainable path in the wake of Western capitalist cities.

By the 1930s, planning had become a tool for promoting an ideology of social equality (Molodikova & Makhrova, 2007), advanced by efforts to establish a functional relationship between production, social equality and Communist ideals, as outlined by Gustov et al. in The Ideal Communist City (1968). As an ideological, political, and social tool, planning was a means of achieving industrialization and dealing with issues of overcrowding.

From the 1920s until the 1950s, architecture and urbanism were tools of the state, utilized by the leader Josef Stalin to realize his visions – resulting in large developments and buildings that had great impact, socially as well as spatially. For instance, the Metro was finally constructed in 1935. After the establishment of the Soviet Union, Moscow entered its major planning era starting post-World War II in 1945. During this era, planning was a state mechanism that increasingly met with resistance from the avant-garde community.

To look at an example of a state planning scheme, the Socialist housing developments known as 'microrayons' are a visible, salient architectural housing feature typical of Soviet typologies in the post-World War II era. As low-budget housing, microrayons were part of the social services allocated to each citizen. Under the political leadership of Nikita Khruschev, and then Brezhnev, prefabricated housing apartments from catalogues became a norm, leading to replication across the former Soviet Union (Ernsten & Gardner, 2010).

Mason and Nigmatullina (2011) argue that controls before 1991 produced controlled and sustainable metropolitan development. This is reflected in Moscow's urban form. Since the 1990s, growth in low-density suburban sprawl has been driven by a demand for single-family homes, leading to a sharp increase in the number of privately owned automobiles. To compensate, roads, highways and transportation infrastructure had to be expanded.

Today, the transformation of post-Communist cities like Moscow is characterized by the expansion of commercial spaces, the transformation of industrial zones, and a demand for new forms of housing (Enyedi, 1998). Additionally, the market economy in Moscow reflects Western-style businesses, services, architecture, and lifestyles.

Moscow's historical evolution from Socialist traditions to contemporary globalization shapes a distinct urban development context, whereby the evolution of revolutionary forces in the past are in line with forms of modern resistance, increasingly appearing as bottom-up development initiatives. Examining Moscow can provide lessons for alternative approaches to development that resonate with similar post-Socialist cities, while also offering comparative insights to any city seeking to adapt and refine urban development practices in a shifting urban landscape.

A right to a socialist city: a greater Moscow?
Russian ideals of urban planning have been experimental and utopian in the past, providing rich lessons from both success and failure. Moscow's current urban trajectory reflects a shift from collectivism to atomization, notably marked by a rising sprawl and individualism, which has created some of the worst traffic congestion in the world.

In August 2011, President Dmitry Medvedev decided to officially double the size of Moscow by developing the southwest regions of the city, now creating the area referred to as 'Greater Moscow'. Expanding Moscow's metropolitan area to include an area known as Moscow Oblast involves federal negotiations. This expansion prompts considerations of historical urban development lessons, and to further reflect on how traditional top-down decisions have worked in the past to navigate a present plan involving diverse actors. These factors make the expansion of Moscow Oblast inherently controversial, catalyzing new avenues of dialogue between citizens, planners and policymakers. For example, the Moscow Urban Forum was organized in 2010 as an annual gathering for public discussion about relevant issues that affect the city. Alongside Socialist traditions, Russia also maintains a tradition of guerilla urban resistance. Many such entities are formed by everyday citizens, who are conscious and inspired to make a difference. For instance, the social movement 'Partizaning' was particularly inspired by Russia's revolutionary and DIY traditions, as they promote 'participatory urban replanning' using 'street art as a tool for civic action in cities worldwide' (Partizaning, 2012). Partizaning is just one example among numerous urban initiatives, media channels and blogs, such as UrbanUrban, Bolshoi Gorod and The Village – all sharing intent to disseminate responses to a globalizing development landscape, while offering innovative solutions and taking action.

The new dialogue created in Moscow's politically and socially charged context of local versus federal politics raises opportunities for collaboration among citizens, businesses and other initiatives to explore a new path for post-Socialist or post-Communist cities. The city's expansion has created a new interdisciplinary forum in which politics and urbanism are debated (Ivanov, 2013; Menu, 2013), and change is experienced by the involvement of new networks of actors (Buernika et al., 2011).

With such a dynamic past, Moscow's future is equally unpredictable. As the city is currently post-Communist, post-Soviet, post-Socialist, (Buernika et al., 2011) it is clear that 'heritage influences actor's decisions regarding urban development'. Further, the literature agrees that Moscow's urban development will be unique. Exemplifying newfound practices, an apparent real estate grab has highlighted people and institutions leveraging each other's strengths through diverse partnerships.

In 2007, Moscow's chief architect Alexander Kuzmin said it was time Moscow opted for a 'plan of necessity' rather than 'a plan of possibility' (Moscow City Government, 2013). On May 5, 2010, after many debates and public hearings, the City Duma, or legislative body, adopted the Urban Development Plan 2025. In the context of Moscow's expansion and the Urban Development Plan 2025, this chapter will examine four case studies of bottom-up urbanism to reveal how institutions and traditional, top-down players both help and hinder progress. First, we review Moscow's process of Cyclification, as a long-term process of urban activism and citizens' resistance to the urban development trajectory, focused on collaborative acts in architecture, ecological urbanism and sustainability. Second, we look at the case of 'Delai Sam' to see how citizens have used multiple event formats and self-organization to collectively address sustainability in an attempt to realize a citizen's vision for the city. Third, we use an example from the district of Mitino to examine experiments in Cooperative Urbanism that highlight governance, transparency and social engagement that support local grass-roots and DIY initiatives. Fourth and finally, we look at the development of the Nagatino co-working space, and the transformation of functions of physical spaces in response

Russia's Avant-Garde:
Art, Architecture and Urban Utopias

❝ Utopia transforms itself into actuality. The fairy tale becomes a reality. The contours of socialism will become overgrown with iron flesh, filled with electric blood, and begin to dwell full of life. The speed of socialist building outstrips the most audacious daring. In this lies the distinctive character and essence of the epoch. ❞

– I. Chernia, 'The Cities of Socialism' quoted in Wolfe, 2011

Between 1928 and 1937, premier representatives of European architectural modernism met in Moscow and other cities throughout the Soviet Union. The leading avant-garde minds of a generation 'gathered to put forth their proposals for a radically new society... from this new built environment, it was believed, would emerge the outlines of the New Man, as both the outcome of the new social order and the archetype of an emancipated humanity' (Wolfe, 2011).

Art and architecture have always played a strong aesthetic and functional/critical role in Russian society, and are linked with ideas of urbanism and social transformation. 'Avant-garde' is a term used to define the large, influential wave of modern art in Russia and the Soviet Union from 1890 to 1960. It includes related art movements such as constructivism and futurism. The avant-garde reached its height between the 1917 Russian Revolution and 1932, when their ideas clashed with the newly emerged state-sponsored direction of Social Realism. Mainly, it is known for involving artists with aspects of society and creating alternative visions of reality, combining life with art in its attempts at radical transformations.

In the 1970s, strong artists movements, in the tradition of Soviet nonconformist art, emerged to challenge the ideas of Soviet Realism. A great example of official Soviet functional art is from 1935: when Moscow's Metro was opened it became central to the transportation system as well as a Stalinist device to force an appreciation of Soviet realist art onto the people. Unlike in the 1920s, the avant-garde of the 1930s and 1940s opposed Stalin's architectural philosophies and rejected their lack of freedom. Most notable was the Moscow Conceptualist art movement, which included the Sots artists and the Collective Actions group. These Soviet artists did not regard their work as political but rather as existential and apolitical, committed to ideas of freedom and the individual imagination: 'For artists living under communism, participation had no such agitationary goals. It was, rather, a means of experiencing a more authentic (because of being individual and self-organized) mode of collective experience than the one prescribed by the state in official parades and mass spectacles' (Bishop, 2011). Artists at this time took to a critical constructive approach to engage with their urban realities. All foreign architects were expelled from the Soviet Union in 1937, which brought an end to the avant-garde's attempt to realize Utopia (Wolfe, 2011). Both then and now, urban planning was either given to international expertise or political leadership rather than fostering an authentic and creative domestic voice.

Art in a Socialist city was meant for all the people and not just the elite. Russian culture also embodied a resistance to authoritarian fascism and capitalism during World War Two and the Cold War. In post-Soviet cities such as Moscow, traditions of DIY-ism are strong because of scarcity in the postwar and Cold War periods. But ideas surrounding the heroism of guerilla and underground struggle are part of the Russian consciousness. It is in this vein that urban activism and resistance emerges, and the contemporary involvement of artists, architects, and now citizens too, speaks to Moscow's traditional way in which the city invites international experts for creative thinking but is now at the same time trying to marry visioning with practicality. New street art and activism movements that are emerging in Moscow signal these traditions of critical, utopian urban re-envisioning.

to changes in the city and its urban development trajectory. We also look at the realization of collective, urban utopias from the bottom-up rather than top-down spatial visions.

The rise of citizen initiatives sparking DIY and of tactical urbanism represents the Russian tradition of resistance, as 'the strong political context and emergence of a new social phenomenon' demands new perspectives into how top-down actors are facilitating bottom-up actors to realize citizens' ideals (Menu, 2013). Each case study demonstrates a bottom-up initiative targeted at one aspect of urbanism-mobility, ecological sustainability, changing uses of space, and governance – to highlight diverse institutional involvement and the ways in which institutions are supporting the idea of 'citizens as experts'. In conclusion, the chapter explores Menu's question of whether or not Moscow's 'urban environment, once an instruction of control, is now being transformed into a subversive instrument' (Menu, 2013).

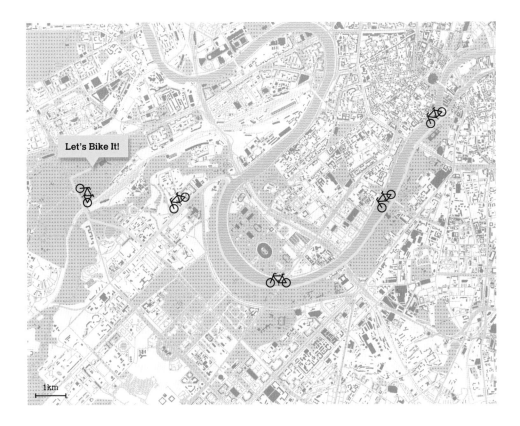

Let's Bike It!

1km

Case 1
The Cyclification of Moscow

❝ Every year there are promises to improve the situation for cyclists. We hope this year it will finally result in something. ❞

– Anton Polsky

Like in many cities, Moscow's rising middle class and suburban expansion catapulted a rise in automobile use. Cycling, once overseen and unused as a mode of urban transport, is now gaining popularity as citizens respond to the congestion and pollution of a car-dominated city.

This case study portrays key initiatives in the 'cyclification' of Moscow, and explores how years of DIY-, tactical action engaged institutions in realizing urban change as traditional institutional and top-down players learn from bottom-up initiatives to build on what works, involving activists as citizen experts.

What we find is that activism, with support from the media and raised awareness and local and international dialogue, facilitated the recognition of and relationship between bottom-up and top-down actors in achieving milestones in the cyclification of Moscow, establishing a movement that is gaining momentum into future development.

Cycling as a mode of transport is growing in Moscow, reflecting a greater shift across Europe toward sustainable, convenient modes of transport. As a result, cycling lanes are now being considered as part of the city's transport network. For instance, at the 2013 Moscow Urban Forum, cycling was a prominent issue and an interview with Department of Transport (DOT) officials revealed that cycling infrastructure is now a main priority. Institutional recognition of cycling and its benefits are largely achieved thanks to years of DIY-, tactical citizen initiatives, culminating in an influential force that affects the trajectory of Moscow's future (re)development. Cycling developments are particularly significant in Moscow, a city marked by idealized Socialist legacies and one of the most affordable and efficient public transport systems in the world (Gutnov et al., 1968).

The beginnings of capitalist Moscow are marked by the collapse of the USSR and the privatization of the Russian economy. As a result, the last twenty years have witnessed a shift from ideas of collectivism to atomization. Moscow's extraordinary traffic jams are evidence of shifting ideals, reflected in urban development and raising questions of access, space and ownership. As Moscow's transport infrastructure struggles to cope with the resulting congestion – traffic jams, packed buses and crowded metros at peak hours – cycling provides a solution.

The grassroots activism that promotes cyclification in Moscow combines issues of sustainable mobility, environmentalism, politics and urban development. The process of cyclification incorporates various individual and local political initiatives and grass-roots activism, catalyzed by local and regional planning decisions, which are affected by international influences and are made in the context of contrasting traditional and modern development approaches in a globalizing city. The process also demonstrates convergent activism as a form of political resistance to capitalism and capital-led urban development by federal and local governments. It reveals diverse citizen efforts that promote cycling in the city as well as the effectiveness of institutions in supporting these efforts to facilitate necessary action.

Citizen resistance: from Critical Mass to crowdsourcing

We will now explore the role of citizens' initiatives in the cyclification of Moscow through a lens that magnifies strategies that changed cycling from an overlooked transport option into an institutionally supported development focus. More specifically, we will examine how persistent, creative advancements mingled with technology and modern media outlets

have led to greater public awareness and has gained the attention and inclusion of institutions in the process of redeveloping the city.

Since the 1990s, Moscow has been home to a growing middle class, characterized by certain consumption and lifestyle choices. As people gain access to new sources of income, their purchases reflect individual identities and pride in private ownership (Coulibaly, 2012). Increased private automobile ownership has been one result, leading to more traffic and pollution. Subsequently, many eastern European cities recognized the immediate and long-term benefits of cycling as a means of everyday transport. In Moscow, two principal initiatives catalyzed the cycling movement: Critical Mass and Velonotte.

Bicycle activists started organizing Critical Mass rides in June of 2002 as a form of eco-resistance in Moscow. Traffic posed a physical threat, so participants used a website (http://crit-mass.by.ru) to organize several anti-car events for World Car-Free Day. Despite initial popularity and a shift toward a participatory, less politically inclined approach, (Wright, 2011) Critical Mass met its demise after several years. Due to their subversive nature, rides were seen as counter-constructive, and Critical Mass participants were criticized for promoting cycling and its culture in a negative manner. Many cycling groups and organizations wanted legal, organized and effective events, while Critical Mass was illegal, spontaneous, rebellious and difficult to control.

Velonotte, an annual ride, was started in 2007 by Sergey Nikitkin, Art Historian, Professor of Urbanism and cycling enthusiast, to celebrate the city's urban and architectural history. The public rides challenged Moscow's elite to explore the city by night – when there is less traffic – and with 80% of the over 150 events on the city outskirts, focused on the periphery, where many live but 'nothing ever happens'. Nikitkin's goal was to reclaim and revitalize these parts of the city, to unite people while addressing the problem of decreasing cultural cohesion. Rather than promoting cycling as transport, Nikitkin wanted to transform people's perception and experience of the city.

The impact of these two movements was to promote the visibility of cycling, but they were hindered by a lack of direct dialogue with authorities and institutions. Instead, the cyclification process in Moscow has been fragmented and disparate, unofficial and independent. An emerging sense of civic ownership was raised in resistance to city changes, while no definitive, significant plans or strategies to alter development were coordinated. Eventually, institutions solicited insights and expertise from recognizable activists in society.

Beginning in the 1990s, under Mayor Luzhkov, the government began promising cycling infrastructure. Cycling activists, however, were skeptical. In response to the drafting of plans for a future vision for Moscow in 2010, a successful initiative arose in response to urban development's environmental impact. 'Let's Bike It!' is a citizen initiative formed by Vladimir Kumov to promote cycling culture. The idea was to revive Russian social life while drawing attention to urban environmental problems, particularly the negative impact of automobiles. To gather materials about positive bicycle culture and systems in Europe, the project documented a cycling trip from Russia to Europe.

In 2010, Anton Polsky, a street artist, designer and avid cyclist, published 'USE/LESS' – a map of his favorite cycling routes – in response to Mayor Luzhkov's conservative, car-oriented fifteen-year urban-planning initiative. In the end, the cycling map became more of a manifesto than a practical tool. It was the artist's way to share his belief that 'It's your city, you can own it, use it any way you want' (McGrane, 2013). Polsky used a website to share the maps, encouraging citizens to download, print, mark favorite routes, and drop them at galleries across the city. In this way, what began as a politically inclined personal art project expanded into a movement to create a participatory, informal bicycle map for Moscow.

Media institutions have played a supportive role. For instance, in 2010, the online magazine The Village hired Polsky as an art director and advisor on urban topics. In 2011, Polsky launched a community project, that became a crowd-sourced map for bicycle racks. As an institution, The Village funded and promoted the project, while a company that offered discounts to small businesses produced the racks. Soon, more businesses began advertising bicycle racks and promoting sustainable lifestyles. With increased public awareness, driven by media, cycling gathered support. Here we have a symbiosis between activists, media and small businesses marking a transition from DIY intervention to jointly developed change.

Leveraging media produced an effective way to elevate cyclification, and to crowd-source ideas, as shown by websites such as UrbanUrban and Partizaning. Since 2011, as part of the Partizaning collective, Polsky has initiated many unsanctioned, guerilla-type cyclification efforts, such as installing navigation for cyclists to mark safe routes and paths throughout the city (Zimberg, 2013; Yerkovich, 2012). Part of this strategy is combining social media and 'tactical urbanism' to raise awareness, attracting news media to formalize public discussion.

Lessons learned from diverse actors and actions
Beyond targeting the media to raise awareness of both the public and institutions in understanding and acting on positive citizen-initiated change, the cyclification of Moscow teaches us that actively engaging local and international dialogue welcomes diverse actors and further facilitates awareness and promotes citizen-institutional collaboration to realize changes.

Emerging relationships between activists, institutions and government are positively correlated to citizens' initiatives that utilized independent media, gained public media coverage and collaborated with institutions. In 2012, in the wake of political protests opposing President Vladimir Putin, a ban was placed against unplanned group cycling. The same year, with official clearance to close roads, the first 'Let's Bike It!' cycling parade was successfully organized, with over 60,000 people involved. Rather than working subversively and organizing flash mobs, the Let's Bike It! parade demonstrated success through legal, organized, collaborative approaches. Also in 2012, cycling activist Alexey Mityaev joined the Department Of Transport, working with the system to advise on their cycling program. When Mityaev and other activists collectively applied for but failed to secure funding to design cycling paths, the resulting media coverage communicated the importance of his ideas to the public. He is now an official adviser to the Mayor on the subject of transportation and road infrastructure.

Success has also come from various local and international actors engaging in discussion. Institutions such as The Village and the Strelka Institute for Media, Urbanism and Architecture, are exploring cycling issues. For now, they are not directly involved, but graciously offer space for discussion. Internationally, in 2012, Mityaev, Kumov, Nikitkin and Polsky were invited to speak with department of transport representatives from New York, and now other cities, about their experience with cyclification in Moscow. They agreed that cycling could no longer be ignored, and that in order to promote safer cycling, the city needed evidence of demand before supporting safe-cycling initiatives. After Mityaev officially involved himself with international experts,

This page
Extract of the USE/LESS
Cycling Map of Moscow, 2010

Next spread (left)
Guerilla cycling navigation
by Partizaning, 2012

Next spread (right)
First cycling parade organized by
Let's Bike It! in Moscow, 2012

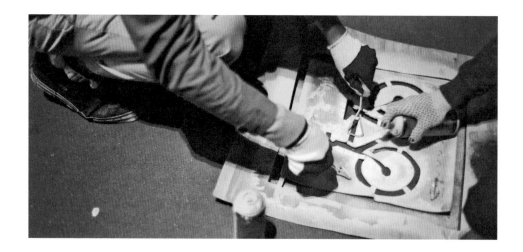

Moscow's cycling infrastructure benefited from these global relationships.

Cyclification therefore helped leading institutions to acknowledge that diverse, small-scale events can be effective. Creative interventions that reached new audiences were important, as was involving multiple players. The Bank of Moscow, a financial institution, and The Village, a private institution, were both involved in the discussion about cycling. This demonstrates that multiple voices and diverse actors are important in urban transformation. In support, Sergey Nikitin sees working with institutions as crucial, as it provides diverse opinions and expertise. For instance, in each city where it is organized,

Velonotte partners with different groups in order to get permission to block parts of the city, while working with varied government departments and media outlets. Apart from the initial illegal and unsanctioned Critical Mass rides, instances of guerilla or insurgent urbanism (Hou, 2010) can be tactical and effective (Lydon et al., 2010) in relation to cycling.

The role of institutions
Here we highlight an overview of this section's central findings from the cyclification of Moscow. To begin with, promoting cycling in Moscow has been a long, disjointed process. Catalyzed by activists, lasting, positive urban transformations were made possible by the support of institutions. The first bicycle lane in Russia was built in Moscow in 1897; however, the majority of original lanes were targeted for recreation, not everyday urban mobility. A 6.6-km bicycle lane built for Moscow commuters in September 2011 was received as more symbolic than practical as it was an unprotected, narrow strip of green running alongside a main thoroughfare. 2013 marked a turning point,

as the Department of Transport (DOT) created 16 km of bike lanes, and plans for 135 km more in 2014. DOT installed 1200 bike racks for 12,000 bicycles and started a bike-share system with 75 stations, set to increase to 350, offering 5,000 bicycles by 2014. Also in 2013, the department organized a 'bike-boulevard', 'Car-Free Day' and set up a website with information and updates about bike infrastructure and related events in Moscow. These grand developments and achievements would not have been realized without active citizen commitment and grass-roots engagement.

The Village was a crucial institution involved in cyclification; it allowed people to write about the issue and highlighted important aspects of cyclification. In 2012, they published an article about how a group of activists, including Polsky, Mityaev and Kumov, had failed to get the contract to fund official masterplans. Following the resulting media buzz, the DOT reached out to activists as consultants, and hired Mityaev.

Through the process of cyclification, urban planning in Moscow became less centrally directed and authoritarian, and found success in more collaborative and user-oriented approaches. Struggling with public space and transportation issues, a DOT representative says they are now focused on improving cycling infrastructure based on international experience. To create such an integrated infrastructural plan, they look for support from citizen expertise. The DOT also finds success in keeping channels of communication open with the public, promoting information online and discussing with activists. Essentially, by supporting the existing projects and efforts of activists, institutions are able to effectively target and address urban issues.

In 2013, many impacts of these various efforts became visible. The City of Moscow introduced a bike share program in collaboration with the Bank of Moscow, installed the city's first bicycle racks, organized events like car-free days, and based on routes suggested in the USE/LESS Map, built one of the first functional official cycling paths in the city. Moscow's DOT has worked with its counterparts in New York, London, and Copenhagen to develop its cycling policies and programs. As a result, it seems that while 'bike sharing may not be as much an immediate step forward for commuting – the program is starting extremely small, both in terms of bikes and miles of bike lanes – as it is a small, concrete triumph for grass-roots political activism' (McGrane, 2013).

With the support of the local government, the media and institutions, a more cohesive cycling ecosystem is now in place. Traditional institutional and top-down players are learning from bottom-up initiatives to build on what works, involving activists as citizen experts. According to the DOT, they are learning a lot from the innovativeness and creativity of citizens: 'bike parades have had a huge resonance with youth and middle-aged people. It is fun, you feel part of a community. Crowd-sourcing resources on the web can engage a lot of people if well promoted. Nothing would have happened without people calling for attention to problems on the city scale'. And so the case of cyclification demonstrates how institutions can partner and support citizen initiatives to create more inclusive cities.

The local government, media institutions such as The Village and activists such as Mityaev and Kumov have been instrumental in creating new forums for dialogue. The first Moscow Urban Forum was organized in 2011. One the speakers invited was

Jan Gehl, famous for orienting cities towards the needs of people. In his report at the Moscow Urban Forum Gehl included recommendations for cycling in Moscow, and further supported cyclification, stating, '[a]s part of their new bike policy, the transport department is working on finding ways to ensure better access to the city by bike and to connect the green park areas in the outskirts of the city with a bike sharing system' (Gehl, 2013). According to activist Mityaev, '[t]his is only the beginning of our work on public spaces. For the last twenty years, Moscow has been perceived as a city designed for cars, but nowadays we are going to put that behind us' (McGrane, 2013).

Part of Moscow's government campaign is now to encourage cycling as an alternative to the city's ever-worsening traffic jams. The promises to make Moscow a cycle-friendly city are a welcome development for cyclists, but more people need to get on their bike to change Moscow's car culture (Bentley, 2011; Moscow News, 2011). Recent amendments to the traffic code mean that cyclists have more rights. Rather than being perceived as rebellious and confrontational, activists are increasingly working together, supporting each other's strengths and leveraging insight and expertise from the community. The implementation of Moscow's bicycle sharing program and its expansion are examples of grass-roots urbanism successfully 'remaking the city' (McGrane, 2013).

Case 2
Cooperative Urbanism in Mitino

❝ [T]he Open City is manifest through three
elements: passage territories (a certain
porosity at the edges between uses,
communities, and districts); incompleteness
of form (buildings and spaces that can
be revised and adapted over time); and
development narratives (an understanding
of how each intervention or development
will shape the future). In this way, the Open
City promotes a more 'democratic ... physical
experience' that allows strangers to encounter
and interact. ❞

– Richard Sennett

In the midst of past Socialist planning and
contemporary urban growth, the line between
traditional public interpretations of space and the
emerging landscape of privatization becomes blurred.
This section emphasizes learning from everyday life
practices and looks at the realization of alternative
spatial uses based on local habits and temporary,

tactical interventions that seek to renew and revitalize space. Mitino, an outer district of Moscow, is selected to highlight an area primed for change as city expansion questions and challenges longstanding traditional infrastructure, such as the cheap housing microrayons.

In this case, we see how community-based protests organized by a forward-thinking organization trigger media coverage, attract attention and raise awareness. This case also highlights innovative forms of communication between citizens and public officials, while emphasizing how tactical, temporary interventions can unite communities and harness their agency to attract and incorporate institutional support in the realization of citizen-initiated developments. From that, we learn that unsanctioned actions can stimulate real change, and may often lead to legitimate, sanctioned actions.

After the fall of the Soviet Union, public began shifting towards private in post-Communist cities. Marked by the shift from a planned economy to a market economy, these cities increasingly came to resemble cities such as London and New York. Moscow transformed into Sassen's (2005) economically strong, networked, command- and control-based 'global city'. Amplified by new economic and political conditions, urban restructuring was further affected by local/global and contemporary/traditional contrasts. Complex legacies in the globalized metropolis facilitated the reinterpretation of public space and identity in the context of Communism and Socialism. Since the 2012 political protests (Barry, 2011) in Moscow, a growing body of analysis and discussion has focused on protests in post-Socialist spaces (Zhelnina, 2014; Malhotra, 2012), and on the difference between the Socialist, post-Socialist, and Russian patterns of urban public space (Zhelnina, 2014).

While some academics have focused on the expansion of the city in general, many areas of Moscow are neglected. Soviet cultural and material legacies contribute to fueling 'spontaneous and highly speculative initiatives, which are disconnected from visionary place-focused policies' (Diodr, 2010). In this sense, the case of Moscow — particularly beyond the center and expanding southwest region — reflects a post-Socialist, post-Soviet, post-Communist city experiencing both top-down and bottom-up influences.

After the Second World War, the Soviet Union built low-budget, mass social housing for a growing urban population. Leaders such as Khrushchev, and later Brezhnev, pushed for intensive construction of high-rise, prefabricated apartment buildings (Ernsten & Gardner, 2010). Social housing formed part of people's basic public services in the USSR. The buildings shared similar standards, and many still exist (Ernsten & Gardner, 2010). As a result, while examining how people live and work in Moscow and how private and public spaces are used and maintained, it is important to look at alternative uses for these microrayon buildings based on local habits, strategies and DIY practices.

Post-Socialist cities and their traditions of public equality are a neglected area of research, though these cities have undergone complex structural transformations (Petrovic, 2005). Neo-Marxist and neo-Weberian historical approaches to understanding the city tend to agree that Socialist legacies get in the way of capitalist development (Petrovic, 2005; Szelyeni et al., 1996). When the line between public and private became blurred after the fall of the Soviet Union, it was reflected in people's maintenance and delineation of their individual spaces (Shomina interview, 2012). To understand bottom-up actors, institutions, and their networks as part of the urban process in Moscow, one must understand the post-Soviet and post-Communist contexts in which they operate (Burneika et al., 2011).

Typically, actors involved in urban transformation processes are 'relatively new, fast changing and hidden from the eyes of researches due to lack of reliable information' (Burneika et al., 2011). Moscow's expansion has gone along with the growth of what is popularly known as insurgent, DIY or guerilla urbanism (Hou, 2010; Lydon et al., 2010; Iveson, 2013). For institutions working in the urban realm, bottom-up initiatives and temporary transformation schemes are untapped assets. Examining how people use space raises questions about the livability and legacy of social housing structures. While many reject remaining aspects of Socialism, some infrastructural realities are unavoidable legacies of Soviet-era urban planning: for example, mass-housing microrayons or the Moscow metro system.

Collaborative engagement
and cooperative urbanism

This section highlights the role of institutions in instigating and supporting bottom-up change. This can occur through the media and through multi-stakeholder dialogue that leads to the implementation of unique and innovative communication between citizens and public officials. This communication utilizes modern technology, of course, but also older technology in the form of hands-on mailboxes located at traditional social housing complexes.

Since 2011, the Moscow-based urban art activist collective 'Partizaning' has become a prominent feature in the media because of their urban re-planning actions. The word 'partizaning' is now used to describe instances of guerilla urbanism, as 'partizan' means guerilla in Russian, and the group operates in 'a tradition of revolutionary struggle' against authorities for social good (Partizaning, 2011). In May 2012, Partizaning performed a series of urban interventions in light of political protests, encouraging people to 'take matters into their own hands' and improve their situation, rather than wait for politicians to change the city (Yerkovich, 2012).

The series of actions, called the May Interventions, ranged from painting DIY crosswalks, placing benches, installing unsanctioned cycling navigation and a public survey mailbox (Partizaning, 2012). These tactical interventions, as a form of community engagement, raised interest from institutions and authorities through media coverage. As a result of these interventions, a Cooperative Urbanism project emerged, including the district of Mitino as a target site to experiment with ideas for DIY and bottom-up urban transformation.

The experimental Cooperative Urbanism project supports place-making and change from the bottom up on the outskirts of Moscow. Specifically, it targets 'sleeping' districts outside Moscow's center. The goal was to involve multiple stakeholders in a collaborative dialogue: activists, residents, government authorities, local media, planning experts and architects. The goal was also to promote the ethos of DIY-ism or urban hacking (Badger, 2012) and that instead of strongly relying on authorities or the government, people should feel the freedom to do things themselves, without worrying about legality or complications.

In the summer of 2012, Moscow was in the midst of many changes. A new generation of young leaders were recently elected, and they saw themselves as progressives working to change the city (Schwirtz, 2012). Since then, the idea of a 'right to the city' has explained an unprecedented citizen presence forming in the streets in reaction to authority. For the first time, this stimulated a discussion on urban public space and corresponding rights in the Russian-speaking discourse (Zhelina, 2014; Malhotra, 2012). Before the 2012 protests, the term 'urban public space' was rarely, if ever, used.

In July 2012, the newly established Strelka Institute (www.strelkainstitute.edu) approached Partizaning (eng.partizaning.org) and offered to be a research and implementation partner on a series of workshops for their 'Agents of Change' summer program. The Strelka Institute wanted to work with urban communities outside the city center and learn from people already engaged in grass-roots urban activism. Partizaning was therefore tasked to organize and implement the workshops, focusing on research, community engagement and urban interventions. The jointly conceived project was an experiment in the ideals

of collaboration, a way to integrate theory with practice and also bring international experts in dialogue with local communities, and connect activists with municipal authorities. From July to August 2012, nine workshops were organized in different districts of Moscow. Partizaning editors served as researchers, collecting data, identifying problems and involving local residents, activists, journalists and municipal authorities in the process of redesigning and reimagining spaces in their district. Each workshop was planned in the periphery, and led by a guest expert or collective.

The workshop planned in Mitino, a district situated on the northwestern edge of Moscow, focused on architecture as a tool for designing social spaces. Mitino is one the farthest districts from the city center, geographically isolated by the Moscow Canal.

Vladimir Demidko had recently been elected to the local parliament for the district of Mitino. Enthusiastic about his job, he wanted to meet activists who needed support at the district level, and so he met with representatives from the Strelka Institute about opportunities for collaboration. To help local government get familiar with community needs, Demidko asked Partizaning to install two mailboxes in the neighborhood, and he pledged to read and respond to residents' letters. With mailboxes in place, local activists were appointed to read the letters and further organize information in order to prepare for an effective place-making workshop. The project used ethnography and mapping, social surveys and research conducted by Partizaning, the Strelka Institute and Norwegian TYIN Tengstue Architects, Demidko's advice and residents' concerns. In one month, residents submitted several hundred letters; many appeals were immediately and directly

resolved by Demidko's municipal office. Moreover, numerous letters demonstrated the willingness of residents to communicate with authorities, and those old-fashioned mailboxes proved an effective communication channel. Demidko was amazed to receive more positive proposals than complaints. As a result, he plans to expand the use of mailboxes to gain feedback from residents.

Ultimately, a parking lot adjacent to the metro station was chosen as a potential transformation site. Demidko obtained permission from the property owner to utilize the space. It was agreed that an event would be organized to involve locals in activities and to create a symbol of change. Residents did not find this parking lot to be a good use of space, as they preferred more plants, benches and opportunities for activities; the goal was to activate and improve the space.

Citizens as experts: lessons learned
Local government involvement was crucial for infrastructural change and the realization of Cooperative Urbanism Mitino's project goals. According to Demidko, residents often submitted mapped, feasible solutions in mailboxes, allowing his department to take immediate action. Many requests were quite simple – for example, small infrastructural repairs to footpaths, sidewalks, playgrounds – and cooperation between residents and government created harmonic efficiency. Demidko emphasizes that residents can improve their lives better than anyone, and often come up with the best solutions.

In this fashion, Cooperative Urbanism Mitino highlighted the challenges and benefits of connecting bottom-up and top-down urbanism, while managing multiple, contrasting interests and stakeholders. The project demonstrates that change does not arise simply because action is sanctioned; unsanctioned actions can be effective – especially with engaged dialogue between actors.

Mitino's innovative urban research method – the mailbox method – presents another successful aspect, which led Moscow's Department of Libraries to utilize the same strategy to survey citizens' needs. Despite its success in this case, responding to letters introduces messy participation (Miessen, 2011) that may not be feasible for larger urban areas. While the project successfully empowered residents and established a temporary spatial transformation, the challenge of involving the community in a long-term, sustainable manner remains.

Regarding the workshop process, a research phase initially mapped the site based on insight into why people perceived the space in a negative way. After mapping, participants began designing modular street furniture to introduce functionality and transform spatial perceptions. Participants occupied the mall-front parking lot for several days, constructing basic, movable modules. Demidko, as well as other officials, participated in the construction process alongside children and parents.

The mailbox's success and the actions of a handful of local residents composed the highest involvement, while sustained community investment waned. In retrospect, working closely with an urban community requires building trust, where a new deputy and new

activists were unable to establish a sound rapport. In this case, mailboxes and the project's constructive nature garnered children's participation. However, adults and teens remained scarce.

Cooperative Urbanism Mitino's success is difficult to gauge; it depends on whether we evaluate structural or value-based transformation. Success is evident in creating a generational group of 'agents of change', who will also inspire others, while Mitino's progressive municipal deputy, Demidko, and resident activist Tony Kolobakhen continue working on local issues. For instance, garages in microrayon developments are ubiquitous, yet researchers found they are generally used for storage (Ernest & Gardner, 2010). In 2012, Kolobakhen set up a cinema theater and social space in an empty garage in his microrayon. Also in 2012, Mitino residents campaigned against the construction of a shopping center in the park, which prompted Moscow's mayor to cancel construction and prepare a park improvement project. In 2013, several on-going district projects now have local government support, including allocation of ten million rubles (appr. 275,000 US dollars) to a resident's proposal to unite people around interests and improve the neighborhood. Through resident-government communication, institutions better understand area-specific needs, the local actors, and provide collaborative, empowering support to create positive change together.

Left
A mailbox letter outlined resident complaints about a 24-hour shop selling cigarettes and beer to children

Centre
A letter received in Mitino's Partizaning mailbox shows a resident's idea for reorganizing the street

Right
A mailbox letter in which a resident requested a children's playground in a specific site

The role of institutions
In Mitino, institutions synchronized with existing change-makers and encouraged and supported community efforts. This collaborative institutional engagement was a central driver of success. Institutions face the challenge of reconciling competing visions and priorities; however, each actor in this case could leverage different areas of expertise and interest to enhance collaborative synergy. The Strelka Institute, comprised of professionals who focus on education and urbanism, provided financial, logistical, expert, and in-kind support. Strelka's involvement in Partizaning's mailbox idea was also significant, leveraging creative activist tactics to engage the local community.

Local government identified active residents that understood the issues in their district, enabling them to realize their ideas. According to Demidko, 'people are ready and willing to help their district'. Supporting initiatives and encouraging projects both during and after the project, Demidko was actively involved throughout. His leadership and support were influential in the project's success and legitimacy. For instance, he worked with a number of communication channels outside the mailboxes: telephones, an open office, community presence and approachability, Internet, and boxes in doorways. In addition, he runs a live journal blog and a Facebook page, and uses social media to connect with constituents, while holding meetings with active residents to mutually benefit from understanding his district's needs, foreseeing

problems and implement solutions. Demidko has said, '[i]f a person needs to contact me, it usually takes him only a few minutes'.

Diverse institutions and actors were able to share expertise and responsibilities. For instance, while Demidko could reach out to residents in Mitino, the younger and professional Strelka Institute was able to involve progressive architects. In general, institutions enabled change, where DIY would be impossible or illegal. Local government upheld their responsibility to support residents and implement infrastructural upgrades and positive changes, while government legitimacy facilitated project goals and led a larger group of local residents to believe and participate in Cooperative Urbanism Mitino. In sum, activism, media coverage and raised awareness contributed to success for Mitino's residents, in ways that are similar to, yet different from the case of cyclification.

Partizaning's institutional role helped instigate citizen initiatives, and then support them via media coverage and the involvement of multiple stakeholders. In terms of local government, Demidko played a key role by actively communicating with and serving the needs of his district in realizing citizen-focused change. Demidko's role in the initiative also generated a sense of legitimacy leading to the involvement of more citizen actors, producing more significant changes and uniting the community. Local governments can mirror similar actions in any city to effectively connect and engage citizens in urban development processes.

Zil Cultural Center

Flacon Design Factory

DIY Crosswalks #1

DIY Crosswalks #2

50m

50m

50m

50m

1 Text for the Moscow 2020 manifesto from:
<http://pixelchannel.ru/moscow2020.htm>

2 Partizaning manifesto as quoted from:
<eng.partizaning.org>

3 Taken from the official website:
<www.delaisam.org>

Case 3
Delai Sam

❝ Moscow: not the most comfortable city for living. Last year, the Moscow authorities presented a masterplan for the city, which ignores a lot of its current problems. We want to live in a green city with convenient public transport, bicycle lanes, beautiful old and new buildings, tolerant mayor, authorities and residents. We must begin to build for ourselves a city in which we want to live. ❞

– Moscow 2020, Manifesto[1]

Urban and historical context:
legacies of DIY and eco-urbanism in Russia
The case of Delai Sam portrays a citizen-driven initiative focused on ecological and sustainable development in response to developments situated in traditional state-led master planning. Delai Sam translates from Russian to English as 'do it yourself', or DIY; the group's central philosophy is a belief in self-organization and action. The idea for Delai Sam emerged in 2010, when a group of citizens comprised of architects, planners, activists and artists collectively wrote an alternative manifesto to the city's 'Moscow 2020', as a form of resistance to proposed urban development plans. Today, they continue to publish greater visions for the city twice a year. This section illuminates how self-organized events of this scale can benefit through connections and collaborations with institutions.

Traditions of activism and DIY practices are etched in Russia's history through the Soviet era, together with utopian principles of Socialism and collectivism. Under Communist rule, Lenin promoted the idea of subbotniks, where people would collectively clean, beautify or maintain public spaces (Malhotra, 2012; McGrane, 2013). While subbotniks and memories of the Soviet past are shunned in contemporary Moscow, ideas of a 'new collectivism' are emerging (Sawhney et al., 2013; Kargina, 2013). We reach a question: can Muscovites overcome capitalist forms of urban development by reformulating traditional Socialist principles of collectivism and activism to generate a contemporary approach towards a sustainable future? Top-down urban development matched by a history of bottom-up resistance appears to have created a space for arts-led grass-roots movements (Menu, 2013).

Moscow is increasingly reflecting 'ecological urbanism' principles that are inherently socially inclusive and environmentally sensitive. They are also less ideologically driven than ideas for green urbanism or sustainable urbanism (Mostavi & Doherty, 2010). A variety of eco-activist protests have formed in recent years, notably against deforestation in Moscow's northern Khimki forest, where the city is advancing construction of a highway connecting Moscow with St. Petersburg.

As street artist activists lead action in Moscow, they reflect a form of DIY urbanism connected to a right to the city (Iveson, 2013; Zimberg 2013), enacted in fashions of artistic urban activism, as seen in the Partizaning collective[2]. This approach prompts a reconsideration of traditional bottom-up and DIY notions, forming socio-political resistance situated in traditions of utopian visions and revolutionary aesthetics.

Delai Sam[3] is a community in Moscow embodying principles of DIY culture and the idea of a 'new collectivism', which is a search for new and effective ways to react and respond to political events in Russia. As stated by Kargina, a co-founder, Delai Sam's philosophy promotes 'an abandonment of any expectation that the government, or someone else, will solve your problems; a rejection of the hierarchical model of society; an attempt at self-awareness and self-organization' (2013). Its founders emphasize that Delai Sam is not a brand, festival or organization; it is an idea that promotes unauthorized and unsanctioned improvements in the city, from the bottom-up. It is known as a marathon, organized by citizens, for citizens, as a multi-format event featuring different urban and grass-roots initiatives each spring and autumn. Events connect people, who can share experiences, ideas and practices with aims to implement concrete, positive urban changes, making Moscow more 'comfortable and eco-friendly'.

Delai Sam's central focus concerns urban ecological issues highlighted in the Moscow 2020 manifesto. What began as an independent, self-organized meeting is now an event, organized every six months with partners seeking to collectively achieve ecological, sustainable goals outlined in Delai Sam's manifesto through free lectures, discussions and workshops. Connected via the Internet, activists horizontally organize events including one-off actions

Left
Delai Sam community
mapping, 2013

Right
Community mapping was part
of an exhibition of Partizaning
tactics during Delai Sam in 2013

4 Partizaning (2012) 'Delai Sam'
Online at: http://eng.partizaning.
org/?tag=delai-sam

as well as year-round work. Emphasizing long-term
planning and action, participants remain committed
throughout the year, involved in various dialogues and
meetings (2013). The DIY ethos is therefore tactically
and strategically targeted at short-term actions with
goals for long-term change (Lydon et al., 2010).
Examples of initiated actions include the collection
and recycling of different waste materials; acting
against the loss of green space due to development
and poor planning policies; addressing traffic jams
and air pollution[4]. While Delai Sam also targets
medium to small cities and towns, this section focuses
on Moscow.

Broaching environmental concerns, Kargina reports
that the Delai Sam's community understands
that ecological problems are closely linked to
socioeconomic issues, as well as to questions of
planning, ethics and aesthetics (2013). In this light, an
ecological approach is one way of approaching urban
issues in the context of the transformation of a post-
Socialist city, especially given the past emphasis on
sustainability and environmentalism (Enyedi, 1998;
Petrovic, 2005; Glazychev, 2008). Specifically, this
case explores how the idea of ecological urbanism,
environmentally sensitive and inclusive, poses a
tangible possibility for Moscow.

In the past, DIY strategies in Moscow have been
understood as coping mechanisms for people
living in cities after the collapse of the Soviet Union
(Ernest & Gardner, 2010). Today, environmentalism
has witnessed the negative ecological impact of a
neoliberal transition, combined with poor policies.
Bottom-up initiatives are now engaging in a public
dialogue between political ideologies and users
(Menu, 2013), and are increasingly influential
(Hou, 2010; Iveson, 2013).

About Delai Sam: from local fest to Delai Film
Delai Sam's cohesive community is composed of
people with diverse backgrounds and expertise.
Institutional support has facilitated the group's growth.
In the beginning, in 2010, Moscow's eco-activists
were preparing their role in the global day of action
planned for 10/10/10, which would focus on reducing
the impact of humans on the environment. This is
when Delai Sam drafted Moscow 2020, their bottom-
up, alternative development plan. To implement
their Moscow 2020 vision, activists decided to hold
meetings every six months to unite people and
develop ideas on improving city life.

Although it was initially organized by activists, Delai
Sam now includes formal and informal institutions.
Kargina believes the 'main value of grass-roots
initiatives lies in drawing attention to what needs to
be done to improve the lives of local people, and the
environment; at the same time, giving a powerful
voice to public opinion and influencing the direction
of change' (Kargina, 2013; interview with Melissina,
2013). Kargina sees many grass-roots initiatives
suffering from a lack of resources, limiting their
ability to influence major infrastructural change –

a job expected of local government. On the contrary, Kargina emphasizes the role of active citizens in 'creating a social mandate, exercising public oversight on the use of resources by local bureaucracy, and the implementation of the changes city council was elected to make' (2013).

Since the inception of the Delai Sam marathons, people-centered urbanism is increasingly valued, as independent groups organize their own Delai Sam-inspired programs and events in smaller cities, including St. Petersburg, Krasnoyarsk, Chelyabinsk, and Nizhny Novgorod. Implementation requires a horizontal, self-organized network of inspired citizens to empower each other and improve urban areas through collective, bottom-up urban transformation. Today, tactical urban interventions by inspired citizens and Delai Sam have included actions such as creating garden plots, recycling, cleaning courtyards, promoting cycling, protecting local architectural heritage, painting crosswalks, building upcycled benches and spontaneous sculptures, cleaning parks, screening films in public spaces, and seed bombing. These temporary, tactical urban transformations are the subject of DIY and guerilla urbanism discussed by Jeff Hou (2010), Mike Lydon (2010) and Iveson (2013). The next Delai Sam is scheduled for April 2014 in Moscow. The event will include an informal conference on urban initiatives focused on the development of select spaces in Moscow, while formulating implementation strategies for specific eco-urban transformation projects.

Lessons from successes and challenges

The group has been facilitated by active outreach to diverse professionals and the maintenance of a core group of individuals committed to successfully advancing the event's goals and overcoming challenges. In this process, diverse events, workshops and leading by example are central assets.

While Delai Sam's localized, small-scale actions are effective and manageable in identifying with particular needs, the challenge remains to uphold their larger, citywide, inclusive vision for Moscow. Small-scale successes do, however, contribute to a greater collective Moscow. These are achieved by consistent participant engagement. Though it is dominated by people in their early to mid-twenties, Delai Sam attracts professionals from diverse fields such as urbanism, urban ecology, architecture and media. A core team has developed, playing a central role in Delai Sam's success. As a community, Delai Sam works year-round, planning lectures and workshops, exchanging information and resources, and developing joint projects. Events are unique to their host city, with a focus and format dependent on local issues. To facilitate the spread of events, standard formats are promoted: for instance, a Do-It-Yourself Summit, concerted Action Day, or Non-action Day, promoting non-consumption.

Similar to temporary, tactical urbanism, testing varied event formats has been key to establishing successful approaches and achieving goals. The Day of Action

is the most successful event. It compiles diverse, specific actions aimed at progressively changing the urban environment. Successful events also include the informal conference on urban initiatives, Delai Summit, which saw over 350 registered participants in 2013, Delai Film, and additional educational workshops, urban tactics exhibitions, and creative activism lectures (Kargina 2013; interview with Melissina, 2013).

Launched in 2013, Delai Film is a festival of activist documentaries intended to become an annual platform showcasing achievements of active citizens and groups, further stimulating Delai Sam principles through examples of self-organized responses to urban problems. According to Kargina, activism is not visible to, and therefore not understood by the majority of society. Therefore, Delai Film strategically incentivizes people to initiate or participate in positive urban and social change themselves, and to document their civic initiatives as well.

Initially called LocalFest, the Delai Sam event has remained affiliated with informal founding institutions like Eco-wiki (www.ecowiki.ru) and the USE/LESS cycling initiative. Delai Sam is now a driver of ecological issues, urban sustainability and self-organization, where active participants and institutions promote group interests. For instance, eco-wiki drives the ecological interests and USE/LESS promotes ideas around cyclification. To manage a multidimensional approach to urban issues and maintain interest and effectiveness, event formats are updated with regards to emerging issues.

Involving multiple interests and stakeholders also facilitates success. For instance, street artists introduce environmental subjects into their work and

eco-warriors develop innovative ways of 'repackaging' a message the public has yet to grasp (Kargina 2013). Since 2011, funding for Delai Sam has also been diverse, coming from multiple institutions and departments for youth and culture.

Direct actions and subsequent city changes characterize Delai Sam's tactical approach (Lydon, 2010), as people-led projects that temporarily convert public space often lead to lasting change. After participants helped set up mobile waste collection systems, initially installed temporarily in ten parks in Moscow, separate waste collection is now permanent in Kuzminki and Bitza parks. In 2012, a one-time workshop by Finnish guerilla gardener Joel Rosenberg led to the establishment of a group of guerilla gardeners in Moscow. Delai Sam thus not only facilitates actions, but also supports new group formation based on collective interest and expertise. The founders of Delai Sam believe they have successfully turned DIY urbanism into a common subject, attracting interest from academics and practitioners, and finding new ways to influence government policy.

The role of institutions
Since the beginning, Delai Sam has been developing a collective vision for Moscow: sustainable, green, healthy and comfortable, with the engagement of citizens and multi-disciplinary coalitions across sectors in planning and implementing tactical, small-scale interventions aimed at long-term changes. For instance, the Department of Culture of Moscow's Multi-Functional Culture Center has given financial support to the initiative since 2012, while creative cluster sites such as Flacon and ZIL provide space to urbanists across Russia to meet at Delai Sam symposiums. Moscow News acts as a media partner

Left
Delai Sam discussions in
Moscow, 2013

Centre
DIY cycling navigation aids

Right
A wall asking people what was
lacking in Moscow

and The Village has helped with outreach and dissemination. Initially about actions, Delai Sam is now more definitively a forum or a conference for sharing.

Institutional funding provided strong support for Delai Sam. The first Delai Sam was sponsored in part by telecom company Megafon, which asked individuals to pledge their support and donate via SMS. Innovative funding mechanisms for subscribers to text/SMS a special number and donate money resulted in a total of 100,000 rubles (app. 2800 US dollars). Furthermore, the Department of Culture and the Moscow Youth Multi-functional Center now financially support the project. Nevertheless, sustainable funding remains a concern. Organizers have tried various financing schemes, including a combination of grants, business sponsorship, and crowd-funded donations. Without a sustainable financial solution, the group relies on institutions for financing.

Despite funding challenges, Delai Sam remains independent, closely associated with numerous creative clusters. Commercial art clusters such as Flacon Design Center and Winzavod Contemporary Art Center have hosted the Delai Sam summit and film screenings. These institutions also share physical spaces where regular co-organizer meetings are held to plan and coordinate annual events. A former industrial cultural center, part of the Department of Culture, has become a permanent partner and recurring site for Delai Sam summit and Delai Film in Moscow.

Visibility, outreach and PR comprise additional attributes of institutional support. Several news and media outlets, such as Moscow News, partner

organizations like Partizaning, The Village and various blogs have also helped with outreach, expertise and visibility. In this case, working with institutions positively impacts Delai Sam by promoting their ideology. According to organizer Melissina, it is, in part, thanks to yearly institutional support that the marathon events are organized, and this has made the organizers more aware of PR strategies, branding, and technical support.

Several municipal authorities recently elected to local government are interested in involving citizens from their district in Delai Sam, which shows that when institutions support ongoing citizen projects, they can increase effectiveness. Also, institutions can lend financial support, space and expertise to raise the information-sharing capacity. Not all institutions are equal: activists note that nonprofits are stronger supporters than commercial institutions.

Delai Sam also builds on tradition, reinventing Lenin's subbotniks through Socialist legacies, contributing to the growing idea of a new collectivism (Kargina 2012; McGrane, 2013), valuing memory and history with a sense of resistance to dominant authoritarianism – a longstanding tradition in Russia.

Case 4
Community Development:
Co-working in Nagatino

In the context of privatization and land ownership
in contemporary urban development processes,
the contrast between capitalist real estate market
values and Socialist principles creates an interesting
dynamic. This section explores co-working as an
innovative spatial use combining citizens' needs
with real estate and commercial interests. Nagatino
reflects the neoliberal urban development taking hold
of Russia in the context of rising entrepreneurship.
Debates are emerging over whether increasing market
pressures destroy social ties or actually stimulate
their creation. Following the collapse of the Soviet
Union, an independent Russia entered a period
of privatization, consequently affecting individual
ownership and property rights issues. Urban land, its
value and real estate in Moscow are complex issues,
particularly outside the city center.

Because of the real estate situation and a combination
of socioeconomic and political forces, Moscow is

Co-working space

50m

Top
Overview of the co-working
space in Nagatino

Bottom left
Coffee area with breakfast bar

Bottom right
Construction of co-working space,
November 2012

1 Ria Novosti. 'Ostozhenka in world's 'top ten' most
expensive streets.' (2011). Online at: http://en.ria.ru/
business/20110309/162926700.html

2 Moscow Urban Forum. (2013). Online at:
http://www.moscowurbanforum.com

3 'Problems Arising from Land Privatization by a
Building Owner.' The Moscow Times. Online at: http://
www.themoscowtimes.com/business/business_
for_business/article/problems-arising-from-land-
privatization-by-a-building-owner/442507.html

undergoing an urban transformation. Ostozhenkae Street, in the heart of Old Moscow, is now more expensive than 5th Avenue in New York.[1] In this light, the city needs to give attention to peripheral areas beyond its center. Moscow's theme at the 2013 Urban Forum was 'Megacities: Success Beyond the Centre'[2], reflecting a focus on microrayons planned outside the center.

In the Soviet era, housing and employment was a priority, but today, real estate development, commercialization and highway development go hand in hand. Spatial use patterns have also been transforming. According to Jaffee and Kaganova (2001), Soviet central planning was in the rankings for having the 'worst legacy in real estate, especially urban housing', particularly due to infrastructural deficiencies. Substantial, necessary improvements require not only changing the policies of local governments, but also the development of market institutions. Shifting notions of public and private space coupled with high migration rates, newly privatized real estate markets and issues dividing land titles[3] are all part of Moscow's contemporary contextual conundrum.

Between 1988 and 1991, Soviet legislation introduced by Mikhail Gorbachev transferred enterprise rights from government to employees, which led to a process of 'spontaneous privatization' enabling industrial assets to be acquired by managers. Urban development and land use were also affected by privatization, which primarily occurred in the early and mid-1990s under the presidency of Boris Yeltsin. Until Gorbachev relaxed restrictions in the late 1980s, private ownership of enterprises and property had been impossible. Privatization facilitated Russia's shift from a planned Soviet economy towards a market economy, but the result was that the national wealth fell into the hands of a relatively small group, dramatically widening the gap in wealth.

The official expansion of the city on July 1, 2012 categorized a majority of land in 'New Moscow' as urban, while allowing room for spatial change.[4] Although land privatization can be a complex process, it is attractive to business owners. Moscow's Mayor, Sobyanin, stated that the government has no plans to move industrial enterprises out of the city. This announcement led to a surge in business activity, as land privatization is not only financially attractive,

but is often a way to provide additional business protection.[5]

Changing notions of ownership and land use: co-working and commercial real estate
The development of co-working spaces signals the changing modes of socialization in Moscow (Borodulino, 2013; Voice of Russia, 2012). Since 2011, numerous co-working spaces have appeared.[6] Recognizing these spaces as incubators for small and mid-sized businesses, the government plans to support co-working initiatives as a means of supporting bottom-up economic development. For instance, the Mayor introduced high-tech co-working as part of Moscow's Technology Incubation Program.[7] The growth of co-working spaces demonstrates a concerted way of addressing commercial, financial and social needs in the city. Previously, few spaces existed for youth to socialize outside their district; now the population is more mobile. Moscow also has a large commuting population – and some of the world's worst traffic jams. Bottom-up social space initiatives outside the center, such as co-working Nagatino, directly or indirectly address these multiple issues. Today, commercial centers and co-working options are common, including the globally present 'HUB', or 'Ziferblat'. Such spaces also emerge at 'creative clusters'[8], or former industrial spaces.

Co-working represents a redevelopment of the commercial use of space, relating to issues of urban mobility and commuting as well as the financial crisis. These spaces also reflect an increasing post-industrial, modern urban trend related to ownership and urban space. Former factory space is being strategically gentrified for real estate purposes, while attracting interest in creating social and community-oriented centers that encourage people to visit. According to representatives setting up community co-working space in Moscow's outer districts, the idea that drives their work is that 'co-working is not simply about the physical space, but about establishing the co-working community'. In this way, the spirit of entrepreneurism, community and bottom-up initiatives become joined.

Moscow's southern district of Nagatino covers an area of 8.17 km with a population of 77,263 (2013). A new co-working space is being opened in one of the district's main business centers. Scheduled to open January 2014, Nagatino's co-working space was founded by Andrew Kompaneets. He believes it should not function simply as a business center, but also as a social space that enhances community cohesion. Located near metro station Nagatinskaya, the center is being built in a former furniture factory. The space is 700 m² and the entire building is 17,000 m². The building itself will be renovated in the coming year, with plans to develop more co-working space.

At different stages of its development, Nagatino's co-working center has informally consulted with institutions, including government and media, as well as the Strelka Institute. The case is an interesting mix of public and private initiative supporting one another, demonstrating the political and economic shift in the city. Projections for the next three to five years show that people in Russia will increasingly have to set up their own businesses, and they will need flexible and reasonably priced working spaces outside their homes. The key to a successful co-working space is not just to rent out tables and chairs, but to generate extra value in the community, and to use business tools to create an incubator that can help people realize their goals.

Best practices and solutions:
community building beyond commercial
Co-working spaces offers innovative avenues for networking, working, and socializing. Additionally, they contribute to urban renewal and the reuse of abandoned and underused spaces. Co-working centers help establish a community feeling.

In Nagatino, private investments facilitated the realization of the space. Institutions mainly lent support via incentives and expertise. Over the past two years, entrepreneurialism has significantly expanded, emerging as a popular trend. Moscow City Government has programs and grants that support small and mid-size businesses. Government itself, inspired by the associated benefits and successes of co-working, has established city networks, and now plans to establish eight to ten government co-working spaces spread across Moscow. In this sense the government appears to adopt Ray Oldenburg's idea of a 'third space' (Oldenburg, 1989), a need for social surroundings separate from home and the workplace. Oldenburg argues that a third place is important for civil society, democracy, civic engagement, and establishing feelings of a sense of place. Third places help anchor community life and facilitate broader,

more creative interaction amongst people. Societies naturally produce informal meeting places; in modern Moscow, the intention is to create these spaces, crucial to societal needs.

Role of institutions
In the case of co-working in Nagatino, government, educational and private or commercial institutions play a significant role, specifically those that are supporting individuals as drivers of economic growth. The Strelka Institute had an informal role by giving PR advice and creating urban business models. They focused on leveraging expertise through valuable personal relationships. Strelka is interested in working with people in the more residential peripheries, and Nagatino presented an opportunity.

Developing a co-working space reveals a contemporary form of participatory engagement with the city. As it supports new socio-economic realities and trajectories, co-working is a rising form of bottom-up urbanism. Entrepreneurship, co-working, community spaces and third spaces demonstrateways in which people are getting involved in the demand and supply of urban real estate transformations.

4 The Moscow Times. (2012). 'Land Law Changes in Moscow and Across Russia.' Online at: http://www.themoscowtimes.com/realestate/quarterly/article/469216.html#ixzz2orcXERL3

5 Lidings. (2011). 'Privatization of Land in Moscow.' October 24, 2011. Online at: http://www.lidings.com/eng/articles2?id=35

6 Neumeyer, J. (2012). 'Office by the Hour.' The Moscow News. Online at: http://themoscownews.com/bizfeature/20120917/190240726.html

7 The Moscow Times. (2013). 'Innovation Center Opens Doors in Downtown Moscow.' Online at: http://www.themoscowtimes.com/business/article/innovation-center-opens-doors-in-downtown-moscow/484360.html#ixzz2nLeZPmo3

8 The Telegraph. 'Creative Clusters- Art Centers Transform Moscow'. Online at: http://www.telegraph.co.uk/sponsored/rbth/culture/8560105/Art-centres-transform-Moscow.html

Conclusions
Visibility Makes
the Difference

❝ The struggle of man against power is the struggle of memory against forgetting. ❞

– Milan Kundera

In the case of Moscow, the role of sustained and strategic tactical urbanism and activism is most successful when it generates media coverage or forms partnerships with media institutions. This is crucial in encouraging bottom-up, citizen initiatives to link with top-down, institutionally supported, government-sanctioned, collaborative efforts. These case studies send a message to institutions: it is time to start paying attention to citizens', urban-user-based initiatives.

Cyclification, Delai Sam, Cooperative Urbanism Mitino and the development of a co-working center in Nagatino demonstrate how a growing, bottom-up urban activism strategy is gaining prominence in Russia's capital city. This new phase of urbanism creates both a crisis and an opportunity. The crisis is that cities are facing huge challenges, and part of the problem is that bottom-up initiatives lack influence and institutional collaboration. Citizens' initiatives today are not only more frequent, but also more innovative, more driven and insightful, which creates the opportunity to connect the means and goals of institutions with those of citizens – where the traditional top-down players start building from the bottom up. Each case in Moscow examines the emerging interplay between institutions and grass-roots actors, highlighting the significance of these relationships in diverse contexts. In contemporary Moscow, the political, economic and social situation is complex and it is further complicated by the amalgamation of past identities. Moscow's historical urban trajectory reflects how urbanism can become a tool of the state or part of market real estate. Top-led urbanization needs to be relevant to citizens' needs, and act on the opportunity to develop an alternative form of city-making: one that is more participative and creates a middle way between utopian ideas and practical necessity (Moscow Times, 2013).

Historically, Moscow has been a site of top-down political decisions, radical experimenting and massive restructuring. After the revolution, post 1920, Communists wanted to pass the responsibility of urban development to elites and artists. By the 1940s, urban development became an instrument of the state agenda, a 'Potemkin style' of urbanism matching a Potemkin style of industrialization, which refers to a top-down and unnatural mode of implementation (Neidhart, 2003). Struggling to surpass its Socialist history in the transition from a post-Soviet to a contemporary global city, Moscow is a unique, complex urban space. It is the site of top-down, elite political aspirations playing out on a massive scale.

Historical systems of planning and bidding for the city's masterplans present a unique participatory trait for future urban engagement. The announcement of a competition calling for designs of the mid-city Zaryadye Park reflects the nature of the city's decision-making ecosystem. President Putin envisioned the project scheme with a group of government officials at the Soviet Hotel Rossiya. After consulting with architectural agencies and the Strelka Institute, it was announced that the 'site will be developed by renowned architects, known for designing the High Line in Manhattan, New York' (Next City, 2013). However, the

High Line emerged from community-led activism, which is not the case here. The park does hold the 'potential to become an extraordinary community space at the heart of Moscow's urban ecology' and as such it is possibly an example of institutions and government enabling citizen involvement in urban development. Moscow's Mayor Sergei Sobyanin, originally appointed by Putin, was reelected in 2013, signaling an era of prominent local politics (Malhotra, 2012). However, skeptics claim that putting local considerations at the forefront strategically distances citizens from federal politics, enabling corruption at the top. The current budget for the city of Moscow is the same as that for the entire Soviet Union in the 1980s, and with plans for expanding the city, the budget allocation for the city and its people remains crucial.

The proceedings of the 2013 Moscow Urban Forum, held December 5-7, further reflect responses to sustainability, activism and the growing citizens' involvement in the urban planning processes. Discussion and dialogue from a formerly elite, professional realm are now opening up to urban users. Overspending on unsustainable, mega-infrastructure projects such as highways is being balanced by redirecting investments on new developments, such as cycling (Gehl, 2013). Reports by The Moscow News on the 2013 Moscow Urban Forum formed a consensus, broadcasting dialogue about decision-making for citizens' needs and prioritizing cycling, pedestrianism and public space (The Moscow News, 2013).

Moscow's grass-roots urban activism emerged as a form of resistance, further realigning citizens' interests with those of decision-makers to enable a discussion of the collective futures. This is best evidenced in the case of cyclification, where guerilla interventions shifted from acts of political resistance to generating a cohesive, critical voice considered by, and finding mutual benefits with, institutions.

Bottom-up, DIY urban activism connects with the idea of the 'right to leaving space for urban experimentation' (Iveson, 2013). According to Iveson, 'DIY experiments will only give birth to a more democratic city if we can find ways to politicize them' (Iveson, 2013). In Moscow, this proves true, where institutions are increasingly involving activists, as they become a voice pushing for widespread community involvement and participation including transparency, civil society, equality and ecological traditions. Each case study offers examples of what institutions did or did not do to enable the implementation of a grassroots, bottom-up initiative. There are numerous ways in which institutions can support grassroots initiatives.

Consider cyclification, where the Strelka Institute worked to involve citizens in new event formats, forums and dialogue. Along with the media, they were able to catalyze experts into discussions and educational programs for citizens. Institutions helped the initiative by facilitating new ideas and by learning what works from bottom-up activists, while also learning from examples in other cities through the organization of events such as Bike Boulevard and Car-Free Day. Cycling activists believe institutions should invest more in urban cycling, such as hiring activists, engaging them in events, moving faster and prioritizing cycling. What is essential is basic awareness-raising. For instance, explaining how cycling can create a safer, more accessible and inclusive urban environment for all. Institutions can have a greater presence in the public eye, which enables them to lead by example. In this sense, Moscow's first cycling racks were strategically located near the Strelka Institute.

Delai Sam displays an evolution from piecemeal beginnings to long-term engagement. Here, institutions enabled activists through financial and in-kind support, addressing needs, raising visibility and helping with outreach. Delai Sam can also hold meetings in spaces made available by institutions. Additionally, institutions found mutual benefit by providing space for film screenings at ZIL Cultural Center and Flacon Design Factory. One of Delai Sam's successes was setting up a small business operating as a living room workshop teaching DIY construction and sustainability through skills in handmade wood-working, fostered in the Flacon creative cluster. In these ways, institutions gave Delai Sam the ability to avoid isolation and stagnation, and provided the capacity to grow, build partnerships and continue their movement.

Cooperative Urbanism Mitino highlights institutional initiatives to overcome communication challenges. Institutions took the initiative in outreach, adapting tactics and ideas, while engaging in direct involvement and communication. Committed leadership from institutions in Mitino reveals commitment and the importance of sustained, engaged dialogue; however, Mitino recognized a lack of synchronicity between activists, residents and planners. The Strelka Institute's involvement of

Partizaning led to the introduction of the successful public mailbox system, which engaged citizens, expanded the capacity for benefits and advanced the overall project. Inter-institutional collaboration was also key, particularly between formal government and education institutions, where leveraging the power of the individual proved significant in all engagements. Working with young institutions like Strelka, as well as local and citywide activists, Mitino was able to respond to and work with a variety of communication tools.

Nagatino's co-working space illustrates how institutions and government can address a specific demand or need in a local context. Formal institutions supported the community demands, leadership initiative and entrepreneurial drive of the founder. This enabled institutions to understand Nagatino's particular needs in order to offer effective, supportive expertise. The nature of institutional relationships here was more formalized and site-specific.

Cyclification and Delai Sam both had the most success when institutions effectively identified, involved and supported citizen initiatives to catalyze or facilitate their own interests through mutually beneficial relationships. Examples of institutions engaging in this fashion range from governmental institutional bodies like the Department of Transportation to creative clusters such as Zil Cultural center and Flacon Design Factory, to educational and specialized institutions like the Strelka Institute, the Center for Economic Resource Use at Flacon Design Factory and Partizaning.

The role of the Strelka Institute demonstrates how institutions can offer expertise and support, particularly for ventures outside the city center, such as Nagatino and Mitino. Also in Mitino, the municipal deputy expressed flexibility and willingness to experiment and collaborate with various groups. In all cases, we learn that support and legal authorization is especially helpful when large-scale changes are required. In the case of Cooperative Urbanism and Cyclification, the media catalyzed efforts by giving visibility to activists and their work. This visibility enabled perceptive institutions to identify key players and common interests among bottom-up activists, sparking new collaborating partnerships.

Recommendations below demonstrate how top-down players can enable bottom-up processes:

Urban planning is a top-down process, given its scale; but it is important for institutions of all types (formal, informal, educational, creative, business, non-profit, non-governmental, etc., as well as government agencies and departments) to maintain a continuous communication with activists and citizens, and to remain aware of citizen initiatives and concerns facing the community. Communication channels can be innovative and unconventional, such as the mailboxes in Mitino, as long as they are effective. Using multiple modes of outreach to maintain dialogue is important. Choose collaboration over opposition.

Collaborating across sectors is an effective way to share expertise and support efforts, while involving new participants and spreading visibility. In the case of cyclification, for instance, the Bank of Moscow, Department of Transportation and smaller city initiatives across the city now work together throughout the year to realize different visions for cycling in the city. Similarly, by partnering with Flacon and ZIL Cultural center, activists from Delai Sam can access spaces for events, funding and can better channel efforts to effective, site-specific locations. Funding, in-kind support, outreach and organization capacity are powerful instruments for institutions to support bottom-up initiatives, as these most commonly lack these capacities. Particularly in Russia, the media play a very important role, despite being largely state-controlled. Institutions with roles in the media can therefore establish collaborative relationships and catalyze the growth of bottom-up initiatives.

Authorities and institutions can sanction and formalize activities. For instance, in Mitino, the municipal deputy's authorization and active role strengthened the initiative by giving it a feeling of legitimacy and thereby attracting less radical, everyday citizens who may otherwise not easily associate themselves with stereotypical urban activists engaging in sometimes illegal DIY, tactical, guerilla interventions. Because of the government's involvement, not only did more people participate, but also a wider demographic of people.

Promoting citizen engagement through inclusive, participatory discussions and events stimulates bottom-up, user-centric urbanism. Engagement means that people are more effectively identifying and addressing issues, and with the support of institutions, citizens can scale up and sustain their efforts and activities. Institutions can further enable citizens by providing opportunities to connect with experts across contexts and countries, expanding inclusivity and thereby supporting the exchange of knowledge.

Think, work and act in context to best evaluate issues and the active responses to them in the urban field. In Moscow, the political history plays a central role in analyzing and understanding the context of present day urban planning, centered historically in a Socialist state and emerging as a contemporary, global city.

The global presence of enterprising urban activism and civic engagement are responses to poor development practices, indicating that top-down players cannot forge ahead by mimicking the development trajectories of the past. In Moscow, reconciling historical foundations is crucial, as Communist cities were known for preservation, while capitalist cities are known for reconstruction and renovation.

Moscow doubled in size in 1961 and is set to repeat this. Bottom-up initiatives will have a strong future, achieving goals and realizing substantial, sustainable and positive urban change with the help of institutions. A new phrase – particularly suited to Moscow – has emerged to reference citizen-involved approaches to urban development defined by a social, political, ecological and equality-oriented trajectory: it is 'new collectivism' (Kargina, 2013; Sawhney et al., 2013).

Is Moscow's urban environment being transformed into a subversive instrument? Yes! The cases of DIY urbanism and bottom-up activism as resistance to top-down development discussed here are signs of Russia's emerging civil society (Kargina, 2013). The active role of street artists and creative urban makers signals a new activation of space. The remaining question is how the city can transform resistance into dialogue and embark on a middle way, reconciling Socialist-oriented planning with an alternative, user-based future.

Bibliography

Badger, E. (2012) 'Street Hacker Officially Embraced'. Atlantic Cities. http://www.theatlanticcities.com/neighborhoods/2012/05/street-hacker-officially-embraced/1921/

Balatzi, A. (2013) 'Bike Sharing Schemes take over Moscow While Becoming A Global Trend'. http://www.ecf.com/news/bike-sharing-schemes-take-over-moscow-while-becoming-global-trend/

Barry, E. (2011) 'Thousands Protest in Moscow Russia in Defiance of Putin'. The New York Times. http://www.nytimes.com/2011/12/11/world/europe/thousands-protest-in-moscow-russia-in-defiance-of-putin.html

Bentley, E. (2011) 'Cycle lanes are fine - but its a cultural change that's needed'. The Moscow News. http://themoscownews.com/blogs/20110426/188617133.html

Bishop, C. (2011) 'Zones of Indistinguishability: Collective Actions Group and Participatory Art'. E-Flux. http://www.e-flux.com/journal/zones-of-indistinguishability-collective-actions-group-and-participatory-art/

Borodulino, E. (2013) 'Anti-cafes develop as Outlets for Youth'. The Moscow Times. http://www.themoscowtimes.com/arts_n_ideas/article/anti-cafes-develop-as-outlets-for-youth/485543.html

Burneika, D. et al. (2011) 'The Problem of Research of Actors of Urban Change in Post Soviet Cities - Vilnius Case'. Annales Geographicae. pp. 43– 44. http://www.geo.lt/geo/fileadmin/failai/43-44/42-53.pdf

Cooperative Urbanism (2012) Online at: coop.partizaning.org

Coulibaly, S. (2012) Rethinking the Form and Function of Cities in Post-Soviet Countries. The World Bank. http://elibrary.worldbank.org/doi/pdf/10.1596/1813-9450-6292

Delai Film (2013) www.delaifilm.ru

Delai Sam (2013) www.delaisam.org

Diodr, P. (2010) Urbanization Trajectories in the Moscow Urban Field: The Case of 'New Moscow'. http://www.academia.edu/1143509/Urbanization_trajectories_in_the_Moscow_Urban_Field_The_case_of_New_Moscow

Dorman, V. (2011) 'Art and Design Creative Centers Transform Moscow'. The Telegraph UK. http://www.telegraph.co.uk/sponsored/rbth/culture/8560105/Art-centres-transform-Moscow.html

Eco Wiki (2012) www.ecowiki.ruEnyedi, G. (1998) 'Transformation in Central European Post-Socialist Cities'. Paper No. 21, Center for Regional Studies of Hungarian Academy of Sciences.

Ernsten, C. & Gardner E. (eds.) (2010) 'Microrayon Living: An Inventory of User Strategies'. Partizan Publik, issuu. com/partizanpublik/docs/ microrayonliving

European Cyclist's Federation (2013) 'Bike Sharing Schemes Take Over Moscow While Becoming Global Trend'. http:// www.ecf.com/news/bike-sharing-schemes-take-over-moscow-while-becoming-global-trend/

Gehl, J. (2013) 'Moscow Recommendations' http:// gehlcitiesforpeople. dk/2013/09/23/moscow-3/

Glazychev, V.L., (2008) Urbanistika. Moscow: Europe.

Grigoryan, Y. (2013) Archaeology of the Periphery.

Gutnov, A. et al, (1968) The Ideal Communist City. http:// americanfreedomwatchradio. com/wp-content/uploads/ downloads/2012/05/The_ Ideal_Communist_City-Gutnov-Baburov-Djumenton-Kharitonove-Lezava-Sadovskij-Moscow_ University-1968-176pgs-COM1. sml_.pdf

Hou, J. (2010) Insurgent Public Space: Guerilla Urbanism and the Remaking of Contemporary Cities.

IndyMedia (2002) 'First Critical Mass Ride in Moscow'. http:// www.indymedia.org.uk/ en/2002/06/34177.html

Itar-Tass (2012) 'Moscow Government to Build Parking Places for Bicycles at Major Transport Hubs'. Mass-transit Magazine. March 26, 2012. http:// www.masstransitmag.com/ news/10682210/moscow-govt-to-build-parking-places-for-bicycles-at-major-transport-hubs

Ivanov, A. (2013) 'Greater Moscow'. Monu Magazine. 19: Greater Urbanism

Iveson, K. (2013) 'Cities within the City: Do it Yourself Urbanism and the Right to the City'. International Journal of Urban and Regional Research. 37 (3) May 2013. pp. 941-956.

Jaffee, D. & Kaganova, O. (2001) 'Real Estate Markets in Russia'. http://faculty.haas.berkeley.edu/ jaffee/Papers/RealEstateMarkets. pdf

Kalinin, I. (2013) 'Russia's Creative Industries'. The Calvert Journal http://calvertjournal.com/ comment/show/1727/russia-creative-industries

Kargina, T. (2013) 'Delai Sam Russian Community DIY'. Open Democracy. http://www. opendemocracy.net/od-russia/ tatyana-kargina/'delai-sam'-russian-community-diy

Karmodi, I. (2011) 'Moscow Builds its Very First Bicycle Lane – or is it an Obstacle Course?'. France 24. http://observers.france24. com/content/20111004-russia-moscow-builds-first-bike-path-obstacle-course-bicycle-cycling-university-video-photo

Kundera, M. (1999) The Book of Laughter and Forgetting. New York: Harper Collins.

Lidings (2011) 'Privatization of Land in Moscow'. October 24, 2011. http://www.lidings.com/eng/ articles2?id=35

Lydon, M. et al. (2010) Tactical Urbanism. Vol 1. Online at: http://issuu.com/ streetplanscollaborative/docs/ tactical_urbanism_vol.1

Malhotra, S. (2013) Interview with Darya Melissina, via email November 22, 2013.

Malhotra, S. (2012) Interview with Elena Shomina.

Malhotra, S. (2013) Interview with Vladimir Demidko, via email,..

Malhotra, S. (2013) Interview with Anton Polsky, Partizaning, on November 27, 2013.

Malhotra, S. (2013) Interview with Olga Maltseva, Department of Transport, via email on November 28, 2013.

Malhotra, S. (2013) Interview with Sergey Nikitkin, Higher School of Economics on November 27, 2013.

Malhotra, S. (2012) 'Moscow Protests Recall Situationists'. Polis Blog. http://www.thepolisblog. org/2012/05/situationists-and-occupy-abai.html

Malhotra, S. (2012) 'Subbotniks for Community Led Urban Restoration'. Pattern Cities. Online at: http://patterncities.com/ archives/1602

Mason, R.J. & Nigmatullina, L. (2011) 'Suburbanization and Sustainability in Metropolitan Moscow'.

McGrane, S. (2013) 'Moscow Tries Bikes'. The New Yorker. June 2, 2013. http://www.newyorker.com/online/blogs/culture/2013/06/moscow-bike-share-political-activism.html

Menu, F. (2013) 'From the Kremlin to Dachas: Traveling into the City's Ideological Layers'. MONU Magazine, 19: Greater Urbanism.

Miessen, M. (2011) The Nightmare of Participation. Berlin: Sternberg Press.

Molodikova, I. & Makharova, A. (2007) 'Urbanization Patterns in Russia in the post-Soviet era'. The Post-Socialist City. http://link.springer.com/chapter/10.1007/978-1-4020-6053-3_4

Moscow 2020, Manifesto. Online at: <http://pixelchannel.ru/moscow2020.htm>

Moscow City Government (2013) 'Urban Development Plan'. http://www.mos.ru/en/about/plan/

The Moscow News (2013) 'Outlook for World Cities'. http://themoscownews.com/business/20130709/191750479/Outlook-for-world-cities-rapid-growth-competition.html

The Moscow News (2011) 'Promises of Pedal Power - but Cyclists Remain Skeptical'. http://themoscownews.com/local/20110425/188612866.html

The Moscow News (2013) 'Restaurant Day'. http://themoscownews.com/food/20130429/191479053/Restaurant-News.html

The Moscow Times (2013) 'New Lanes Hope to Improve Bike Safety'. August 07, 2013. http://www.themoscowtimes.com/news/article/new-lanes-hope-to-improve-bike-safety/484213.html

The Moscow Times (2013) 'New Lanes Hope to Improve Bike Safety'. August 7, 2013. http://www.themoscowtimes.com/news/article/new-lanes-hope-to-improve-bike-safety/484213.html

The Moscow Times (2013) 'Innovation Center Opens Doors in Downtown Moscow'. http://www.themoscowtimes.com/business/article/innovation-center-opens-doors-in-downtown-moscow/484360.html#ixzz2nLeZPmo3

The Moscow Times (2012) 'Land Law Changes in Moscow and Across Russia'. http://www.themoscowtimes.com/realestate/quarterly/article/469216.html#ixzz2orcXERL3

Mostavi, M. & Doherty, G. (eds.) (2010) Ecological Urbanism. Harvard Graduate School of Design. Cambridge: Harvard Press.

Moukine, G. (2013) 'Innovation Center Opens Doors in Downtown Moscow'. The Moscow Times. http://www.themoscowtimes.com/business/article/innovation-center-opens-doors-in-downtown-moscow/484360.html

Myers, J.C. (2008) 'Traces of Utopia: Socialist Values and Soviet Urban Planning'. http://clogic.eserver.org/2008/Myers.pdf

Neidhart, C. (2003) Russia's Carnival: The Smells, Sights, and Sounds of Transition. Lanham: Rowman & Littlefield.

Neumeyer, J. (2012) 'Office by the Hour'. Moscow News. http://themoscownews.com/bizfeature/20120917/190240726.html

News.au (2013) 'Moscow Opens Bike Sharing Network'. http://www.news.com.au/travel/travel-updates/moscow-opens-bike-sharing-network/story-e6frfq80-1226654899540

Next City (2013) 'Wild Urbanism in the Middle of Putin's Moscow'. http://nextcity.org/daily/entry/wild-urbanism-in-the-middle-of-putins-moscow

Oldenburg, R. (1989) The Great Good Place: Cafes, Coffee Shops, Community Centers, Beauty Parlors, General Stores, Bars, Hangouts, and How They Get You Through the Day. New York: Paragon House.

Partizaning (2011) 'Manifesto', http://eng.partizaning.org/?page_id=2

Partizaning (2013) www.partizaning.org

Petrovic, M. (2005) 'Cities After Socialism as a Research Issue'. Unpublished manuscript. Centre for the Study of Global Governance, London School of Economics and Political Science, London, UK http://eprints.lse.ac.uk/23378/1/DP34.pdf

Pfeifer, L. (2013) 'Tactical Urbanism and the Role of Planners'. Supervised research project, School of Urban Planning, McGill University, Montréal, Canada.

Prentice, A. (2013) 'Traffic-clogged Moscow switches gear with bike-hire scheme'. Reuters. http://www.reuters.com/article/2013/05/31/us-russia-transport-cycling-idUSBRE94U0QB20130531

Restaurant Day (2012) www.restaurantday.org/ru

Sassen, S. (2005) 'The Global City'. http://www.saskiasassen.com/PDFs/publications/The-Global-City-Brown.pdf

Sawhney, N., De Klerk, C. & Malhotra, S. (2013) 'Mikroact: Designing for Collective Urban Actions'. University of Delft conference on ICTs, governance and participation. (Forthcoming proceedings)

Schwirtz, M. (2012) 'Opposition, to Its Surprise, Wins a Bit of Power in Moscow'. New York Times, March 8, 2012. http://www.nytimes.com/2012/03/09/world/europe/russian-voters-surprise-many-first-time-candidates.html?_r=1

Sennett, R. (1970) The Uses of Disorder: Personal Identity & City Life. New York: Knopf.

Sennett, R. (2008) 'The open city'. In The Endless City, R. Burdett & D. Sudjic, (eds.) pp. 290-297. London: Phaidon.

Szelyeni, I. et al. (1996) Cities After Socialism: Urban and Regional Change and Conflict in Post-Socialist Societies.

The Telegraph. 'Creative Clusters-Art Centers Transform Moscow'. http://www.telegraph.co.uk/sponsored/rbth/culture/8560105/Art-centres-transform-Moscow.html

Voice of Russia (2012) 'Time is More than Money in New Moscow 'anti-café''. http://voiceofrussia.com/2012_05_16/74881641/

Wolfe, R. (2011) 'The Graveyard of Utopia: Soviet Urbanism and the Fate of the International Avant-Garde'. http://rosswolfe.files.wordpress.com/2011/09/ross-wolfe-the-graveyard-of-utopia-soviet-urbanism-and-the-fate-of-the-international-avant-garde.pdf

World Bank (1995) 'Russian Housing Reform and Privatization: Strategy and Transition Issues', Vol. 1: Main Report. Washington, DC.

Wright, M. (2011) 'The Changing Mood of Critical Mass Bike Rides'. The Guardian. http://www.theguardian.com/environment/bike-log/2011/dec/02/critical-mass

Yerkovich, V. Telegraph (2012) 'Russia's Urban Guerillas Creating Safer and Greener Streets'. http://www.telegraph.co.uk/sponsored/rbth/society/9713887/russia-urban-guerrillas.html

Zhelnina, A. (2014) 'Hanging out', Creativity, and Right to the City: Urban Public Space in Russia Before and After the Protest Wave of 2011-12 // Stasis. No. 2 (forthcoming)

Zimberg, A. (2013) 'Artful Dodgers: Urban Interventionists Partizaning are Taking Back the Streets'. The Calvert Journal. http://calvertjournal.com/comment/show/433/partizaning-street-art-protest

New York

Case 3

Contextualization:
The Real Estate Capital Turning Toward its Community?

Written by Beatriz Pineda Revilla

The four institutionally supported bottom-up initiatives presented in this chapter are located in Brooklyn. The history of Brooklyn as a borough of New York City starts in 1898, when Brooklyn stopped being an independent city. This introduction serves as a contextualization of the urban planning and socio-political situation of New York City in the twentieth century in order to better understand the four initiatives that will be presented throughout the chapter. New York City has been dubbed 'the real estate capital of the world' by some authors (Angotti, 2008) and even by the City's own marketing and tourism agency, NYC & Company.
The financial and real estate sectors play a crucial role in local urban planning policies that normally follow the principle of 'highest and best use of land', by which the real estate market determines which uses are most profitable for a given location. At the same time, New York City has a growing civic movement and many organizations are working hard toward an integrated approach to urban planning that includes residents in the process of city building.

One of New York's crucial planning tools is zoning, a means of organizing the way land is used and a powerful tool used by the local government to exercise authority over privately owned real property. In the late nineteenth century, technological improvements allowed for the construction of high-rise buildings that decreased the quality of the living conditions for citizens, due to the loss of light and air. In response to that, the City enacted the Zoning Resolution of 1916, which introduced controls on building heights and setbacks as well as separate zones for land uses. These rules are used to separate industrial and incompatible uses from residential districts and create a distinction between residential, commercial and manufacturing uses. This ordinance was later used as a model to guide development in the rest of the country's city centers.

Following successive waves of immigration, New York City's population grew from five million inhabitants in 1916 to more than eight million in 2010 (NYC Department of City Planning, 2014). In the same period, evolving technology led to lifestyle changes that encouraged the construction of mass transit routes and the use of the car. The Housing Act of 1949, which aimed at providing an updated and modernist vision to the urban planning of the time, led to the destruction of the substandard housing through the clearance of slums and blighted areas, and the construction of 'good' (Short, 2006) and decent housing. This urban renewal program was later consolidated by the Housing Act of 1954, with the end result being the destruction of many inner city communities that were seen as 'slums'. This, in turn, increased segregation and the so-called 'white flight' to the suburbs (Mollenkopf, 1991). Many white households left the inner city, which was becoming in most cases black and poor, to go to the suburbs. The federal government stimulated this suburban growth and car culture by investing in highway construction and encouraging suburban home ownership with attractive mortgage programs (Aalbers, 2011).

Robert Moses was one of the most influential personalities during this period of New York's urban renewal process. For more than forty years, he held several non-elected positions including park commissioner, construction coordinator, member of the City Planning

Board, and chair of the Slum Clearance Committee and of the Housing Committee (Short, 2006). He is best known today for the region's major road construction projects that cut through many neighborhoods in the 1950s. Moses himself said in a television interview, 'We wouldn't have any American economy without the automobile business... [T]his is a great industry that has to go on [...] and there has to be a place for them to run, there have to be modern roads, modern arteries. Somebody's got to build it'.

These new circumstances, along with modernist theorists such as Le Corbusier and his 'tower-in-the-park' model, led planners to update the 1916 Zoning Ordinance. In 1961, the current Zoning Resolution was enacted, incorporating parking requirements and emphasizing the creation of public space. The concept of incentive zoning, according to which developers could build additional floor area in exchange for incorporating public amenities and squares into their projects, began implementation (NYC Department of City Planning, 2014). Despite the good intentions behind the guidelines, the resulting public spaces were not always as successful as was hoped. Decades later, implementation of this zoning ordinance has proven that the 'tower-in-the-park' model of lower city densities does not contribute to a vibrant streetscape.

In the 1960s, the 'City Livable Movement' emerged in opposition to the modernist planning that had prevailed for four decades. This new approach encouraged a city made for ordinary people, identifying human-scaled streets and blocks and the mix of residential, commercial and working spaces as the main ingredients in a livable city (Berg,

1999). One of the most important defenders of this movement was Jane Jacobs. She advocated for New York City's communities and proposed rehabilitation rather than renewal (Jacobs, 1961). Her resistance to Robert Moses' renewal plans saved communities from being destroyed and planted the first seeds for better organized and better connected communities.

Building on this new civic awareness and the social movements that arose in the 1970s, not only in the United States but also all over the world (Angotti, 2008), in 1969, the City of New York, under Mayor Lindsay's administration, presented the NYC Masterplan. It was a comprehensive plan that aimed at dealing with the challenges the city was facing with a focus on improving housing conditions, reducing unemployment and boosting community participation. This masterplan was never implemented, but it nonetheless spurred some major changes. Before 1969, the city was divided into three basic zoning districts: residential, commercial and manufacturing. One of the goals achieved in 1969 was the implementation of a special zoning district that allowed the zoning ordinance to recognize and preserve the diversity and history of different neighborhoods. Another important achievement took place in 1977, during the last year of Mayor Abraham Beame's administration, which was the division of the city into 59 Community Districts, each with its own Community Board. This division, which still remains today, helps the local community boards to better address local issues within their own districts (NYC Department of City Planning, 2014).

Mayor Beame was succeeded by Mayor Edward I. Koch. During his three terms as mayor, from 1978 to 1989, Koch led New York City from fiscal insolvency to economic boom. It was during his administration that a crucial shift with a major impact in urban planning took place, the consolidation of neoliberalism. In 1981, Ronald Reagan became President of the United States, and throughout his administration he replaced the Keynesian political economy and the interventionist state by encouraging privatization and market-driven development, as well as delegating federal government functions to local governments, nonprofits and civil society in general. The increasing political power of capital, together with post industrialization and the rise of globalization, made public-private partnerships the main urban development strategy (Angotti, 2008).

A clear example in this direction was the change to the City Charter approved in 1989, which authorized community plans (under section 197a). The '197a plans' were created to improve the city and its boroughs by encouraging dialogue between local communities and City agencies (NYC Department of City Planning, 2014). In 1990, David Dinkins became the first African American mayor and under his administration the first community plan, Bronx Community Board 3, was implemented, in 1992. Crime rates started to decrease drastically during those years, a trend which continued under Rudolph Giuliani in the 1990s. In 2001, Michael Bloomberg became NYC's mayor, and the four case studies analyzed in this chapter were implemented under his three-term administration. Therefore it is worthwhile

to examine the urban planning strategies developed during these twelve years. Before becoming mayor, Bloomberg was the CEO of the media and financial services company Bloomberg LP, hence he was known as the 'business-mayor' (Brash, 2011), embodying a neoliberal and entrepreneurial approach. Some authors (Eisinger, 1988; Hall & Hubbard, 1998; Harvey, 2001) define 'entrepreneurialism' as a form of neoliberal governance that prioritizes the stimulation of corporate investment and real estate development by exercising speculative and activist governmental means. During the description of the cases, this aspect will be further elaborated. Mayor Bloomberg's environmental concerns were also influential during this time. In 2007, he enacted a plan called PlaNYC to fight global warming and prepare the city for the projected one million more people expected to be living in New York by 2030. Environmental issues are one of the many aspects of civic life that the City regulates through its agencies. New York City relies on forty agencies that manage the City's resources in fields such as education, housing, health and transportation, among others. Four of these agencies, together with their programs, will be analyzed in detail in the following sections.

All four New York case studies share a common setting: Brooklyn. As the most populated borough of New York City, Brooklyn has developed in its own way while at the same time reflecting the major changes that the nation and the city experienced in the twentieth century. During the first two decades, transportation improvements, such as the construction of major bridges and subway lines, together with the remarkable industrial role of

Brooklyn's waterfront, helped Brooklyn to flourish. After World War II, especially during the 1960s and 1970s, the shift from manufacturing to containerization left many residents unemployed. The borough declined in population as many middle-class people moved to the suburbs, but by the 1990s some signs of renaissance began to appear. Neighborhood associations worked hard to preserve Brooklyn's diverse ethnic identity and the historical character of its brownstone–lined streets. These efforts brought new businesses and housing construction to the borough, reducing crime rates and creating a new image for Brooklyn (Kenneth & Manbeck, 2004). During the last few decades, these processes of revitalization and gentrification have been shaping the character of the borough's distinct neighborhoods, especially those closest to Manhattan, in the northwestern part of Brooklyn.

The cases that follow will outline some of these neighborhood initiatives and the communities behind them. In order of presentation, the four cases are as follows:

Garden of Eden is a community garden on the grounds of one of the New York City Housing Authority's (NYCHA) housing developments. Supported by NYCHA's Garden and Greening Program, Garden of Eden has gone through a process of beautification and environmental education that benefits residents, seniors, and the community.

BRIC and UrbanGlass are two cultural nonprofits built through a partnership with two City agencies, the New York City Department of Cultural Affairs (DCLA) and the New York City Economic Development Corporation (EDC). They are providing artists of all ages and levels and the local community with resources and free or low-cost cultural programming.

New Lots Triangle Plaza is a community-led public space implemented through the New York City Department of Transportation's (DOT) Plaza Program in collaboration with the nonprofit New Lots Avenue Triangle Merchants Association, established by the merchants located around the square. The ultimate goal is to enhance neighborhood streets and support local businesses.

Manufacture New York is a fashion incubator/factory hybrid dedicated to providing independent designers with the resources and skills to streamline their production processes and to transform local manufacturing into the most affordable, innovative option for all.

Case 1
Garden of Eden -
Planting the Seeds of
a Sustainable Community

" It is hardly possible to overrate the value...
of placing human beings in contact with
persons dissimilar to themselves, and
with modes of thought and action unlike
those with which they are familiar... Such
communication has always been, and is
peculiarly in the present age, one of the
primary sources of progress. "

— John Stuart Mill

This first case study features Garden of Eden, a
community garden on the grounds of one of the New
York City Housing Authority's (NYCHA) housing
developments. A first section will contextualize the
case study. Secondly, a short overview on the role
that NYCHA plays in the New York housing context
will be provided together with a description of the
program run by NYCHA in order to support community

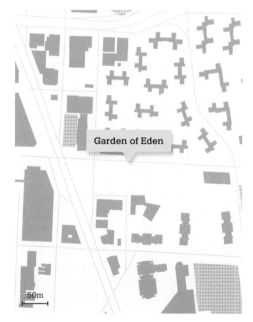

1 Census 2000 recorded the highest median income in one census tract as $112,414 while the lowest was $9,876 (NYC Department of City Planning).

gardens. Thirdly, an overview of the other institutions involved in supporting Garden of Eden will highlight the multiple partnerships at hand in order to better understand the process.

Placing Garden of Eden in context

Garden of Eden is located in Fort Greene, a neighborhood in the northwestern part of Brooklyn, which belongs to the Community District No. 2. The City of New York currently has 59 Community Districts, each of them with its own Community Board. Every Community District encompasses several neighborhoods and advises the City on issues related to the welfare of the district and its residents.

When looking at this Community District, and specifically at Fort Greene, it is striking to see the disparities in income between different census tracts.[1] According to the Furman Institute, the unemployment rate in the District in 2010 ranked 28th when compared with the the other city districts, whereas the median income of the District was ninth. This is a clear indication of the unequal wealth distribution in the neighborhood (NYC Department of City Planning, 2014).

Today Fort Greene is an effervescent neighborhood that attracts artists inspired by the many cultural facilities that the area offers. It has a rich and well-preserved history, and a large African American community whose roots go back to the beginning of the nineteenth century. At that time the Brooklyn Navy Yard, once the largest naval construction facility in the United States, opened its doors and provided opportunities for skilled workers. By the 1870s more than half of the African American population of Brooklyn lived in this particular neighborhood, alongside Irish, German and English immigrants (Kenneth & Manbeck, 2004).

During World War II, the Brooklyn Navy Yard increased its workforce, and in 1944 the NYCHA built two public housing developments for the wartime workforce: the Raymond V. Ingersoll Houses and the Walt Whitman Houses. These high-rise developments occupied 38 acres (15 hecatres), which represented 20% of the area of the neighborhood, and accommodated 14,000 people in 3,500 units (Kenneth & Manbeck, 2004). In 1966, the shutdown of the Navy Yard due to the shift towards a more service-oriented economy left many residents unemployed. During the 1970s the

Previous spread (left)
Garden of Eden after
implementation, 2013

Previous spread (right)
Before the implementation
of Garden of Eden, 2007

Left
Due to 2004 rezoning, the area
underwent a rapid transformation,
including the development of
new luxury high-rise residential
buildings

area showed signs of decline and the neighborhood lost businesses and residents, but the residents' strong sense of belonging and community within the public housing developments, together with the close collaboration between residents, police and elected officials, helped improve the quality of the public housing (Kenneth & Manbeck, 2004). Garden of Eden, a local community garden and our object of study, was implemented on the grounds of one of these housing developments, the Ingersoll Houses, in 2009.

Public housing and the New York Housing Authority (NYCHA)

Public housing is the most widely known form of subsidized low-income housing in the United States. The phrase 'public housing' evokes many negative images in the collective imagination – crime, bad quality architecture, extreme poverty – but in fact this is not the reality of most public housing developments nationwide (Schwartz, 2010).

NYCHA is the largest public housing authority (PHA) in the United States. It was founded in 1934 and it controls nearly 180,000 units of housing, which represent 15% of the approximately 1.2 million units owned by the 3,000 PHAs in the country (Schwartz, 2010). Those 180,000 units are divided into 334 developments (many of NYCHA's facilities are known popularly as 'projects' or 'developments') that provide community facilities such as senior, community, health care, and daycare centers to 400,000 residents living in NYCHA-owned housing, and to another 225,000 residents who receive a rental subsidy to live in privately owned housing.

Despite public and private efforts to provide affordable housing in New York City, there is still a growing need for public housing as the cost of housing in the city continues to rise. NYCHA was a crucial partner in Major Bloomberg's New Marketplace Plan to increase affordable housing. In order to achieve its mission and provide safe and affordable housing for low- and moderate-income citizens, NYCHA receives revenue mainly from the rental income of its buildings as well as from federal subsidies and private grants. The fact that the governmental funding has been drastically cut and that NYCHA's building stock is aging is leading NYCHA to develop new financing options and to build partnerships with the public, private and nonprofit sectors in order to continue fulfilling its mission.

NYCHA's Garden and Greening Program: supporting gardening initiatives

Despite NYCHA's difficult economic situation, urban agriculture initiatives, and community gardens in particular, are strongly supported at NYCHA's developments. The benefits that gardening activities provide to the communities are seen to be worth the extra effort and resources that it takes to implement them. Community gardens are nothing new in the United States: there is a long tradition that began during the World Wars and the Great Depression, when community gardening participation became almost universal (Lawson, 2005). 'Victory gardens' flourished during World War II and provided a way for communities to produce food in times of crisis (Saldivar-Tanaka et al., 2004). As the United States recovered from war, community gardens diminished in number, but they made a comeback in the early 1970s when food prices increased and an environmental consciousness arose (Lawson, 2005).

At this point it is important to make clear the distinction between community gardens in general and the community gardens located in NYCHA's developments. According to Ferris, Norman & Sempik (2001, 560), 'what distinguishes a community garden from a private garden is the fact that it is in some sense a public garden in terms of ownership, access, and degree of democratic control'. It involves the convergence of multiple individuals, joining together in diverse settings, to grow food, among other things. NYCHA's gardens, although implemented in land owned by the City, are separated from the public space by a short fence and the access to the gardens is restricted to NYCHA's residents due to liability issues. Also the gardeners do not own the garden but lease the space from NYCHA through an annual registration process. Despite these circumstances, which confer a sense of private ownership to these spaces, these gardens help build community and neighborhood residents and visitors can enjoy the beauty that these spaces provide.

The Garden and Greening Program was established by NYCHA in 1963 to beautify residences, educate the population and support residents interested in gardening. At the beginning, NYCHA distributed flyers inviting tenants to garden and a contest was organized. The initiative was warmly welcomed and 105 gardens were planted in over 65 NYCHA developments. Fifty years later, the program supports

745 individual and community gardens at over 200 developments. It is an application-based program and the residents need to approach NYCHA with a location and a vision for their future garden. The gardeners must reapply annually at their property management offices to register their gardens. Although NYCHA prefers registered gardens and works to ensure that registered gardens receive resources, it understands that some gardens do not get registered for a variety of reasons and aims to provide resources to all gardeners. NYCHA encourages the participants in the registered and non-registered gardens to combine efforts and organize themselves. Registered gardeners are provided with free seeds in spring and bulbs for the fall planting season. They also receive technical assistance and compost for the garden. An extra annual $40 is reimbursed to the gardeners who register their gardens. Gardeners are also invited to the educational workshops and events that the Garden and Greening Program organized such as the Annual Citywide Garden Competition Award Ceremony, which recognizes the effort of the most dedicated gardeners. This contest started strictly as a Flower Garden Contest but expanded in the early 2000s to include vegetable and theme garden categories.

Many scholars have focused on the motives that drive people to participate in a community garden (Glover, 2004; Glover et al., 2005; Alaimo et al., 2010; Draper & Freedman, 2010). The most common motives are health benefits, access to food, neighborhood beautification and social interactions (Draper & Freedman, 2010; Rosol, 2010). These are also the main reasons behind the creation of NYCHA's gardens and the motivations that drive Garden of Eden's gardeners.

Garden of Eden: a shared partnership
Garden of Eden is located near the intersection of Myrtle Avenue and Flatbush Avenue, in close proximity to Downtown Brooklyn, the third largest central business district in New York City. In 2004, the area was rezoned to retain jobs that were at risk of leaving the city. Since then it has been undergoing a quick transformation including the development of new luxury highrise residential buildings. Another consequence of the rezoning was the loss of local affordable commercial retail space, as local small business owners and low- to moderate-income consumers have been excluded while national chain

retailers have been encouraged to move in (NYC Department of City Planning, 2014).

In this context, the contribution of local nonprofit organizations is very important to address local needs. The Myrtle Avenue Revitalization Project (MARP) is a nonprofit established in 1999 that aims to restore the economic vitality of Myrtle Avenue, one of the main streets of Fort Greene. The strategies implemented to achieve this goal are providing cultural, entrepreneurial and employment opportunities for its residents, and they also assist the small businesses along the avenue. The Ingersoll and Walt Whitman Houses stretch along Myrtle Avenue for nearly 3,000 feet (1 km), and therefore MARP has offered a lot of support to these residents since its beginnings. In 2009, during one of the meetings between MARP and the residents, the lack of affordable and fresh food in the area arose as a crucial issue. The residents came up with the idea of gardening to tackle this shortage. A group of six African American women, supported by Meredith Phillips Almeida, Deputy Director at MARP, approached NYCHA with the idea of creating a community garden at the Ingersoll Houses. The proposal for the Garden of Eden was approved by NYCHA and the implementation process started.

Since its establishment, the relationship between MARP and this group of gardeners has been growing as the garden has been expanding. MARP started working on the program 'Myrtle Eats Fresh', run by Kassy Nystrom, Director of Food & Health Initiatives, in order to improve access to healthy and affordable food in the neighborhood. Community gardens are just one of the strategies in place to achieve this goal and the Garden of Eden is not the only garden in the area. The neighboring NYCHA developments, Walt Whitman and Farragut Houses, have also initiated their own community gardens following the steps of Garden of Eden, in 2011 and 2012, respectively. Other strategies within this program are the Myrtle Avenue Farm Stand, where local farmers can sell affordable, fresh produce to the neighborhood, and the Community Chef Program, which trains residents to conduct cooking demonstrations at local events, sharing tips and recipes on how to cook healthfully on a budget.

Having a nonprofit organization such as MARP in the area is one of the aspects that distinguish Garden of Eden from other NYCHA's gardens. The role of MARP was crucial during the implementation phase, when

MARP hired a consultant to help the gardeners with the initial layout. The group has also been helpful during the development phases that have taken place since then. The garden started with eight planting boxes and now has 40 plus a long waiting list that continues to grow. In Spring 2014, NYCHA and the residents will start a new garden at the Ingersoll Houses to satisfy demand. The gardeners have become more self-sufficient over the years, but still MARP continues to provide them with support such as field trips that allow the gardeners to learn about other similar initiatives and exchange experiences, skill building workshops and planting materials seasonally. Another local nonprofit organization, Families United for Racial and Economic Equality (FUREE), also helped the gardeners during the implementation stage. FUREE is a Brooklyn-based multiracial organization formed almost exclusively by women of color that aims at empowering low-income families. Some of Garden of Eden's members are also part of this organization.

Garden of Eden has benefited from several grants provided by Citizens Committee for New York City (CCNYC), one of the oldest micro-funding organizations in New York City. CCNYC conducts workshops and awards micro grants to resident-led groups to support their self-determined neighborhood improvement initiatives. In order to do that, CCNYC raises funds from donors, including foundations, corporations, and individual donors, among others. Environmental projects such as community gardens have an important role within CCNYC. In 2012, Garden of Eden received a grant that helped them with the expansion of the garden and provided the resources to purchase a compost barrel. In 2013, the gardeners applied again, helped by MARP, and with that grant they installed an irrigation system.

Garden of Eden is a good example of how a community initiative can benefit from multiple partnerships. In this case the project has succeeded in part because it has received combined support from an organization that is familiar with the hyper-local context and has an interest in creating partnerships with the NYCHA Garden and Greening technical support.

Lessons learned from Garden of Eden
In order to measure the success of Garden of Eden in these first four years since its implementation,

three indicators will be used: social, economic, and institutional. The focus will be on the actions undertaken by the local institutions (Cutter et al., 2008).

First, the social dimension of the garden plays a crucial role (Adger, 2000; Abesamis et al., 2006). One of the indicators that measure this social aspect is diversity (Holling, 1973; Carpenter et al., 2001; Resilience Alliance, 2002; Folke, 2006; Okvat et al., 2011). The many stakeholders involved in Garden of Eden have strengthened the community garden by contributing to the decision-making process (Tidball & Krasny, 2007; Osbahr, 2007). Also, the gardeners themselves embody the diversity of the community, encompassing people of African American, Bangladeshi and Chinese descent and all different age groups. The rich variety of vegetable crops and flowers grown by the members reflects, in some cases, their cultural preferences.

Another social indicator is the active participation of the gardeners. During these four years since the implementation of the initiative, trusting relationships have been developed, creating a strong network between the gardeners and the institutions involved (Mayunga, 2007). The clear set of norms from NYCHA and its close support to the gardeners have contributed to increase what Putnam (1996) describes as 'social capital', defined by trust, cooperation, reciprocity and networks. Many scholars including Glover (2003) and Worden et al. (2004) among others, have analyzed how community greening creates human, natural, physical, and financial capital, which together lead to social capital. Some authors have established a distinction between horizontal and vertical social capital. The former refers to the relationships that occur among individuals with equal or similar demographic characteristics (Gittell & Avis, 1998), while the vertical aspect, called 'linking' by authors such as Fox (1996) and Heller (1996), can be defined as the capacity to leverage resources, ideas, and information from institutions. 'Linking' plays a crucial role in the success of this initiative. First, linking is happening since the beginning among the gardeners and the institutions. This dialogue has allowed the gardeners to receive support in every step taken. Equally important, linking has occurred between the institutions, which have been in continuous contact and are aware of their respective weaknesses and strengths.

Secondly, the economic dimension is crucial to the success and longevity of the initiative (Rose, 2006). Diversity is key here. The several sources of economic support in the case of Garden of Eden greatly improve the chances that this community garden will successfully continue in the future. Economically, each of the institutions involved supports the initiative in different ways. While CCNYC provides the gardeners with grants, NYCHA and MARP contributions are focused mainly on providing services for the gardeners, such as the Annual Award or skill building workshops. Both NYCHA and MARP provide the gardeners with some of the practical resources needed, such as seeds, compost, and raised planting beds. These services and resources are a very important part of the support that the gardeners receive, as well as the educational programs that all the institutions involved offer to the

gardeners. Another important economic indicator is the security of land tenure, which is one of the biggest challenges that urban agriculture initiatives face (UN Development Program, 1996). The fact that NYCHA owns the land gives sufficient stability to the garden and ensures its continuation and even its expansion, planned for next year. Each one of the institutions involved is aware of the importance of 'linking' with the other institutions. Especially in economic terms, NYCHA's economic situation benefits from the strong local institutional support that Garden of Eden receives, which distinguishes this garden from other NYCHA gardens.

Thirdly, there is the institutional dimension (Cutter et al, 2008), which can be measured by looking at the capacity for self-organization and leadership among the gardeners. Learning by themselves how

Left
Participants had to build new garden boxes because of the increase in demand

Right
Garden of Eden benefited from several grants provided by the nonprofit Citizens Committee for New York City (CCNYC)

to grow food, establish participatory rules, organize activities, advocate with city government (Hynes, 1996; Pinderhughes, 2001; Tidball & Krasny, 2007), as well as having a clear leader (Abesamis et al., 2007; Tierneyan & Bruneau, 2007) strengthens the community and contributes to the resilience of the garden.

To summarize and focus on the role of the institutions, the importance of the process of 'linking' (Fox, 1996; Heller, 1996) developed among NYCHA and the nonprofits involved has been essential. The regular communication and awareness of their respective roles has provided Garden of Eden with complementary social and economic support. The openness of NYCHA to support community gardens through the Garden & Greening Program also contributes to the success of these gardens and assures their replicability.

Case 2
BRIC Arts | Media | Bklyn + UrbanGlass -
Toward a Synergetic Partnership

This case analyzes the partnership between the two
cultural nonprofit organizations, BRIC Arts | Media
| Bklyn (BRIC) and UrbanGlass, and the two City
agencies involved in this initiative, the New York
City Department of Cultural Affairs (DCLA) and the
New York City Economic Development Corporation
(EDC). The first section presents a context for the
case study. The second part describes the role that
the City agencies played in renovating an old theater
to provide the two cultural organizations with an
upgraded headquarters and how they continue
supporting their cultural programming. The third
section describes the role played by both cultural
nonprofits. The final section provides an overview
of the strategies implemented in this initiative in order
to achieve an effective partnership.

Downtown Brooklyn cultural district
The two nonprofit organizations featured in this case
study, BRIC and UrbanGlass, are located in the same

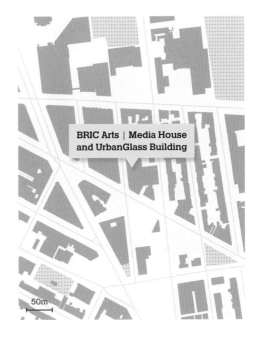

BRIC Arts | Media House
and UrbanGlass Building

50m

Previous spread (bottom)
The renovated BRIC Arts | Media House and UrbanGlass building

Previous spread (top)
BRIC Arts | Media House and UrbanGlass, with the Williamsburgh Savings Bank Tower in the background

Top
Before the renovation of the Strand Theater

Bottom
Urban Glass facilities

neighborhood as the community garden analyzed in the previous section: Fort Greene, Brooklyn. These groups are two of the nearly fifty world-class arts and cultural organizations that constitute the Downtown Brooklyn Cultural District. This area of Fort Greene, bordered by Flatbush Avenue and Atlantic Avenue, around the intersection of Fulton Street and Lafayette Avenue, has a long cultural history. In the 1860s, members of the Philharmonic Society of Brooklyn founded the Brooklyn Academy of Music (BAM), which presented its first performance in 1861 and became a major performing arts venue in Brooklyn. After this first step, soon Fort Greene started welcoming many theaters to the area. In the mid-twentieth century, arts and cultural organizations began to move into the area's abandoned buildings. In the late 1990s, Harvey Lichtenstein, at the time BAM's Executive Director, had the idea to create a Cultural District to combine the efforts of the many grassroots initiatives that were taking place in the area. That is how the Downtown Brooklyn Cultural District was initiated.

Today, the Downtown Brooklyn Partnership (DBP) is the Business Improvement District (BID)[1] for the area that includes the cultural district. BAM is one of the best-known cultural venues in the area, but many other smaller organizations, such as BRIC and UrbanGlass, are part of this cultural ecology and contribute to the success of the neighborhood. DBP's oversight and management in coordination with the cultural organizations and other community groups are critical to maintaining the vibrant street life of the Downtown Brooklyn neighborhood.

The role of the City in the renovation of the Strand Theater

In the beginning of the 2000s, under the administration of Mayor Michael Bloomberg, the City delivered a development plan to revitalize the Downtown Brooklyn Cultural District in partnership with the neighborhood's cultural organizations. Responsibilities for cultural affairs and investments are normally divided across multiple local public sector agencies, such as cultural affairs, city planning and economic development (Markusen & Gadwa, 2010). This was also the case for the Downtown Brooklyn Cultural District, where the New York City Department of Cultural Affairs (DCLA) and New York City Economic Development Corporation (EDC) were the main agencies involved.

At that time, both BRIC and UrbanGlass had already occupied the historic Strand Theater, at the corner of Rockwell Place and Fulton Street, for nearly a decade. UrbanGlass, the first and largest artist-access glass center in the United States, moved into the Strand building in 1991. Previously located in the SoHo neighborhood of Manhattan, the organization came to Brooklyn looking for a bigger and more affordable space for its glassworking facilities. A call for proposals by EDC to reuse abandoned theaters provided them with the opportunity to rent this city-owned property at an affordable price. A few years later, BRIC moved into the old theater building. Since it was established in 1979, BRIC has supported contemporary art, performing arts and community media programs that reflect the borough's creativity and diversity.

In the early 2000s, BRIC and UrbanGlass approached DCLA with the idea of renovating the old Strand building, which is owned by the City, to upgrade their respective spaces. No longer a functional theater space, the Strand building had a foreboding, bricked-up facade, and was not a welcoming facility. This request fit well with the City's interest in improving the Downtown Brooklyn Cultural District and the proposal was approved. EDC is a nonprofit organization – with a President and majority of board members appointed by the mayor – that operates under contract with the City, acting as its official economic development agency. In this capacity, EDC conducts land sales and manages capital projects and properties on behalf of the city. DCLA was the funding City agency, and together with the Brooklyn Borough President, and the City Council it provided $40 million for the restoration of the building. Leeser Architecture was selected to design the new headquarters of BRIC and UrbanGlass. Representatives from EDC, DCLA and the two nonprofits were involved in weekly meetings with the project architect, Thomas Leeser, during the two years of participatory design process to develop the plans that would meet the programmatic needs of each organization. One of the biggest challenges during the design process was upgrading a former theater into a modern center that could accommodate the diverse array of programming while also incorporating each organization's identity. The role of EDC, as the project manager, was crucial during the renovation process, which took place between 2011 and 2013. The result was the renovated BRIC Arts | Media House and UrbanGlass, which opened its doors

Right
Glass-blowing workshop
organized by Urban Glass

in October 2013, with new performance spaces, a new television recording studio, art galleries, state of the art glass-blowing facilities, and classrooms for these two organizations. Both BRIC and UrbanGlass resumed their activities in the renovated space, and the cultural center welcomes many artists, visitors and local people from the neighborhood. The design enhances the street-level-presence of the building with large openings on the ground floor that increase the visibility of both organizations in the neighborhood. This contributes to one of the goals of the newly renovated building, which is to connect this cultural center with the local community.

After the completion of the renovation process, the building was transferred to the jurisdiction of DCLA, which serves as landlord of BRIC and UrbanGlass. Although DCLA no longer provides capital funding to the groups, the agency still provides annual support for the programming of both organizations, helping them to protect and realize their respective visions. This support and the long-term agreement with DCLA, allows BRIC and UrbanGlass to plan ahead securing their respective missions and allowing them to grow over time.

The role of the nonprofits. BRIC Arts | Media and UrbanGlass as cultural co-tenants

As Markusen and Gadwa (2010) have stated, cultural nonprofits have a significant impact on city and state cultural planning. Most museums, artists' centers, theaters, and community arts facilities serve as nonprofits (Heilbrun & Gray, 1993; Wyszomirski, 1999; Gray & Heilbrun, 2000) which is also true in the case of BRIC and UrbanGlass.

BRIC, which once was an acronym for 'Brooklyn Information and Culture', has been operating for three decades in various venues throughout Brooklyn. Founded under a different name in 1979, The Fund for the Borough of Brooklyn (FBB), BRIC started organizing events and exhibition programs, such as the Celebrate Brooklyn! Festival in Prospect Park, or the exhibitions in the rotunda of Borough Hall. The goal was to provide platforms for the growing number of artists that were settling in Brooklyn. This civic and cultural mission has been part of BRIC's philosophy since the beginning. At the moment, free and low-cost programming and resources are offered to audiences, media makers, and artists of all ages and levels, from emerging to mid-career, as well as established professionals. BRIC presents concerts, dance, and other performing arts presentations by artists from around the world and also by artists that have a tie to Brooklyn. Different types of residencies are offered, providing artists with the space to work in multidisciplinary teams and the stage to share their creations with the public.

The new BRIC Arts | Media House has reunited BRIC's three programs under one roof: Community Media, which was located in the Strand Theater before the renovation, Contemporary Art, based previously in Brooklyn Heights, and Performing Arts, which historically presented events in Prospect Park. Within these three categories, many of the initiatives undertaken by BRIC engage with the local community. For example, BRIC's Brooklyn Free Speech public-access media initiative offers Brooklyn residents the opportunity to put content on television. The goal of this initiative is to truly reflect the needs of the local community and to give residents a voice. Another free event is BRIC's Stoop Series on Tuesday nights, when the public and the community are invited to participate in storytelling, performing, singing and poetry events, among others. Also a monthly House Party is organized by BRIC, which opens its doors to the community to offer different daytime activities that are planned around a theme, culminating in a live performance at night. BRIC also reaches into the community through the many partnerships established with local nonprofits, such as public libraries and the neighboring NYCHA developments, the Ingersoll and Walt Whitman Houses. The local libraries act as intermediaries between BRIC and the residents, presenting an outpost for BRIC's community media programming. In the case of the partnership with NYCHA, free dance and media classes have been offered to Fort Greene's public housing community. The success of these initiatives has paved the way for many more events. BRIC's desire to engage with the established residents in the area, as well as to provide access to art and culture is clear.

UrbanGlass started in 1977, under the name of New York Experimental Glass Workshop. It was an initiative of a group of artists who wanted to work with glass but did not have access to the necessary equipment. Since then, the organization has continued to grow and has become the largest artist-access glass center in the United States. UrbanGlass fosters community and serves as an incubator for creation

and innovation by providing affordable classes to students of all levels interested in working with glass. Scholarships and residencies are also available to local and visiting students. UrbanGlass maintains partnerships with different universities in New York City that provide students with the opportunity to experiment and work with glass. Over 500 students per year study and work with the UrbanGlass faculty, which includes world-renowned artists and designers. UrbanGlass also rents its studio and equipment, by the hour or the day, to artists who work in the field. Even though the studio is not open to the public, UrbanGlass offers scheduled tours of its facility. In addition to all these activities, UrbanGlass provides a scholarly forum for the contemplation of glass as an artistic medium through the publication GLASS: The UrbanGlass Quarterly, and in the public exhibition space and retail space on the ground floor.

The two organizations have a common goal of providing access to art and culture, and offer rich and varied educational programming. As nonprofits, both BRIC and UrbanGlass rely on the economic support of both public and private funders and accept donations that help them pursue their missions and provide free or affordable programs and activities for the public. For both organizations, one of the goals has been to transform the lobby of the building into a successful public space. To this end, BRIC created the 'stoop' (stairs), an interior programming and social space that resembles a rooted characteristic of Brooklyn's culture, which is to sit on the stoop of your house

and talk to your neighbors. For the first time since they moved into the building in 1991, UrbanGlass' presence is now also visible from the exterior through the ground floor gallery space that provides the organization with a dynamic street-level presence, inviting the community into the space and generating a wider interest in the art of glass. Since the opening of the renovated building in October 2013, the new home of BRIC and UrbanGlass has proven to be a vibrant arts center that encompasses different disciplines within one building, and attracts a culturally engaged audience. Both BRIC and UrbanGlass are working hard to include local residents in their programming, so that the center is attractive for all community members.

Since the building opened, BRIC and UrbanGlass have organized some common events, such as the opening party and a 'block party', when they closed the streets around their building to vehicular traffic in order to invite the community to come and visit the new space. BRIC and UrbanGlass also work together in the advertising of their renovated headquarters, maximizing their individual efforts. Although by design certain spaces belong to BRIC and others to UrbanGlass, they have a joint management agreement for the operation and maintenance of the common spaces, including the elevator, lobby, stairway, and so forth. On the ground floor, UrbanGlass manages the exhibition space and retail store that face Fulton Street, while BRIC manages the lobby space and the cafeteria and has hired a Brooklyn-based coffee bar to take care of it. Although the organizations have separate entrances, both use the lobby as the main entrance. All in all, this cultural co-tenancy can be defined as a symbiotic and harmonious partnership.

Public, private and nonprofit: a synergetic partnership

The rationale behind this project is that the concentration of cultural organizations and activities enhances the appearance, safety, and appeal of public space and those cultural districts can stimulate investment and encourage new uses, attracting visitors and contributing to the revitalization of an area (Markusen & Gadwa, 2010). In the mid-1980s, the creative city and cultural economy buzz emerged in Europe, and many states and cities used this cultural strategy to approach urban planning and to contribute to the economic development of neighborhoods, communities and downtowns. By the mid-2000s, interest in this type of cultural strategy increased, and many communities commissioned cultural plans to build and expand their cultural capacity. In the United States, the cultural sector's ability to stimulate economic development is well-recognized and widely employed in urban planning. This strategy started already in the 1960s, with the creation of the National Endowment for the Arts (NEA) and the increase of public arts funding among City cultural affairs departments, philanthropic arts programs, and state arts boards, etc. (Markusen & Gadwa, 2010).

Despite the studies that link culture with economic and regenerative impacts (Bianchini et al., 1988; Landry, 2003; Landry et al., 1996), in the last decade this causal relationship has been questioned (Markusen & Gadwa, 2010; Glaeser, 2004; Markusen, 2006). The fact that art and culture contribute to the creation of jobs, property revaluation, and public sector revenue has not been proved by these aforementioned studies, nor do they show what would have happened in the absence of these cultural initiatives (Markusen & Gadwa, 2010). Therefore the explanation of this causal relationship does not follow only one pattern, and the role of external factors that could influence each specific case should be taken into consideration.

In the Downtown Brooklyn Cultural District, Harvey Lichtenstein's grassroots vision for the area, together with the public support received from the City, the private investment leveraged by this support, and the work of the many nonprofits organizations located in the District, has successfully contributed to a renaissance over the last decade that has revitalized the neighborhood, a former urban renewal area. In 2004, the City approved the rezoning of the area to help facilitate the growth of the new cultural district. Since then, the City has committed more than $100 million in capital funding for new facilities and renovations, public spaces and affordable housing projects in the neighborhood. These new facilities include several performing arts venues, including the renovation of the Strand Theater. Together with this public effort, private investors have been active in recent years, building hundreds of new apartments and office spaces, as well as changing the retail character of the area. Culture and art have played a crucial role in this process, but it is the mix of residential, commercial, cultural and retail spaces together that makes this area so attractive, spurring processes of gentrification.

In the case of BRIC and UrbanGlass, the support provided by the City, through its agencies, DCLA and EDC, is remarkable. Thanks to this support both organizations have upgraded their facilities and continued to expand their respective programming and involvement in the community. BRIC and UrbanGlass exemplify a successful partnership between two cultural organizations that are dedicated to different artistic and cultural fields, but can nonetheless share their headquarters and the common goal of providing affordable access and education to artists and to the local community. It is this joint mission that has kept them together for nearly twenty years. Cohabiting under the same roof makes them stronger and provides employees and participants with multiple opportunities to exchange ideas in the cafeteria or in the lobby, profiting from each other's experiences. In the case of BRIC, the fact that its three main programs now share the same space allows for a synergetic interaction between them. In this way, the circle closes: the City helps cultural nonprofits that in turn help the community by providing access to cultural and artistic facilities, further contributing to the successful revitalization of the area and thereby advancing the City's original goal and Harvey Lichtenstein's vision.

Case 3
New Lots Triangle Plaza –
Sharing the Decision Making Process

New Lots Triangle Plaza is an urban square
improvement project implemented by the NYC
Department of Transportation (DOT) in cooperation
with the nonprofit New Lots Avenue Triangle
Merchants Association. The first section of this
case study will provide a contextualization of the
neighborhood where the square is located. Next
will come an analysis of the roles of the Merchants
Association and DOT. Finally the partnership will
be examined in order to identify the strategies
implemented during this initiative.

Placing the New Lots Triangle Plaza in context
New Lots is a subsection of the East New York
neighborhood in the eastern part of Brooklyn. It is
a neighborhood whose current character has been
influenced by waves of immigration beginning in
the late seventeenth century. At that time, Dutch
settlers gave the area the name New Lots, as they
found enough land here to expand their agricultural

New Lots Triangle Plaza

50m

activities. New Lots remained rural until the beginning of the nineteenth century when it gradually started to attract industrial enterprises and its name was changed to East New York. In the early years of the twentieth century, transportation improvements made the area more accessible, attracting German, Italian, Russian, Polish and Lithuanian immigrants. In the 1950s, many African Americans moved into East New York after being pushed out of neighboring areas affected by urban renewal policies, or after moving from the southern U.S. states. This newly unbalanced and overcrowded situation, combined with high rates of unemployment, caused friction that contributed to the decline of the neighborhood. In the 1980s, East New York became home to many blue-collar immigrants from Central and South America who arrived in New York trying to improve their living conditions and achieve the American dream (Kenneth & Manbeck, 2004).

Since the late 1970s, local organizations, church congregations and homeowners associations have been working to rebuild and redevelop the community. Thanks to this communal effort, soaring crime rates and drug-related activities have been reduced and throughout the last decades the neighborhood has regained its vitality. The construction of affordable housing and the development of commercial areas in the neighborhood have also contributed to this renaissance (Kenneth & Manbeck, 2004). New Lots Avenue Triangle is one of these retail areas centered on the New Lots Triangle Plaza.

New Lots Avenue Triangle and its Merchants Association: creating community
During the last two decades, there has been a growing interest in the study of 'community' among scholars, mirroring the shift in the provision of social

services that began in the late 1970s and early 1980s (DeFilipis, Fisher & Shragge, 2006). During these years the public sector began transferring responsibilities to public-private partnerships and the nonprofit sector.

This shift has been most prominent in the United States, Canada and the United Kingdom, where community-based nonprofit organizations are playing an important role in local development and social provisions in fields such as health, housing, economic development, and education. This shift, which is one of the results of neoliberal urban governance, has been called 'neocommunitarianism' (Jessop, 2002) or 'neo-liberal communitarianism' (DeFilipis, 2004).

In the case of East New York, the community has proved to be a vital arena for social change. Trust, cooperation, reciprocity and networks are crucial aspects in the social capital of a community (Portes, 1998; Glover, 2004; Alaimo et al,, 2010). Robert Putnam (1996) reviews the benefits that living in a well-connected society, where trust and cooperation are present, can bring to individuals. Temkin and Rohe (1998) further point out the cyclical aspects of social capital: the more people get together, the more they will trust each other, benefitting the socioeconomic system that will also function better because of closer ties between the citizens.

One of the nonprofit organizations that is helping to increase the social capital of this neighborhood is the New Lots Avenue Triangle Merchants Association. Co-founded in 2006 by Eddie DiBenedetto, owner of Caterina's Pizzeria, and Reverend Leonard Hatter, the organization is loyal to its mission statement to 'bring together local merchants, community and religious leaders and residents for the purpose of improving the New Lots Triangle area'. The association is composed of twenty-five merchants located in the New Lots Avenue Triangle commercial district, which encompasses a three-block radius around the New Lots Triangle Plaza.

The primary objective of the Merchants Association is to develop a comprehensive plan to revitalize the neighborhood surrounding the commercial district. Some of the main strategies to achieve this goal include creating strategic partnerships with local community groups and organizations, programming events, running a website where local businesses can share their contact information, and beautifying the area by removing graffiti and installing planters. The $360 annual fee that each merchant pays allows the association to organize annual events for the community such as a turkey giveaway at Thanksgiving, and a toy donation and Christmas tree lighting during the winter holidays. In this way, the merchants contribute to the community in return for the support that their clients offer them throughout the year.

The Merchants Association saw a perfect opportunity in the New Lots Triangle Plaza to create a quality public space for the community. And so, in 2010, the Merchants Association reached out to the DOT and applied to the Plaza Program.

Department of Transportation's (DOT) Plaza Program

DOT is the New York City Agency in charge of providing for the safe, efficient, and environmentally responsible movement of people and goods, as well as maintaining the transportation infrastructure in New York City. DOT is the largest real estate holder in the entire city with streets accounting for 80 percent of all

the land that the City owns. Hence the importance of the Public Space Unit, one of the departments within DOT, which runs several successful programs for civic improvement. One of them is the City Bench Program, which is an initiative to increase the amount of public seating in the streets. Another program is the Weekend Walks, in which DOT partners with community groups to close specified areas to vehicles and temporarily allow other activities.

The main program of the Public Spaces Unit is the Plaza Program, which was launched in 2008 as part of the City's long-term plan, PlaNYC 2030. The aim was to enhance the public realm and provide all New Yorkers with quality open space within a ten-minute walk. Since then, this initiative has been creating new neighborhood squares throughout the city by transforming underused streets into public, open and flexible spaces that can facilitate community events and trigger economic activities in the surroundings.

Similar to other programs in the Public Space Unit, the Plaza Program is application-based: nonprofit organizations may apply to DOT and propose locations for new squares. The reason why DOT targets nonprofit organizations as partners is because, as opposed to developers or single local business owners, they have a bigger-picture public mission that may be supported or kept alive with the help of a public space. DOT evaluates each application and rates each proposal based on a 100-point scale.

Sites in low- or moderate-income neighborhoods that lack open space are given priority, as are organizations that can demonstrate experience in organizing community initiatives. Applicants must also prove that they have an active Board of Directors and that they have the capacity to maintain the space.

Once a plaza site has been selected, DOT and the nonprofit association sign an agreement according to which DOT holds responsibility for the design and construction of the square, including all the costs involved, and the partnering association agrees to acquire insurance as well as maintain, manage and program the public space so that it remains not only clean and safe, but also becomes an active and successful open space.

As these arrangements show, sustainability is considered an important aspect of the Plaza Program. DOT uses recycled and standardized materials in all the squares to make maintenance easier and more economically feasible. Additionally, DOT provides each nonprofit association with the opportunity to sign a second agreement, called a concession agreement, by which it gives the community the right to generate revenue in the space as long as that income is used to maintain the plaza.

Partnership between the Merchants Association and DOT

In 2009, the merchants in the New Lots Triangle community got together and decided to transform the 800-square-foot triangular concrete island on Ashford Street and Livonia and New Lots Avenues into a meeting place. The Merchants Association contacted DOT Brooklyn Borough Commissioner Joseph Palmieri, and they presented him with their vision for the square. The Commissioner encouraged them to apply for the Plaza Program, which they did in 2010.

The suggested site is a busy transportation hub due to its strategic location at the end of the elevated 3 train line and as a crossing point for the main bus routes in the area. This, combined with the strong role of the Merchants Association as a community organizer and the lack of public space in the surroundings, helped the proposal score very high on the Program's 100-point scale and to be accepted by DOT.

Before and after of the New Lots Triangle Plaza: from a space to a place

After the application was approved, both parties, DOT and the Merchants Association, agreed to implement the development of the square in two phases: first they would install a temporary plaza to evaluate and test the original design, and later they would replace it with the permanent renovation.

The participatory design process took approximately one year. Several workshops were organized by DOT and the community was able to give their input and ideas about the future space. It was not a smooth process, in the beginning, as there was some strong opposition from the community. Concerns included the possibility of loitering and losing parking spaces.

The idea of diverting the bus route was also a main complaint among the residents of the area. Eddie DiBenedetto, President of the Merchants Association played a crucial role in leading this process. He had been running his business, Caterina's Pizzeria, at the entrance of the train station for more than forty years; he knew his neighborhood and his community very well. Eddie had a strong relationship with the Police and the Sanitation Department, which led to Chief Officers from both departments attending community meetings to alleviate doubts and concerns. This helped to convince many skeptics. Local organizations such as ARTs East New York and United Community Center were also invited to these workshops and actively supported the new plaza. Ronda Messer, from the DOT Brooklyn Borough Commissioner's office, and Emily Weidenhof, the Plaza Program Director, also contributed to the success of the process. Finally, Community Board 5, the advisory group for East New York and neighboring districts, approved the proposed design and the implementation process started.

In October 2011, the temporary plaza was inaugurated. One of the local bus lines was rerouted, which made it possible to close Ashford Street between Livonia Avenue and New Lots Avenue. The 800-square-foot concrete island was joined with nearby sidewalks, making the landing area for passengers coming out of the train safer and simplifying the turn for the buses. The result was a 3,800-square-foot space. DOT provided movable chairs, tables, and umbrellas, as well as planters and granite blocks to create a safe perimeter. The square at this time is maintained and cleaned by volunteers like Eddie, who puts the tables and chairs out every day and takes them back into his pizzeria at night for storage. The temporary plaza has proven to be successful and the community is already enjoying the new space.

DOT expects that the permanent plaza will be open in 2015. As part of the design, several trees will be

planted in the ground, replacing the planters, and fixed furniture will be located in the square, including the City's standard benches along the perimeter. The main paving material will be scored concrete and cobblestones will be used to define the edge. In addition to the current activities organized by the Merchants Association, a weekly farmer's market is also envisioned in the square. Residents will be invited to hold events as well, upon seeking approval from the Mayor's Street Activity Permit Office (SAPO), which is part of the NYC Office of Citywide Event Coordination and Management's (CECM).

The New Lots Triangle Plaza is a perfect example of how a space can become a place. Many scholars (de Certeau, 1984; Lefebvre, 1991; Harvey; 1996; Gieryn, 2000) have analyzed this distinction between space and place. Gieryn (2000) states that there are three main characteristics that define a place. First, places are attached to a geographic location, and they have boundaries that delimit them. Secondly, a place has physicality; it is an assemblage of things (Bijker et al., 1987; Latour, 1996; MacKenzie, 1990) that allow social processes to happen. Thirdly, a place has some meaning or value attached to it. As Soja (1996) states, places are interpreted, narrated, perceived, felt, understood, and imagined. The initial 800-square-foot traffic island and its surrounding was just a space, but following this argumentation it can be stated that the current temporary plaza is now a place. It has acquired a meaning and a value for the New Lots Triangle community. All of these characteristics will be enhanced during the next, permanent phase of the project.

Working towards a common goal: sharing the decision-making process

The partnership of the Merchants Association, as representative of the New Lost Triangle community, and DOT successfully exemplifies what Fung & Wright (2003) call 'empowered participatory governance'. They define it as a form of 'collaborative governance that distinctively combines public participation, decentralized decision-making, practical focus, continuous deliberation and engagement and cooperation between parties and interests that frequently find themselves on opposite sides of political and social questions' (ibid., 263). Wainwright (2003) refers to this concept as 'embedded bargaining power'. There are several key aspects that make 'empowered participatory governance' successful: first, the ability of the community organization to negotiate with the state institution; secondly, the governmental institution's openness to share the decision-making process and to respect the autonomy of the community organization. In the case of the partnership at hand, these requirements were met from the beginning. To monitor the status of the plaza, meetings with both representatives of the Merchants Association and DOT are held monthly. Eddie also reports once per month to the DOT on the events and provides updates related to the plaza and the New Lots Triangle community.

During the participatory design process, while talking about how to design a public space, bigger issues that concerned the community arose, such as fear of crime, conflict of interests among homeowners, etc. Throughout the different workshops and thanks to the cooperation of local groups and organizations, many of those concerns were communally addressed and even solved. This is an indication of how a relatively small public square with community support can become a catalyst of social change (DeFilipis et al., 2006). Places and not spaces spawn collective action and can turn into the scenarios where collective action takes places (Tonkiss, 2005; Gieryn, 2000). Still, building a strong community with high levels of social capital is a lengthy process. By promoting local consumption, community corporations, and the use of local inputs, communities can become more powerful (Shuman, 1998), but in order to have a bigger impact, communities should create linkages that go beyond the local. It is at this stage that the state must be present to support community initiatives to allow them to have an impact beyond a local successful story (DeFilipis et al., 2006). In this case, DOT's Plaza Program supports local initiatives and creates a network of plazas and strong communities throughout New York City. Two other plazas have been already implemented in the nearby areas of Brownsville and City Line. In the case of this last plaza, Eddie was the person who informed the local community of City Line of the existence of the Plaza Program. Eddie DiBenedetto is an example of how the social capital of a group can also become concentrated in one individual (Bourdieu, 1980).

In summation, communities cannot be seen as a 'Third Way' (Etzioni, 1993; Etzioni, 1995), an alternative to the market or to the state, because they play an important role in both (DeFilipis et al., 2006). The New Lots Avenue Triangle Merchants Association, as the advocate for its community, is successfully creating linkages with local organizations and governmental institutions. The merchants aim at using this plaza as a springboard to create new programs for the community, such as summer youth activities or prisoner reintegration programs. Another future goal might be to form a Business Improvement District (BID). New York City now has 68 BIDs, which are areas where commercial tenants and property owners pay an additional tax (or levy) that is collected by the City and returned to the BID to pay for improvements and services beyond those provided by the City, such as branding, sanitation, and safety.

The implementation of the New Lots Triangle Plaza has already put this community on the map. This case helps us to recognize that a place, such as this plaza, has 'an active dimension of movement organizing' (Wilton & Cranford, 2002). This is also a good example of how the will and commitment of one single person, in this case Eddie DiBenedetto, backed up with the support of the community, can spark the transformation of a whole neighborhood. DOT's wish to bridge the gap between institutional support and community needs is remarkable here, and has contributed to the trusting relationship between the New Lots Triangle community and DOT. All these aspects, together with the strategic implementation of the square in two phases, have contributed to the success of this initiative, which DOT uses as a model for the implementation of future plazas. gap between institutional support and community needs is remarkable here, and has contributed to the trusting relationship between the New Lots Triangle community and DOT. All these aspects, together with the strategic implementation of the square in two phases, have contributed to the success of this initiative, which DOT uses as a model for the implementation of future plazas.

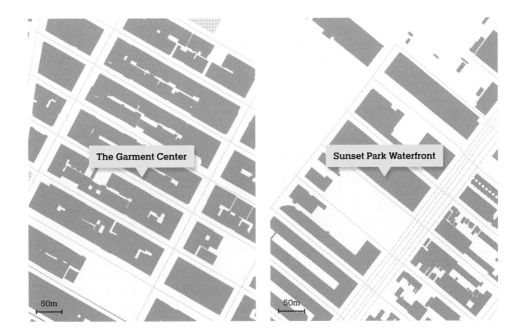

The Garment Center

Sunset Park Waterfront

50m

50m

Case 4
Manufacture New York –
An Inclusive Stakeholder Approach

Manufacture New York is a fashion incubator and factory with the mission to provide independent designers with the necessary support and resources to streamline their production process, from concept to customer. The case study will begin with an explanation of how this concept originated and describe its first steps, followed by an overview of the future plans for Manufacture New York and a description of the different stakeholders involved in this inclusive initiative.

The Garment Center Pilot Program
The idea of creating a space where emerging designers could afford to work and grow in the apparel business came to Bob Bland, CEO and Founder of Manufacture New York, as a vision. Bob's experience as a NYC designer for over a decade helped to crystallize the idea. After working for big labels such as Tommy Hilfiger and Ralph Lauren, and then creating her own firm in 2006, she realized that there was a gap between the big brands and the individual designers. Well-known companies profit from extensive networks and pre-existing factory relationships while emerging talented designers are working in small studios or from their homes, and in most cases are struggling to make a living doing what they love.

Driven by this motivation to transform local manufacturing into an affordable, innovative and sustainable option for all designers, Bob started to look for support and raised enough money through crowdfunding to start making this new model a reality. The first step was to choose a location. With the help of her team, she found a 2,000-square-foot (185 m²) space in Midtown Manhattan, in the core of the Garment District. The place was completely rundown when they arrived and the team of Manufacture New York transformed it with their own hands in less than two months.

The result of this collective effort is the Garment Center Pilot Program, which opened its doors in September 2013. High-quality production facilities including sewing machines, pattern and cutting tables, dress forms, and steamers are set up in the working space. The $300 monthly membership also allows members to use the common spaces, computer workstations, and conference room to have meetings with clients and buyers. Manufacture New York also acts as a consultant and provides designers with workshops on business development and marketing. The opening of the Pilot Program has received a warm welcome and the first designers have already moved into the space and are benefiting from the new installations.

Starting point, the Garment District in Midtown
Choosing the Garment District in Midtown as a location for the Pilot Program was not coincidental. Since the early 1880s, New York City has been a

hub for making clothes, and for almost a century the production has been localized in the Garment District to such a degree that today it is considered to be the research and development hub for American fashion.

The history and character of this area has been continuously reshaped by zoning ordinances and as a result, manufacturing in Midtown has witnessed many ups and downs in the last decades. In the late 1960s and early 1970s, this area hosted a generation of New York-based, high-end designers including Calvin Klein and Donna Karan, among others, who made New York a global fashion capital. In the late 1980s, the rise of mass production hubs overseas and the demand for low-cost clothing contributed to the decline of the manufacturing sector both nationally and citywide. From 1985 to 2007, manufacturing jobs decreased drastically from 105,000 to 26,000 (County Business Patterns, 1990-2008). As a response, in 1987, the City created the Garment Center Special District to retain factories and manufacturing jobs in the Garment District and discourage property owners to transform manufacturing spaces into offices and other uses. This was a crucial moment for the manufacturing sector, as clothes at this time were increasingly designed in New York but produced overseas. The way designers were trained was also affected by this shift. During those decades, students had a strong design background, but lacked the skills to produce clothes themselves, which discouraged entrepreneurial ambitions and led many designers to work for established firms.

In the late 2000s, a renaissance of manufacturing took place in U.S. cities where companies and factories clustered in close proximity, benefitting from complementary businesses, as well as knowledge and innovation spillover (Scott, 2008; Wial et al., 2012). Some economists state that this manufacturing renaissance has helped to lead the country out of recession (Hagerty, 2011). Although the Garment District is benefiting from this clustering, other factors have played an important role in its current status. Midtown is one of the areas with the highest real estate values in the whole country and these industrial spaces in Midtown are appropriate to host other tenants, such as accounting firms, architectural offices, etc., who are willing to pay higher rents than manufacturers for this central location. Therefore, in recent years, the City has rezoned the Garment District as residential/commercial, which has accelerated the influx of new uses in the neighborhood, such as hotels and offices (Design Trust for Public Space in partnership & CFDA, 2012).

Next stop: the Sunset Park Waterfront in South Brooklyn

All these circumstances are encouraging manufacturers to relocate in the outer boroughs such as Brooklyn. Manufacture New York is not an exception. Even though the group will keep the Garment Center Pilot Program in Midtown as a sales showroom, event space, and domestic sourcing library, by the end of 2014, they will open the headquarters of Manufacture New York in South Brooklyn, on the Sunset Park waterfront. Its strategic location near the ports of New York and New Jersey, as well as the area's large amount of renovated and affordable long-term space for designers, artists and manufacturers, make this location one of the best in Brooklyn for industrial manufacturing.

Sunset Park has successfully remained loyal to its industrial past. Even though manufacturing has changed over the years, the industrial waterfront has adapted to the new needs together with the neighborhood. Sunset Park is one of the most ethnically heterogeneous parts of Brooklyn. During the 1880s and 1890s, the area attracted many shipbuilders from Ireland, Poland, Norway and Finland, who made Sunset Park their new home, creating their own communities like 'Little Norway' and 'Finntown', which have now largely disappeared. In 1890, a 200-acre (810 hectares) complex of piers and warehouses, known as the Bush Terminal, was built along the Sunset Park waterfront. It soon started to compete with Manhattan's ports, and due to its success, it expanded in the early 1900s, attracting many Italian immigrant dockworkers to the area. They in turn contributed to the flourishing of the neighborhood in the early twentieth century. During the years of the Great Depression, in the 1930s and the 1940s, the neighborhood entered a decline. The construction of the Gowanus Expressway on Third Avenue, in the early 1950s, cut it in two and made the distinction between industrial and residential use, established by the zoning ordinance, even clearer. The area along the waterfront to the west of the Gowanus Expressway was defined as industrial while the zone to the east of the expressway was considered residential – a division that remains today. Many residents moved to the suburbs and a new wave of immigrants from Puerto Rico took over the houses and the waterfront jobs (Kenneth & Manbeck, 2004).

The 1950s and 1960s witnessed the start of a period of economic restructuring that signaled the end of the postwar economic boom and the beginning of a new era of capitalist development in large industrial countries. The consequence for the Sunset Park waterfront was a process of deindustrialization. Containerized shipping made Brooklyn's once-thriving waterfront facilities obsolete and most of the maritime industry moved to the New Jersey shore, where large plots of land were available for container storage. Accompanying this deindustrialization was a process of 're-industrialization' (Soja, 2010, 116), which reshaped the nature of industrial production and the relationship between labor and corporate management. Far from disappearing, industry adopted a new information-intensive, flexibly organized and spatially reconfigured form and it continued to be the main driving force of urban development.

The main industrial complexes on the Sunset Park waterfront followed this approach. The Bush Terminal, renamed Industry City in 1960, was revived as an industrial campus, and the Brooklyn Army Terminal reopened in 1987 as a center for light industry. During the 1980s and 1990s, many immigrants from Latin America and China settled down in the neighborhood, providing the workforce for the 'new' waterfront jobs, including warehousing, distribution, apparel production and printing. This marked the beginning of the revitalization of the area. However, it was still a challenge to re-use and adapt the antiquated 19th-century industrial infrastructure to a 21st-century industrial model. In 2009, the New York City Economic Development Corporation (NYCEDC), together with the NYC Department of City Planning and the NYC Department of Small Business Services, among other parties, launched the Sunset Park Waterfront Vision Plan. Much of the property on the industrial waterfront, west of Third Avenue, is city-owned and managed by NYCEDC. These industrial facilities provide a unique opportunity to develop projects and create new jobs that will benefit the overall City and the local neighborhoods. The aim of this long-term vision is to develop Sunset Park into a 21st-century model for diverse, dense and environmentally sustainable industry (Sunset Park Waterfront Vision Plan, 2009).

Liberty View Industrial Plaza and Salmar Properties
As part of this coordinated and strategic vision, and in cooperation with state and federal government stakeholders, the City has been selling some of the vacant industrial building stock to real estate developers. This was the case of Federal Building No.2, renamed as Liberty View Industrial Plaza by its new owners, the real estate company Salmar Properties. This is the building that will host the new headquarters of Manufacture New York by the end of 2014.

In 2011, Salmar Properties bought the building for approximately $10 million from New York City Industrial Development Agency (NYCIDA). Since then it has invested about $100 million to renovate it and transform it into a modern building that will provide a high-tech and sustainable infrastructure for its future tenants, including central air conditioning, backup generator power, a fiber optic network, and broadband and cable services, among other facilities. The renovation was completed in 2013 and Liberty View Industrial Plaza will welcome the first companies by spring 2014.

Liberty View Industrial Plaza, a former naval supply building, has 1.2-million-square-foot (11.15 hectares), distributed over eight floors and is one of the largest vacant buildings in the entire city. Salmar Properties foresaw the potential of the space and decided to renovate the building while maintaining its historical appearance following the preservation and renovation guidelines of the National Park Services, a U.S. federal agency that manages national parks, national monuments, and other conservation and historical properties. This approach contributes to preserving the waterfront's industrial heritage. The massive structure of the old building is one of the few elements that has remained, preserving the building's character.

The vision for Liberty View Industrial Plaza and a requirement by the City, as part of the initial purchase agreement, is to provide 1,300 industrial jobs over the next thirty years, bringing manufacturing back to the city. Over time the definition of manufacturing has changed and there is now a broader range of companies that can use these industrial buildings. Therefore, the real estate developers aim at leasing the space to tenants in the high-tech field that are interested in large floor plates. This industrial use

Left
The new headquarters of
Manufacture New York in Liberty
View Industrial Plaza under
construction

will occupy 85% of the total capacity of the building
and will be complemented with 15% of retail space.
Salmar Properties' idea is to create a synergy so that
different companies can benefit from sharing the
same working space. The ultimate goal, as foreseen
by the Sunset Park Waterfront Vision Plan, is to
transform the waterfront into a modern industrial and
manufacturing cluster, a process that has already
started. The neighboring buildings of Industry City
have recently been purchased by the real estate
company Jamestown, which will soon start with the
renovation process.

**Manufacture New York in Liberty
View Industrial Plaza**
Manufacture New York will occupy 160,000 square
foot (14,800 m²), one entire floor in Liberty View
Industrial Plaza. Within that space, 40,000 square foot
(3700 m²) will be dedicated to the Manufacture New
York fashion incubator and a small production line.
The facilities will include a shared industrial sewing
room, conference rooms, computer lab, showcase
factory, and photo studio for over fifty incubator
members. Manufacture New York will also have a
technology annex for fashion innovation that will host
over twenty fashion tech companies that will be able to
work side by side with designers to develop innovative
solutions. Operating in a vertically integrated
structure, Manufacture New York will be the master
tenant organizing the remaining 120,000 square
foot (11,100 m²) among different manufacturers
working on apparel, accessories, specialty, furniture,
metalworking, etc. There will be approximately
thirty manufacturers that will employ more than
300 employees. The aim of this innovative model
is to create a sustainable fashion ecosystem where
manufacturers can work together with designers.

Stakeholder involvement: an inclusive approach
The top-down strategies implemented in the fashion
and manufacturing industry during the last decade
have had little success. The team of Manufacture
New York, aware of that reality, has worked toward
an inclusive approach, bringing together emerging
designers, real estate developers, nonprofit
organizations, City agencies, and architects.

This innovative approach has made more progress
in one year toward the goal of bringing domestic
manufacturing back to New York City than any
other initiative.

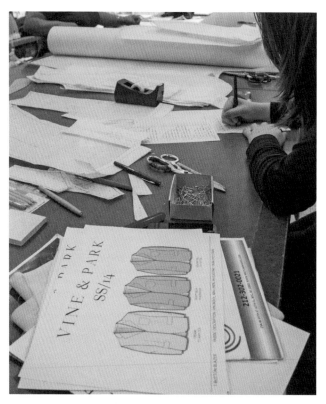

Top and bottom
The Garment Center Pilot Program
in Midtown Manhattan

Designers: Manufacture New York will not only provide support at a grassroots level for emerging designers, but also for established firms that are interested in taking part in this initiative. Manufacture New York aims to welcome a broad range of designers. One approach is providing flexible rental options for the new spaces and facilities, and affordable fees for the designers.

Real estate developer: Salmar Properties is interested in bringing manufacturing back to New York and in contributing to the emerging brand 'Made in Brooklyn'. Their interest in organizations such as Manufacture New York led Salmar Properties to provide long-term leases for at least ten years to its tenants. This will give companies a certain stability and allow them to grow their businesses and plan ahead.

The architects: From the beginning, the team of Manufacture New York was aware of the importance of building both an economically and socially sustainable organization. The importance of choosing energy efficient equipment and sustainable materials, among other requirements, is key to achieve a high Leadership in Energy and Environmental Design (LEED)[1] rating. The sustainable architecture firm Thread Collective was in charge of the initial floor plan and the renderings for the incubator. Currently, a request for proposals among seventeen companies is being conducted to select a final firm that will design the headquarters of Manufacture New York at Liberty View Industrial Plaza. The team of Manufacture New York is confident that the final design can achieve a LEED Gold rating.

Nonprofit organizations: Manufacture New York has received financial support from Fractured Atlas, a national nonprofit artist service organization that supports the independent arts community. Fractured Atlas has become a fiscal sponsor and through them Manufacture New York is accepting tax-deductible donations.

City government: Manufacture New York is seeking financial support in 2014 from the City of New York, through the New York City Economic Development Corporation. The NYCEDC has an industrial desk that funds capital investment projects that support manufacturers in the city. Another funding source is the Empire State Development program from the State of New York. The City runs several economic development organizations in each borough that help build a network between employers and real estate developers, and bring together ideas and perspectives. Manufacture New York contacted Salmar Properties through one of these organizations, the Southwest Brooklyn Industrial Development Corporation (SBIDC), which provides advocacy and services to help businesses in the Sunset Park and adjacent neighborhoods grow and create jobs for local residents. In addition, the New York City Industrial Development Agency (NYCIDA) has an agreement with Salmar Properties in which the real estate developer buys the city-owned property and then leases it back for thirty years for one dollar, providing the developer with some tax advantages during the renovation and tenant build-out process. In return the real estate developer has to ensure 1,300 industrial jobs over thirty years.

This integrated approach bridges different perspectives and interests, and it makes Manufacture New York an interesting example of a bottom-up initiative that has been able to successfully implement its business model. The trust of the different stakeholders involved in the project is crucial if this new and innovative business model is to succeed. In the case of Manufacture New York, this trust has been built upon two main pillars. The first pillar is Bob Bland's strong vision and acute knowledge of the apparel business, which has enabled her to create a fashion ecosystem that provides designers with resources at a grassroots level. Equally important is the collective energy and hard work of the whole team behind Manufacture New York, the people who will ultimately be responsible for bringing this initiative to life. The second pillar is the shared goal of bringing manufacturing back to New York City to create industrial jobs. Based on these two pillars, the City and the nonprofits involved have placed their trust in Manufacture New York and are willing to financially contribute to the initiative. The same trust can be observed when looking at the real estate developers who, thanks to the financial support provided by the City and their vision to transform the Sunset Park waterfront in a modern industrial and manufacturing cluster, are willing to provide Manufacture New York with the space to make this initiative happen. This case study exemplifies the important role that trust plays in a multi-partner relationship.

1 Leadership in Energy and Environmental Design (LEED) is a set of rating systems for the design, construction, operation, and maintenance of green buildings, homes, and neighborhoods. There are four levels of certification: certified, silver, gold and platinum.

Conclusions
Learning How to Improve Collaborative Efforts

As presented in the contextualization section of this chapter, the neoliberal and entrepreneurial governance that has characterized New York City in the last decades has influenced the urban development strategies applied. As Harvey (1989) states, the shift from a 'managerial' approach, typical or the 1960s, has given way to 'entrepreneurial' forms of action in the 1970s and 1980s. This is especially visible in New York City, where public-private partnerships, privatization, the boosterism of local governments, and the role of nonprofits and civic society play a crucial role in city making. When looking at this new active role of citizens, it is worth looking at how the idea of citizenship has changed over time. The old idea of citizenship that consisted of the right or possession of something was transformed by neoliberalism into a form of citizenship that needs to be 'self-worked' and 'self-attained' (Brand, 2007). This 'active citizenship' locates the individual within the processes of social change, which was limited until recently to unusually active citizens and civic elites. 'Under generalized active citizenship, all citizens acquire a certain autonomy and with it, responsibility. They are not only encouraged to participate in the government of others through state or other programs, but also required to be active in their own government: the citizen as self-governing individuals' (Brand, 2007, 626).

All these aspects that characterize an entrepreneurial society can be recognized in the four cases analyzed in this chapter. By analyzing each of these initiatives, the aim is to find strategies that can help institutions to bridge the gap between their support and the citizens who are willing to take responsibility and be part of the process of making their own city. The cases chosen differ considerably in scale, ranging from a small community garden to a 160,000-square-foot (14,800 m²) space in a renovated industrial building. Also the types of spaces that host these initiatives are different, two of them in outdoor spaces and the other two inside. Whether these initiatives are creating new public spaces, beautify their communities, or provide access to education or work, what all these initiatives have in common is the willingness of citizens to create a better community and a better city for all. A short overview of the main aspects that define each project is presented below:

Garden of Eden is a community garden initiated in 2009 by a small group. The garden, located on the grounds of one of the many public housing developments in the city, belongs to the New York City Housing Authority (NYCHA). NYCHA leases the space to the gardeners, who need to renew the contract every year. Since its implementation, the garden has been very successful and it has been expanding every year to satisfy the high demand for gardening space from the NYCHA residents. The gardeners grow both flowers and vegetables, beautifying their neighborhood while at the same time enjoying fresh produce from the garden. One of the main factors that has contributed to the success of this initiative is the institutional support that the gardeners receive, not only from NYCHA, through its Garden and Greening Program, but also through several local nonprofits that provide the gardeners with services and resources. The regular communication between the gardeners and the institutions involved, and also between the institutions themselves, is a key point contributing to the success of the initiative.

This dialogue allows the institutions to be aware of their respective roles in this garden, complementing each other's support. More importantly, this initiative demonstrates how NYCHA changed to promote this program and respond to citizen demand. NYCHA's Garden and Greening Program, through an application-based process, is supporting over 750 community gardens at over 200 public housing developments in the city.

The power of a City/nonprofit partnership is evidenced in the **BRIC and UrbanGlass** case study. Due to the City's desire to revitalize Downtown Brooklyn Cultural District, some City agencies, such as the New York City Department of Cultural Affairs (DCLA) and New York City Economic Development Corporation (EDC), are economically supporting the cultural nonprofits established in the area. BRIC and UrbanGlass are two of these cultural organizations that have been in the neighborhood for nearly twenty years, cohabiting under the same roof. This cultural co-tenancy has proven to be successful and has helped them to preserve their common goal of providing access and education to artists and to the local community. The inclusiveness fostered by both organizations contributes to the success of the cultural center in the area. Another key factor in this initiative is the long-term agreement between the City and the nonprofits, which secures the headquarters of both organizations and allows them to plan ahead and develop their missions the future.

New Lots Triangle Plaza is an urban square developed in 2011 thanks to a partnership between the DOT and a nonprofit created by local merchants. This initiative exemplifies another successful 'public-nonprofit'

partnership. There are several aspects that make this initiative successful. First, the implementation of the square in two stages, temporary and permanent, helps all the stakeholders to gain a better understanding of the needs of the space and the community before final decisions are made. Secondly, the agreement established between DOT and the merchants delegates the responsibilities of maintaining, managing and programming the new public space to the nonprofit. DOT's openness to sharing the decision-making process with the nonprofit encourages a considerable autonomy of local action, empowering the community. Thirdly, the case study illustrates the powerful role that an individual can take to help transform an entire neighborhood. The voluntary work done by individuals has contributed to keeping the square clean and alive. Finally, the replicability of these initiatives through the application-based Plaza Program positions this square in the growing network of public open spaces that have been created since 2008.

Manufacture New York, a fashion incubator and factory, is an example of how a powerful idea together with an innovative business model can bring a bottom-up initiative to life. Part of the success of this business model is its inclusive approach, which combines the interests of designers, real estate developers, nonprofits, City agencies and architects. What makes this inclusive approach successful is the trusting relationships built among the stakeholders, who are willing to take the risks that come with innovative entrepreneurial activity (Harvey, 1989). The City economically supports the idea of bringing manufacturing back to New York and this support gives enough security to the developers that are willing to back this innovative concept by providing Manufacture New York with the space. Another aspect that contributes to this success is the implementation of the idea in different phases, starting small with the Pilot Program in Midtown, and going big later, with the eventual goal of occupying a space of 160,000 square feet (14,800 m²) on the Sunset Park waterfront. Finally and equally important, the fact that the idea comes from a person who herself is a designer and knows the struggles and requirements of her profession helps to keep the concept realistic and pragmatic.

The four initiatives covered in this section stretch over a period of time that ranges from just a few months to four years (or nearly twenty years if we take into consideration the length of the total co-tenancy between BRIC and UrbanGlass). Despite these differences, there are some common factors between these four cases that contribute to the success of these initiatives. To help with developing some guidelines and strategies for future initiatives, a few key points are identified and explained in more detail below:

Crucial role of the nonprofits

Strong public support to bottom-up initiatives through application-based programs and long-term agreements

Trust and 'linking' between the stakeholders

Implementation in phases

Importance of locality

Leadership: 1 person, 1 idea

Replicability

Establishing a nonprofit helps citizens organize themselves around a mission statement and increases the visibility and capacity of the organization. This legal status has many advantages, as it facilitates users in finding the services provided by the organization and makes application for funding easier, among other things. Therefore many citizens with an idea to improve their community have chosen to create a nonprofit to better pursue their goals. Equally important to the crucial role of the nonprofits is the strong public support of these bottom-up initiatives. During Bloomberg's administration, many application-based programs were implemented by different City agencies, which allowed citizens to have an active role in the process of city making. By establishing application-based programs, the City shows its willingness to listen to citizens' needs, delegating to the citizens the responsibility to reach out to the different City agencies and present their proposals. The short- and long-term agreements that characterize those programs allow these initiatives to grow strong over time. Typically those long-term contracts secure the location of these projects, contributing also in that way to their resiliency.

It is also important to build relationships among the stakeholders based on trust. Building trust is a lengthy process that is normally based on a frequent communication, the establishment of clear norms, and the awareness of the respective roles that the different actors play. This process of 'linking' (Fox, 1996; Heller, 1996) between the initiators and the institutions and among the institutions is itself an important aspect in achieving a successful initiative. Also the implementation in phases of the idea has proven to be key to better manage the resources and to learn from experience what the real needs of the community are. Together with the progressive implementation of the initiative, the importance of locality appears to be key to achieve resiliency. Citizens and organizations that are involved in their neighborhoods are better prepared to understand the real needs of their communities and to suggest local and realistic approaches. The same applies to projects that require a good knowledge of a specific profession. The closer the initiator is to that field the more successful the initiative will be. Normally these projects have a strong leader behind them, a person with a strong goal or idea who is able to inspire and lead the community towards that goal. Nonetheless, there is always need for a strong team that supports that person. Finally, better than just creating one successful bottom-up initiative is to conceive a model that can be replicated and applied in different locations and with different residents. This replicability is supported most obviously by the different application-based programs analyzed during this chapter.

Despite the important strategies identified in the cases analyzed here (Role of Nonprofits, Strong Public Support, Trust, Implementation in Phases, Locality, Leadership, Replicability), there is still room for improvement. For example, the local '197a plans' introduced in 1989 in order to allow for civic engagement in urban planning issues did not achieve their full potential and only eleven community plans have been implemented since then. These plans could be better used as a tool for grassroots

development to empower citizens in the process of shaping their own city.

Also the institutional support provided by the City could be complemented with other non-governmental programs that also include the community as a main actor in the process of city making. The creation of programs that help citizens to develop leadership skills could also be encouraged, as well as the improvement of visibility for application-based programs in order to include all segments of the population, from the high to the low ends of society. All of these identified and suggested strategies aim at contributing to this worldwide dialogue with the ultimate goal of informing institutions how to better approach bottom-up initiatives and to support the citizens behind them.

Bibliography

Aalbers, M. (2011) Place, exclusion, and mortgage markets. Wiley-Blackwell.

Abesamis, N.P. et al. (2006) 'Social Resilience: A literature review on building resilience into human marine communities in and around MPA networks.' MPA Networks Learning Partnership, Global Conservation Program, USAID.

Adger, W.N. (2000) 'Social and ecological resilience: Are they related?' Progress in Human Geography, 24 (3) pp. 347–364.

Alaimo, K., Reischl T.M. & Allen, J.O. (2010) 'Community Gardening, Neighborhood Meetings, and Social Capital.' Journal of Community Psychology. 38 (4). pp. 497-514.

Angotti, T. (2008) New York For Sale: Community Planning Confronts Global Real Estate. Cambridge, MA: MIT Press.

Berg, T. D. (1999) Reshaping Gotham: The City Livable Movement and the Redevelopment of New York City, 1961-1998. Purdue University.

Bianchini, F., et al. (1988) 'City Centres, City Cultures: The role of the arts in the revitalisation of towns and cities'. Manchester, UK: Centre for Local Economic Development Strategies.

Bijker, W.E., Hughes, T.P. & Pinch, T. (eds.) (1987) The Social Construction of Technological Systems. Cambridge, MA: MIT Press.

Bourdieu, P. (1980) 'Le capital social'. Actes de la recherche en sciences sociales. 31 (2-3).

Brand, P. (2007) 'Green subjection: The politics of neoliberal urban environmental management.' International Journal of Urban and Regional Research. 31 (3). pp. 616-632.

Brash, J. (2011) Bloomberg's New York : Class and Governance in the Luxury City. University of Georgia Press.

Carpenter, S., Walker, B., Anderies, J. & Marty, A. N. (2001) 'From metaphor to measurement: resilience of what to what?' Ecosystems. 4 (8). pp. 765–781.

County Business Patterns, 1990-2008.

Cucca, R. (2012) 'The Unexpected Consequences of Sustainability. Green Cities Between Innovation and Ecogentrification'. Sociologica 2.

Cutter, S.L., Barnes, L., Berry, M., Burton, C., Evans, E., Tate, E. & Webb, J. (2008) 'A place-based model for understanding community resilience to natural disasters'. Global Environmental Change. 18. pp. 598–606.

de Certeau, M. (1984) The Practice of Everyday Life. Berkeley: University California Press.

Declaration of Policy, Housing Act of 1949, 63 Stat. 413, 42 U.S.C. 1441 (1958).

DeFilippis, J., Fisher, R. & Shragge, E. (2006) 'Neither Romance Nor Regulation: Re-evaluating Community'. International Journal of Urban and Regional Research. 30 (3). pp. 673-89

DeFilippis, J. (2004) Unmaking Goliath: Community Control in the Face of Global Capital. New York: Routledge.

Draper, C. & Freedman, D. (2010). 'Review and Analysis of the Benefits, Purposes and Motivations Associated with Community Gardening in the United States'. Journal of Community Practice. 18. pp. 458-492.

Eisinger, P.K. (1988) The Rise of the Entrepreneurial State: State and Local Economic Development Policy in the United States. Madison, Wisconsin: University of Wisconsin Press.

Etzioni, A. (1993) The Spirit of Community: Rights, Responsibilities, and the Communitarian Agenda. New York: Crown Publishers.

Etzioni, A. (ed.) (1995) New Communitarian Thinking: Persons, Virtues, Institutions, Communities. University Press.

Ferris, J, Norman, C. & Sempik, J. (2001) 'People, Land and Sustainability: Community Gardens and the Social Dimension of Sustainable Development'. Social Policy & Administration. 35 (5). pp. 559–568.

Folke, C. (2006) 'Resilience: The Emergence of a Perspective for Social-Ecological Systems Analyses'. Global Environmental Change. 16 (3). pp. 253–267.

Fox, J. (1996) 'How Does Civil Society Thicken? The Political Construction of Social Capital in Rural Mexico'. World Development. 24 (6). pp. 1089-1103.

Fung, A. & Wright, E.O. (2003) Deepening Democracy: Institutional Innovations in Empowered Participatory Democracy. London: Verso,.

Gieryn, T. (2000) 'A Space for Place in Sociology'. Annual Review of Sociology. 26. pp. 463-96.

Gittell, R. & Avis, V. (1998) Community Organizing: Building Social Capital as Development Strategy. Thousand Oaks, CA: Sage Publications.

Glaeser, E. (2004) Review of The Rise of the Creative Class by Richard Florida. Available from: http://www.creativeclass.com/rfcgdb/articles/GlaeserReview.pdf. [Accessed: 12th February 2014].

Glover, T. D. (2003) 'The story of the Queen Anne memorial garden: Resisting a dominant cultural narrative'. Journal of Leisure Research. 35. pp. 190–212.

Glover, T. D. (2004) 'Social Capital in the Lived Experiences of Community Gardeners'. Leisure Sciences: An Interdisciplinary Journal. 26 (2). pp.143-162.

Glover, T.D., Parry D.C. & Shinew, K.J. (2005) 'Building Relationships, Accessing Resources: Mobilizing Social Capital in Community Garden Contexts'. Journal of Leisure Research. 37 (4). pp. 450-474.

Gray, C. M. & Heilbrun, J. (2000) 'Economics of the Nonprofit Arts: Structure, Scope and Trends'. In: J.M. Cherbo & M.J. Wyszomirski (eds.) The Public Life of the Arts In America pp. 202-25. New Brunswick, NJ: Rutgers University Press.

Hagerty, J. (2011) 'U.S. factories buck decline'. Wall Street Journal.

Hall, T. & Hubbard, P. (eds.) (1998) The Entrepreneurial City. Chichester: Wiley.

Harvey, D. (1996) Justice, Nature and the Geography of Difference. Blackwell Publishers.

Harvey, D. (1989) 'From Managerialism to Entrepreneurialism: The Transformation in Urban Governance in Late Capitalism'. Geografiska Annaler. Series B, Human Geography (1). The Roots of Geographical Change: 1973 to the Present. pp. 3-17

Harvey, D. (2001) Spaces of Capital: Towards a Critical Geography. Edinburgh University Press.

Heilbrun, J. & Gray, C.M. (1993) The Economics of Art and Culture: An American Perspective. New York: Cambridge University Press.

Heller, P. (1996) 'Social Capital as a Product of Class Mobilization and State Intervention: Industrial Workers in Kerala, India'. World Development. 24 (6). pp. 1055-1071.

Holling, C.S. (1973) 'Resilience and Stability of Ecological Systems'. Annual Review of Ecology and Systematics. 4 (1-23).

Hynes, P. (1996) A Patch of Eden: Americas Inner City Gardeners. p. 185. White River Junction, VT: Chelsea Green Publishing Co.

Jacobs, J. (1961) The Death and Life of Great American Cities. New York: Random House.

Jessop, B. (2002) 'Liberalism, Neoliberalism, and Urban Governance: a State-Theoretical Perspective'. In: Brenner, N. & Theodore, N. (eds.) Spaces of Neoliberalism: Urban Restructuring in North America and Western Europe. Oxford: Blackwell.

Kenneth, T.J. & Manbeck, J.B. (2004) The Neighborhoods of Brooklyn. Yale University.

Landry, C. (2003) The Creative City: A Toolkit for Urban Innovators. London: Earthscan.

Landry, C. et al. (1996) The Creative City in Britain and Germany. London: Anglo-German Foundation for the Study of Industrial Society.

Latour, B. (1996) Aramis, or the Love of Technology. Cambridge, MA: Harvard University Press.

Lawson, L.J. (2005) City Bountiful: A Century of Community Gardening in America. p. 363. Berkeley, CA: University of California Press.

LEED certification. Available from: http://www.usgbc.org/leed/certification. [Accessed: 13th January 2014].

Lefebvre, H. (1991) The Production of Space. Oxford: Blackwell.

MacKenzie, D. (1990) Inventing Accuracy: A Historical Sociology of Nuclear Missile Guidance. Cambridge, MA: MIT Press.

Making Midtown. A new vision for a 21st century Garment District in New York City. Design Trust for Public Space & Council of Fashion Designers of America (CFDA) (2012)

Markusen, A. (2006) 'Urban Development and the Politics of a Creative Class: Evidence from the Study of Artists'. Environment and Planning A. 38 (10). pp. 1921-40.

Markusen, A. & Gadwa, A. (2010) 'Arts and Culture in Urban or Regional Planning: A Review and Research Agenda'. Journal of Planning Education and Research. 29 (3). pp. 379–391.

Mayunga, J.S. (2007). 'Understanding and applying the concept of community disaster resilience: A capital-based approach.' Draft working paper prepared for the summer academy, Megacities as Hotspots of Risk: Social Vulnerability and Resilience Building, Munich, Germany, 22–28 July 2007.

Mill, John Stuart (1848) Principles of Political Economy with some of their Applications to Social Philosophy. London; Longmans, Green and Co.

Mollenkopf, J.H. (1991) Dual city: Restructuring New York. Russell Sage Foundation.

NYCEDC, 2009. Sunset Park Waterfront Vision Plan. Available from: http://www.nycedc.com/project/sunset-park-vision-plan. [Accessed: 13th January 2014].

NYC Planning. Department of City Planning. City of New York. Community Districts Profile: Brooklyn Community District 2. Fiscal Year 2014 Statement of District Needs. Available from: http://www.nyc.gov/html/dcp/pdf/lucds/bk2profile.pdf. [Accessed: 13th January 2014].

NYC Planning. Department of City Planning. City of New York. Zoning. Available from: http://www.nyc.gov/html/dcp/html/subcats/zoning.shtml. [Accessed: 13th January 2014].

NYC Planning. Department of City Planning. City of New York. 197a Plans. Available from: http://www.nyc.gov/html/dcp/html/community_planning/197a.shtml. [Accessed: 13th January 2014].

Okvat, H.A. & Zautra, A.J. (2011) 'Community Gardening: A Parsimonious Path to Individual, Community, and Environmental Resilience'. American Journal of Community Psychology. 47 (3-4). p. 374.

Osbahr, H. (2007) 'Building resilience: Adaptation Mechanisms and Mainstreaming for the Poor.' Human Development Report Occasional Paper.

Pinderhughes, R. (2001) 'From the ground up: The role of urban gardens and farms in low-income communities.' Environmental Assets and the Poor. Ford Foundation.

Portes, A. (1998). 'Social Capital: Its Origins and Applications in Modern Sociology'. Annual Review of Sociology. 24. pp. 1-24.

Putnam, R. (1996) 'The Strange Disappearance of Civic America'. American Prospect. 24 (Winter).

Resilience Alliance. (2002) Resilience. Available from: http://www.resalliance.org/index.php/resilience. [Accessed: 13th January 2014].

Rose, A. (2006) 'Economic resilience to disasters: towards a consistent and comprehensive formulation'. In: Paton, D. & Johnston, D. (eds.) Disaster Resilience: An Integrated Approach. Springfield, IL: Charles C. Thomas.

Rosol, M. (2010) 'Public Participation in Post-Fordist Urban Green Space Governance. The case of community gardens in Berlin'. International Journal of Urban and Regional Research. 34 (3). pp. 548-563.

Saldivar-Tanaka, L. & Krasny, M. (2004) 'The Role of NYC Latino Community Gardens in Community Development, Open Space, and Civic Agriculture'. Agriculture and Human Values. 21. pp. 399-412.

Schwartz, A.F. (2010) Housing Policy in the United States. Routledge.

Scott, A. (2008) Social Economy of the Metropolis; Cognitive-Cultural Capitalism and the Global Resurgence of Cities. Oxford: Oxford University Press.

Short, J.R. (2006) Alabaster Cities: Urban U.S. since 1950. Syracuse University Press.

Shuman, M. (1998) Going Local: Creating Self-Reliant Communities in a Global Age. The Free Press, New York.

Soja, E.W. (1996) Thirdspace: Journeys to Los Angeles and Other Real-and-Imagined Places. Cambridge, MA: Blackwell.

Soja, E.W. (2010) Seeking Spatial Justice. University of Minnesota Press.

Temkin, K. & Rohe, W. (1998) 'Social Capital and Neighborhood Stability: An Empirical Investigation'. Housing Policy Debate. 9 (1). pp. 61-68.

Tidball, K.G. & Krasny, M.E. (2007) 'From risk to resilience: what role for community greening and civic ecology in cities?' in: Wals, A.E.J. (ed.) Social Learning: Toward a Sustainable World. Chapter 7, pp.149-165.

Tierney, K. & Bruneau, M. (2007) 'Conceptualizing and Measuring Resilience: a Key to Disaster Loss Reduction'. TR News. May-June, pp. 14-17.

Tonkiss, F. (2005) Space, the City and Social Theory: Social Relations and Urban Forms. Polity Press.

U.S. Department of Housing and Urban Development (2009) Picture of Subsidized Households.

Wainwright, H. (2003) Reclaim the State: Experiments in Popular Democracy. London: Verso.

Wial, H. et al. (2012) 'Locating American Manufacturing: Trends in the Geography of Production.' Metropolitan Policy Program. Brookings.

Wilton, R.D. & Cranford, C. (2002) 'Toward an Understanding of the Spatiality of Social Movements: Labor Organizing at a Private University in Los Angeles'. Social Problems. 49 (3). pp. 374-394.

Worden E.C., Frohne, T.M. & Sullivan, J. (2004). Horticultural Therapy. University of Florida. [Online] Available from: http://edis.ifas.ufl.edu/pdffiles/EP/EP14500.pdf#search='horticulture%20therapy%20war. [Accessed: 13th January, 2014].

Wyszomirski, M.J. (1999) 'Creative Assets and Cultural Development: How Can Research Inform Nonprofit-Commercial Partnerships?'. Journal of Arts Management, Law, and Society. 29 (2). pp. 132-41.

Taipei

Taipei's History, Democratization, and Neoliberalism

Written by Ying-Tzu Lin,
Shu-Mei Huang, Jia-He Lin
and Wei-Hsiu Chang

Taipei is a relatively young city with a turbulent history. Over the past 140 years, three different regimes have governed the city – the Qing dynasty, Japanese colonizers and the nationalist Kuomintang government (hereafter KMT) in exile from Mainland China. Each regime left its footprint on the urban fabric. This chapter will outline four milestones of community development and participatory planning in the not-quite-postcolonial city.

To offer a basic framework for understanding Taipei, the chapter's introduction explores the city's history and how processes of democratization have been linked to urban development. Taipei citizens are currently grappling with an urban crisis in the shadow of globalism and neoliberalism, and dealing with issues such as the privatization of state-owned properties, housing inequality, lower living standards and an impoverished urban nature. To counter these crises, an emerging social movement is reclaiming citizens' right to the city.

This introduction will outline three periods of development in Taipei: 1) Colonial urbanization during 1900s-1970s; 2) The rise of an urban social movement and participatory planning during the 1980s-2000s; 3) City on sale: the neoliberalizing city under globalization since the late 1990s.

Colonial urbanization
in the 1900s-1970s

The first official administration in Taipei was established in 1709 under China's Qing dynasty, but the region of Taipei was not identified as a development center until 1875, when an inner fortified city called Chengnei (城內) was built. Later, it became the capital of Taiwan province. In 1895, Taiwan was ceded to Japan as reparation after the First Sino-Japanese war. Taipei was retained as the capital and political center under Japanese rule, and the colonial regime implemented a series of modern urban planning moves from 1897 onwards. Initially, the regime focused on improving basic infrastructure for sanitary and military purposes. A five-year urban development plan was issued wherein geometric urban grids replaced the outlines of the Chinese walled city. Street blocks were reshaped, and roads were widened. The second phase of urban development began in 1901, when large numbers of street houses were constructed along the newly laid-out streets. Neoclassical and Baroque architecture were introduced to the city. Controls on urban form, such as the building heights of shop houses, were enforced for the first time. Land tenures, a zoning system, public parks, and transportation plans had been laid out efficiently by 1936 as part of the Taiwan Urban Planning Act (Huang, 2003). Under colonial planning, Taipei was a city that could accommodate 500,000 people. Before the end of the Second World War in 1945, Taipei had become a modern city.

After World War II, Taiwan was returned to China. After China's civil war in 1949, the KMT government retreated to Taiwan, and an era of dramatic changes began. In the early 1950s, Taipei's population rapidly grew from 300,000 to 600,000. The influx of migrants resulted in serious housing issues that had already been compromised because of the government's military focus: at that time, 85% of the national budget was allocated to defense (Gold, 1985) and long-term urban planning took a backseat to short-term military defense plans for the urban areas (Zeng, 1994). Refugees were left to build their own housing as best they could.

A decade later, the KMT gradually realized that they were unlikely to take back Mainland China anytime soon. Development intentions were thus transformed from military projects to economic projects, which caused another rapid expansion of the urban population. Between 1962 and 1972, one million people arrived in Taipei. The lack of long-term planning immediately brought about another housing crisis and many planned infrastructure developments were postponed or changed. By the end of the 1980s, urban development in Taipei was out of control (Huang, 2003).

At the same time, the political tensions between the KMT and the Communist Party had obstructed the democratization of politics and planning in Taiwan. Between 1949 and 1989, the KMT had imposed the longest period of martial law the world had seen. Public meetings, demonstrations, civil organizations and democratic elections were not allowed. Mounting social problems influenced the government to abolish martial law in 1989, ending 38 years of dictatorship. The democratization of the country finally liberated the city of Taipei to its citizens.

The rise of an urban social movement and participatory planning during the 1980s and 1990s

After the abolishment of martial law, civil initiatives and community groups rapidly emerged. Citizens wanted to participate in urban planning instead of accepting directives from the top. While there were only

seven environmental protests in Taipei City from 1986 to 1990, forty-six protests took place between 1991 and 1996 (Hsiao & Liu, 2002). It is clear that the planning system and the development regime dominated by the government were challenged by this vigorously transforming society. Borrowing Manuel Castells' (1997) argument about civil society, Li-Ling Huang (2003) has argued that the interweaving of 'proactive' and 'reactive' social, political and cultural movements were important forces reshaping the urban landscape at this time.

In this time of transition, the KMT's rival Democratic Progressive Party (DPP) became increasingly influential in Taipei. The DPP candidate, Chen Shui-Bian, was elected as mayor in December 1994. The DPP's inclination toward direct democracy was in line with participatory planning, and after that time the Taipei City government started a series of reforms to promote community-based projects. A variety of small grants were established to fund projects such as public space improvements or to revitalize abandoned sites. Although these projects did alleviate the problem of public space shortages, the practices of participation were mainly confined to space-making actions instead of policy-making procedures (Huang, 2003).

The 1995 case of Jung-Kang Park was widely regarded as the first victory of the citizens: in this case, they successfully rejected a proposed road-widening project in favor of preserving the community park and its old trees. Instead, the community developed a park through participation with the help of progressive planners and designers (Huang, 2003). The renewed

Jung-Kang Park later became a cultural hub in the city, demonstrating how participatory planning could generate lively urban landscapes.

While participatory planning seemed to take a leap forward because of changing party politics, city government continued to want an orderly, prosperous, and grand city. Under Chen's tenure, the forced eviction of the Kang-Le neighborhood in 1997 was one of the most memorable moments in the history of Taipei's urban social movement. A squatting community of over 300 households that had been residing on the proposed site of two parks for several decades, was ruthlessly displaced by the government despite firm opposition and widespread public attention. Urban parks are valuable public facilities, without question. But in this case, in the name of a 'green' and 'fine' environment, the government turned its back on vulnerable citizens. This tragic event revealed the pro-development ideology of the government as a 'Green Bulldozer', a term coined by Sun-Quan Huang (2012). Moreover, it vividly forewarned of the upcoming struggles of bottom-up urbanism in the new century.

City on sale: the Neoliberalizing city under globalization from the 1980s onwards

In the 21st century, Taipei has been both a liberal and a capitalist city. On the one hand, it is one of the examples of capitalist urbanization that is criticized by the geographer David Harvey. Harvey argues that 'capitalist urbanization tends to destroy the city as a livable, political and social commons' (Harvey, 2012, 68) Even the seemingly successful action in the Jung-Kang neighborhood has not prevented gentrification leading to commercial displacement. The fact that Taiwan has been trapped in economic stagnation since the late 1990s has contributed to a twisted, neoliberal political economy that is hostile to democracy. The privatization of state-owned properties and the promotion of private-led urban regeneration have been adopted by both the central and local governments. Large quantities of state-owned lands were either sold or rented to private developers through Build–Operate–Transfer (BOT). On the other hand, the government has abused incentive zoning to attract private investment. As a result, countless spaces were transformed into unaffordable real-estate commodities that only the rich have access to. Worse still, social exclusion and gentrification have overwhelmingly changed, if not dissolved, a lot of old neighborhoods in the inner city.

The Daan District and its neighboring areas in the south of the city, where the Jung-Kang neighborhood and the following selected cases are located, have the most typical middle-class neighborhoods. Residents of those neighborhoods tend to be economically better off but socially passive and indifferent to public affairs and community politics. Even in those neighborhoods with a stronger sense of self-identity, the power of gentrification still takes a toll. It is difficult to retain community power because many shop owners or long-time residents are likely to be pressured out as a result of rapidly increasing rent. Speculative urbanism has destabilized once lively communities.

The trend of community participation in the 1990s changed Taipei city's ethos from 'we do not own the city' to 'we own the city'. This belief, however, is struggling to survive in the neoliberalizing city in the 21st century.

Who owns the city?
The following chapter presents four case studies, each of which marks an important moment of bottom-up urbanism in Taipei. Despite the aforementioned challenges, community planners and civic groups have continuously and creatively devoted themselves to putting the city back in citizens' hands.

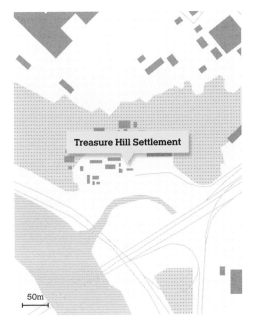

Treasure Hill Settlement

50m

Case 1
The Treasure Hill 'Symbiotic' Settlement

Written by Ying-Tzu Lin

The case of Treasure Hill Settlement has marked an important stage of bottom-up place-making in Taipei over the past decade. The post-Chinese Civil War landscape was marked by informal settlements where low-ranking veterans accommodated themselves in self-constructed houses on state-owned properties. The democratization of Taiwan in the early 1990s was the first time that bottom-up initiatives had the chance to work with institutions and change the system to some degree. This resulted in the preservation of Treasure Hill Settlement, a story of negotiation and cooperation among multiple stakeholders. This case study examines the development of the preserved Treasure Hill Community. It pinpoints significant transitions that contributed to an urban informal settlement beyond everyone's expectations and offers lessons for both grassroots groups and institutions to better address the inevitable conflicts that arise during cooperative projects.

Socio-spatial context of the case

According to a report released by the Organization of Urban Re-s (OURs, 2004), the Treasure Hill Historical Settlement is located on the borderlands between Taipei City and its satellite city New Taipei City. With one side facing the Xindian River, the whole settlement sprawls along the hillside. It was a military post from the 1950s to the 1970s, and then became a self-constructed village where veterans, political refugees of the Chinese Civil War, and immigrants from the countryside lived. By the 1980s, there were already over 200 households living in this ten acre (four hectare) settlement. Those residents were mostly underprivileged, economically as well as socially. They used whatever was available to them to build houses, such as pebbles from the riverbanks, recycled bricks from deserted fortifications, etc. Over time, these individual homes , developed into an informal settlement that accommodated the city's most underprivileged.

For a long time, the settlement was overshadowed by its neighbor Gongguan, a thriving commercial district in the service of students of National Taiwan University (NTU) and National Taiwan University of Science and Technology (NTUST). Gongguan is considered part of Taipei City and its satellite towns Xindian and Junghe. In contrast, the informal buildings in the Treasure Hill Settlement were disowned as urban slums, and were once slated for demolition by the Taipei City Government because of concerns over flooding. The planned slum clearance would have led to a new waterfront park but thanks to numerous protests, Treasure Hill was named a historical settlement in 2004 (Lin, 2013). In 2006, the settlement underwent restoration and refurbishment. It was divided into three areas: a rehousing quarter for the original residents, a new artists' village, and a youth hostel. The restoration was completed in March 2010 and the site re-opened in October 2010. Nowadays, it is one of the most popular cultural hubs in the city.

The formalization of the Treasure Hill settlement

At first, Treasure Hill served as a refugee camp for veterans and rural immigrants. The government turned a blind eye to their illegal occupation of the land and their informal buildings, because the settlement helped to take care of the refugees. The informality was even sanctioned to a degree, as residents in Treasure Hill were granted water, electricity, and legal addresses through household registration, which partially legalized the status of the housing.

In fact, these kinds of informal settlements were not uncommon in the past; they used to spread out in the periphery of the city during the 1950s-70s. Most of them gradually disappeared in the course of modernization. Among these semi-legal settlements, Treasure Hill was relatively lucky. The community existed on its hill without being disturbed until the late 1980s, when the city government rezoned the area as reserved parkland in an updated masterplan. Between 1993-1995, the government tried to enforce the demolition several times but was flummoxed by nonstop protests in every instance (Kuo, 2007).

Given the settlement's semi-legal status and the more open political atmosphere brought about by the newly elected mayor of Taipei City, Chen Shui-bian, a better future seemed in store for the Treasure Hill community (Chang, 2005). Mayor Chen decided that the future of the settlement should be reconsidered with a comprehensive survey and rehousing plan. Between 1995 and 2001, various members of the public and academic sectors released research and surveys; the urban development department, social welfare department, public works department of Taipei City government and the National Taiwan University Building and Planning Graduate Institute (hereafter NTUBP) all participated. Among them, NTUBP played a key role in the preservation movement, as it was the first group to build a trusting relationship with the residents. The group published a thorough investigation and a community-based proposal that integrated preservation, adaptive reuse, and development in 2001. There were several components: 1) a multi-functional park with ecological, cultural, and community functions; 2) Adaptive reuse of existing buildings for an art village; 3) Social housing. After lengthy negotiations, the city government finally chose the second one and selectively adopted parts of the first and the third proposal. The final plan was summarized as follows:

The settlement would be largely preserved and refurbished. Temporary housing would be built to house the original residents during the refurbishment process.

After the refurbishment, properties in the settlement were all assumed by the city government

The Treasure Hill Settlement would be reopened as an 'international art village' with a mixture of artist studios and cultural institutions alongside social housing (available only to the original residents)

The original residents could return to the houses through applying to the social housing plan

Thus, the Treasure Hill settlement became the first officially designated historical settlement according to the Cultural Heritage Preservation Act in Taipei City in 2004.

The making of a symbiotic community
The Treasure Hill Settlement preservation movement can be read on multiple layers. First, it is a story of various socio-economic levels working together. The residents in the community were mostly at the bottom of the urban socio-economic ladder. Generally, they were the poor, the elderly, the disabled and new arrivals to the city. Treasure Hill offered them affordable housing in the city. For them, preservation was a matter of survival.

Although there were a few students from NTU who rented houses there, in general students were detached from the settlement, yet they nonetheless contributed greatly to the research and the new proposals. Secondly, for advocates of equality and social justice, the preservation of Treasure Hill – an organic settlement and heterogeneous urban cultural landscape – is an example of a 'just city' (Fainstein, 2010). As for the authorities, the preservation was an inevitable choice in response to mounting social pressure.

Though many people are attracted by the informality and complexity of the physical landscape of Treasure Hill, most people would agree that it is the social network of the community that makes it a lively place (OURs, 2004; Kuo, 2007). Therefore, the question of how to retain original residents in the changing settlement became an important goal of the preservation movement.

From the very beginning, NTUBP was quite aware of this issue. The institute placed a strong emphasis on engagement with the local residents. Through community participatory planning they learned about residents' needs, their personal histories and life stories and collective memories. These marginalized people did not have much social and cultural capital, but with NTUBP's help, they gained the confidence to fight for a more desirable future.

For twenty years, NTUBP has maintained a close relationship with the community. Formal interactions occurred in community meetings about designing strategies for protests and community planning. Informal social interactions were even more important to this long-running partnership. For example, there were weekly outdoor movie screenings in the main square. Moreover, residents living in the temporary housing without access to private kitchens developed relationships with one another by sharing food. They cooked in the common terrace and organized weekly potluck gatherings. A particular point to mention is that food sharing lies at the very center of Taiwanese socializing, and inviting people to share food can be regarded as the first step to build social relationships; food often links people together as part of the process of community organizing in Taiwan (Huang, 2011).

The movie and food parties were important events in a weekly routine that not only gathered residents into a community but also allowed outsiders to meet the group. In almost all of the community events, the chief of the borough, eighty-year-old Mrs. Chen, acted as the key person who pulled people together. As she had lived in the area all her life, she knew all the people, history and stories of the community. In formal public events, she was highly participative as a community representative and a negotiator between the community, public sector and NGO groups. In the informal events, she always cooked a pot of fried rice noodles that could serve everyone. The significance of this dish is rooted in the Taiwanese tradition of serving food in front of the temple square during fairs, and so this particular dish is a metaphor of sending blessings to people.

Despite strong opinions in favor of keeping the settlement, the authorities searched for more persuasive reasons for a comprehensive preservation. Through the historical investigation of Treasure Hill, preservationists found that this area used to be

Left
Ms. Chen and her food
contributions (fried rice,
tea and fresh vegetables)
at a community event

1 Matt Gross. (February 12,
2006). Going to Taipei.
http://www.nytimes.
com/2006/02/12/travel/12going.
html?pagewanted=all&_r=0

associated with moviemaking, especially Taiwanese
New Wave movies in the 1980s. This cultural aspect
gave strong support for preservation and further
supported the idea of using/reusing Treasure Hill
as a cultural hub. Now, through cultural events,
the public can better understand the stories of the
community. It is also important to note that different
cultural events can provide opportunities for people
to experiment with programming and reorganization
of the community for a different future.

Many local cultural events and international art
activities have been brought to Treasure Hill since
2003. There was an artists' cafe called Pao Wo that
served as a meeting place for cultural exchange.
In 2003 and 2004, the Global Artists Participation
Project (GAPP) invited artists from various countries
to create landscape artwork with the local residents
at Treasure Hill (Kang, 2005). The German art group
id22 identified a riverbank vegetable patch as a form
of 'alternative urban agriculture' (LaFond, 2008).

The Finnish architect Marco Casagrande (2010; 2012)
came up with his notion of 'urban acupuncture' after
conducting field research in Treasure Hill. Through
close observation and design research, Casagrande
noticed that this was a place full of human energy
but stigmatized by the government. He argued that
through careful design and planning interventions
at a small but pivotal scale through a project like
Treasure Hill, hidden energy flows could create a
positive and energetic urban landscape. He compared
this design and planning approach to the needles
used in traditional acupuncture.

Over the years, numerous cultural events were
held at Treasure Hill even before it was refurbished.
The settlement became increasingly famous and
eventually, the authorities were convinced that
preservation was the path to follow given its potential
for diversifying urban culture and nurturing creative
industries.

On the negotiating table, the concept of a 'symbiosis
community' came up. The word 'symbiosis' carried the
expectation that diverse activities and a population
can coexist in one settlement, creating a lively
atmosphere (OURs, 2004). Under the promise of
keeping the physical settlement, residents had to
give up their properties, temporarily move out for
several years until the refurbishment was completed.

The public sector offered financial support for the
refurbishment, though all the property would be
retaken by the government afterward. This is not a
perfect solution, but it was the best one available at
the time. At the same time, parts of the settlement
were turned into the international art village and
youth hostel, as a profitable component of the project.
Nowadays, Treasure Hill has become popular and
it is often recommended as one of the 'must visit'
places in Taipei in travel guides[1] and international
media such as the New York Times. The municipality
is happy about the unexpected marketing effect.
However, the international reputation does not really
help to boost the internal dynamics between the
residents and other sectors in the community, which
can be difficult at times. Lacking communication and
interaction between local residents and the art village,
the community is now eager to find a sustainable
co-managing relationship rather than just coexisting
in the same physical territory; they seek to be truly
symbiotic in the sense of contributing jointly to overall
well-being.

**A critical overview of the
conservation of Treasure Hill**
It is helpful to consider Bruno Latour's (1987; 2005)
Actor-Network Theory to review this case study, in
which subjectivity has shifted from the community
to the art village. This analysis aims to explore better
network dynamics and help institutions learn about
how to develop more symbiotic urban development
plans.

At the start of the movement, it was an issue of
legitimacy of urban informal settlement. The
complexity of the postwar socio-spatial context
was embodied in the ambiguous land and property
ownership situation that existed between the
government and the veterans. It was clear who were
the stakeholders in the network. During the second
phase, more and more actors, especially NTUBP and
the artists who organized the Pao Wo cafe, diversified
the network. For example, NTUBP's investigation
revealed stories and histories of the settlement.
NTUBP introduced community-based planning and
cultural events as a method to empower the local
residents and sought publicity through the media. In
so doing they presented a more engaging story of the
Treasure Hill community to the public, and more and
more actors were drawn to support the preservation
movement. On the other hand, NTUBP also served

as a negotiation platform and a professional workforce. Meanwhile, the artists brought in a series of events that were carefully curated to match with the physical landscape. Art became central to the emerging imagination of the settlement.

The vision of 'symbiosis' gradually took shape during the second phase, leading to a new picture of residents coexisting with artists. However, the shifting focus from taking care of local residents to creating a new art village was not fully resolved. This problem was left unsolved at the start of the third phase. Now the plan is that the Taipei International Art Village (under the governance of Department of Cultural Affairs, Taipei City Government), the youth hostel, and the original residents will become three major communities cohabiting in the settlement. Under functionalist planning, the physical space has been restructured into social housing, the art village, and a youth hostel. Unfortunately, the neighborhood's spiritual leader, Mrs. Chen, passed away in 2012, leaving the original community without a binding element. The city government hired the Tsuei Ma Ma Foundation for Housing and Community Service to act as a rental manager to serve the original residents, but community development demands organization and coordination beyond rental administration. Gradually, the organization of the original residents has declined in contrast to that of the thriving art village.

The refurbished Treasure Hill Settlement developed into a new settlement that was not quite the same as planned. New actors, such as artists and the Taipei Art Village, have not found a balanced way to reside with the old residents so far. Obviously, residents and artists have different lifestyles. Moreover, the fact that artists tend to stay for short periods of time in the art-in-residence program makes is impossible for them to build up relationships with the original residents. Currently, the concept of 'symbiosis' only exists in the abstract – the art village and the old community coexist in the same physical settlement, but do not contribute equally to its success. Different actors in the settlement have not formed meaningful relationships with one another, and Treasure Hill is still looking for a pivotal communicator to facilitate and fill the role of leader.

In addition, the implementation of the social housing program presents certain problems. Without new residents being accepted into the social housing program, 'symbiosis' will quickly degenerate as older people pass away one by one. Eventually, the art village and the youth hostel will dominate the settlement. By then, the spirit of this self-built community will have disappeared, and Treasure Hill will become another 'cool' site occupied by artists and tourists. Since the core value of the preservation movement was to keep the contextual human landscape intertwined with the physical landscape, the spirit of handmade place-making should be sustained. Both bottom-up and top-down stakeholders must collectively work out a feasible long-term plan to manage the social housing. This crisis has unfortunately been ignored by the city government, but stakeholders need to build a more inclusive network with shared agendas across different city agencies and other partnerships if they want to realize the vision of a symbiotic settlement.

Lessons learned
This preservation movement started from a core belief that residents of the urban informal community should be able to live without fear of displacement. Instead of wiping out the informal urban landscape, this case demonstrates an alternative model for the authorities to keep informal urban settlements with an experimental planning scheme to create a new urban cultural landscape. Nowadays, the area's former stigma is gone and the settlement has transformed into one of the most popular cultural sites presenting the creativity of Taipei City. The case of the Treasure Hill preservation movement offers some insightful lessons about the collaborative planning experience and how it can engage bottom-up civil groups and top-down public institutions:

First, it is useful to engage with outsiders such as NTUBP and OURs who can provide communication platforms and professional consultants over the course of the project. With the assistance of professional groups, local residents in this case gained more social and cultural capital.

Secondly, it is important to recognize that 'story creation' requires considerable collective work. Connecting pieces of memories into a coherent story is not easy, but it is helpful in defining the character of a place. In this case, personal histories were stitched into a collective memory of the postwar community struggle that gave rise to the informal settlement originally.

Below
Residents meeting each other
at the community space

The case of Treasure Hill also offers lessons about shared space and leadership. It is important to have leadership emerging from shared space and shared events.

Mrs. Chen was such a key person who brought the community together while she was alive, and her loss has been strongly felt. It is a pity that locals' voices became gradually invisible after the art village came to dominate the representation of Treasure Hill. This does not live up to the original concept of a symbiotic partnership of residents and artists. The municipality

should be more proactively sustaining a balanced interaction between the two parties. It such a case it may be helpful to find another community leader who can reactivate or recalibrate the dynamics of the community.

Lastly, it is clear that a rigid bureaucratic system cannot match the complexity of the city. There should be a creative cross-agency platform to involve different public and private groups, integrate resources, satisfy the different needs of the community and enable a sustainable city.

Case 2
They Almost Owned the City –
The Transient Life of the Qing-Tien
Community

Written by Wei-Hsiu Chang, edited by
Mehdi Comeau and Shu-Mei Huang

While community building has emerged through
several movements in Taipei, most actions were
limited to small-scale design projects or incidental
initiatives, such as community potlucks or thematic
parties. The case of Qing-Tien is one of the few
cases in which the community was able to initiate a
downzoning plan that set a limit for development in
order to preserve urban nature and historic fabric. In
a city where property speculation is taken for granted,
it was a unique bottom-up action that demonstrated
how 'creative destruction' could be countered. This
case study begins with a review of the history of
Qing-Tien, and then traces how the tree conservation
movement brought about a special designation for
the cultural landscape of the neighborhood and

elaborates on how the community effort resulted in an unprecedented revision of zoning. Finally, the section concludes with lessons learned from this constantly changing community.

A brief history of Qing-Tien

The Qing-Tien neighborhood is one of the few places in Taipei where one can still see the wooden houses built by Japanese craftsmen during the occupation of six decades ago. The gardens are full of big, old trees that, as of 2003, were nonetheless neglected as green assets of the city (DYZ Studio, 2003). The neighborhood's development is closely tied to the history of the nation.

In 1928, the colonial government established the Taihoku Imperial University (hereafter TIU) in southeastern Taipei as the most privileged academic institution in Taiwan. A few years later, a group of professors from TIU and scholars of the Taihoku College of Commerce together formed 'the University Credit Cooperatives' to develop a private village that could better meet their housing demands. The project site was part of the Showa-cho administrative region, surrounded by extensive paddy fields. Based on

the 'Taiwan house building code', those professors developed an ideal housing typology inspired by traditional Japanese architecture, combined with certain Western attributes such as sun-filled living rooms. In contrast to the colonized population living in the muddy, crowded western region of the city, the professors' private housing village at Showa-cho featured wide streets and a proper drainage system, with a low building coverage ratio of approximately 20 percent. In addition, there was well-designed landscaping around the houses, which provided tree shading and groundwater management to mitigate the subtropical climate.

After World War II, TIU was renamed National Taiwan University (NTU). Most buildings that had been inhabited by the Japanese were transferred into the possession of the state. These private houses also became state-owned, managed by NTU as faculty housing. Eventually the whole village fell into a new administrative district, called Qing-Tien. The transformation was accompanied by massive reconstruction: wooden houses were sold to private developers and redeveloped into four- to five-story walk-up apartments. A few remained as housing for

retired public servants or their descendants. Those that had been preserved as staff housing maintained their original style, with trees in the gardens and traditional dark-tiled roofs. Today those houses are managed by several public institutions, including NTU, NTNU, Taiwan Railway Administration, and the Taiwan Power Company. Some of them are vacant or even half wrecked, however, becoming 'beautiful ruins', as Chu Tian-Xien wrote in her famous novel The Ancient City, in which she draws a contrast with the rapidly transforming modern landscape of Taipei.

Community building in the Qing-Tien neighborhood

Those old trees are at the center of the community building process in the Qing-Tien neighborhood. Residents sharing a neighborhood do not necessarily form a community; community empowerment is concerned with the making of citizens through social processes that enhance the autonomy of civil society. Furthermore, citizenship is formed through lived urban experience, and the process of forming a community consciousness brings community 'in itself' to community 'for itself' (Hsia, 2007). In other words, community does not exist naturally; community is born from social processes as a result of a mix of interaction and initiatives. In the case of Qing-Tien, both top-down and bottom-up initiatives contributed to the process. Two tree-related projects funded by Taipei's city government are especially worth noting.

The first project was organized by the Department of Cultural Affairs (hereafter DCA, established in 2000) of Taipei city government. It was a pilot program aimed at promoting tree conservation, a project that the then-young entity carried out under the directorship of the founding chief, Ms. Long Ying-Tai. In mid-2002, the DCA chose Qing-Tien neighborhood as the site to demonstrate the significance of urban greening. A press conference was held in the Qing-Tien neighborhood to raise awareness about urban tree conservation. There, Long made remarks about the cultural meanings of urban trees, and their integral role in social sentiment and collective memory (Long Ying-Tai, 2004). In the same year, another 'community empowerment project' funded by the Department of Urban Development (hereafter DUD) carried on the momentum. The project engaged the residents in investigating natural resources available in the neighborhood. The participants collectively produced a neighborhood map and a mobilization action plan, organizing events such as a photography exhibition. The series of actions were organized by a few relatively enthusiastic Qing-Tien residents with the intention of involving middle-class residents in public conversation. These latter residents were primarily public officials and school employees who were indifferent to public issues. The success of those actions also attracted politicians, e.g., city councilors. The two projects mentioned above set up the foundation for community mobilization of Qing-Tien in the following years.

In July 2003, a tree-cutting incident in the Qing-Tien neighborhood turned the residents into activists. At that time, a private garden owner tried to remove old trees without addressing DCA or informing the residents. It was a violation of the bylaw of Taipei City Tree Conservation, which had just been enacted in April 2003. The DCA issued its first ticket to the owner in the very neighborhood where they once declared a commitment to protecting urban trees. The incident was not the only case; NTU itself repeated the violation when it attempted to reconstruct a residence for visiting scholars without regard for existing trees or plants. Again, it attracted lots of criticism from the residents in the Qing-Tien neighborhood. After that, every problematic tree removal became a neighborhood crisis, which brought residents together in their fight against inappropriate development. With these struggles, a sense of community was raised, gradually turning the self-interested individuals into a community.

In response to the community protests, NTU and DCA asked the Institute of Building and Planning at NTU to carry out a comprehensive survey of neighborhoods like Qing-Tien in order to make an inventory of existing Japanese wooden houses and old trees. An action group called Da-Yuan-Zi studio (hereafter DYZ studio) was formed to take on the project. With the survey the DYZ studio found out an ongoing crisis of land sale that was much larger than the issue of tree cutting. Behind the scenes, as DYZ pointed out, a nationwide privatization of public lands was going on.

The central government was planning to gradually sell off 'vacant' properties, including many state-owned Japanese wooden houses, in order to bring in much-needed funds (EY, 2003).

The privatization of state-owned land had a huge impact on the existing historic landscape composed of green spaces and wooden houses. Private developers obtained those lands for profitable real-estate projects, which changed the low density of those lands and, in the process, the land required by those old trees. How can a tree exist without its base? When the Qing-Tien community discovered the linkage between local trees, Japanese wooden houses and conservation issues, the community movement expanded from a socio-cultural mobilization into one with a strong political-economic focus. Beyond trees, houses and historical stories, it was a matter of the commons and the public.

The community successfully brought attention to these disappearing Japanese wooden houses and historical trees. According to the Cultural Heritage Act enacted under DCA, both houses and trees could be considered 'cultural heritage' to be preserved upon designation. The community created the 'Qing-Tien Think Tank' to collect and exhibit the Japanese professors' academic contributions during the colonial era, which, as the think tank argued, were well represented by the trees and Japanese houses as an interconnected built environment. The government's policy of land sale was denounced as

1 The first downzoning case in
Taipei took place in Yi-lan
county in 1998.

threatening the cultural heritage of the communities and the city. The community wanted to preserve as many existing trees as possible regardless of land ownership because they considered trees as integral to the community's identity. Trees, in this light, became interesting elements that transgress the border between the private and the public.

The community effort brought about the designation of 'Qing-Tien Historical District' in 2004 and 2005. In response to the community's request, DCA and DUD rezoned the Qing-Tien neighborhood, including every Japanese wooden house in the conservation area. In order to keep the density low to retain enough sunlight and space for the trees, the community asked DUD to stop transferring development rights (TDR) and to cancel the floor area ratio bonus (FAR bonus) on parcels near those Japanese wooden houses. Construction in the area was prohibited for two years before the rezoning plan was finalized (from March 2005 to March 2007). During these two years, DCA designated four historic monuments and six historic buildings at Qing-Tien.

The climax of community building: a magic moment when the community prioritizes culture over profit

In July 2007, the urban planning commission approved the rezoning plan – an unusual move that had the potential to compromise the private property's value. It made Qing-Tien the first and only case of bottom-up mobilization that would prioritize cultural values over private property development rights in Taipei City.[1] The rezoning would have ensured the lushness of Qing-Tien. It embodied an unusual antidevelopment moment that sacrificed profit in order to conserve the environment.

However, this success was relatively short-lived. In the following years, concerns over private property rights gradually emerged, related to the fact that 2007 also witnessed a trend of urban renewal promoted by the government in Taipei. Through the lens of redevelopment, property owners at Qing-Tien realized that private developers were avoiding Qing-Tien because the profitability of the place had been largely limited by the downzoning. As a result, local property owners could not enjoy the benefits of TDR and FAR bonuses as people living outside of Qing-Tien could. The perception of the downzoning dramatically changed from 'good environmental

management' to 'urban renewal killer'. Increasingly, residents along with realtors who were eyeing the neighborhood complained to local councilors and Taipei city government concerning the downzoning. The opponents then called for a new rezoning plan that would restore their general rights to development. After serious debates in private conversation and public meetings, the plan and boundary of Qing-Tien Historical District were seriously revised. A smaller conservation area was drawn to exempt many properties from the building limits. In 2013, the city government approved the new plan. The success of the private property owners, in a way, suggested the disintegration of the once lively Qing-Tien community that was eager to protect its urban nature and history.

Reflecting on the transient success of the Qing-Tien community

The transient life of the Qing-Tien community illuminates two issues that the community organizers did not foresee. First, the dynamics of community could be largely changed by urban renewal policies that basically encouraged property owners to compete. This problematic incentive resulted in many urban renewal projects in places where the market may be strong but the built environment is not necessarily as dilapidated and useless as the urban renewal policy implies (Hsu & Chang, 2013). Yet, at this time no urban renewal projects were proposed in Qing-Tien, which is surprising given that the price of real estate in Qing-Tien community had more than doubled since 2003. It is in this context that the property owners in Qing-Tien blamed the 2007 rezoning, which led to the 2013 rezoning. What was neglected is that an excessive floor area bonus is indeed an accepted alternative form of public subsidies paid by the public (Chang, 2012). In a way, the urban renewal policy redeveloped not only properties but also the mindset of residents.

Secondly, the gentrification and commercialization of the designated Japanese wooden houses went beyond the community's expectation. The managing institutions, such as NTU, tend to let the highest bidders operate those historic houses, even if they have no intention to connect with Qing-Tien community's daily life. For example, one of the Japanese wooden houses became a famous restaurant, which brought additional traffic and noise that actually compromised the resident's quality of life. With these unexpected problems, and the

Top
One of the Japanese style houses
in the Qing-Tien community

Bottom
Community tour of old trees
and historical buildings in
Qing-Tien, 2003

aforementioned issue caused by downzoning, more and more residents came to consider the historic preservation a disaster rather than a community success.

A significant landscape change can be expected to emerge in Qing-Tien, a place where the residents almost owned the city as a community. The role of the public sector, including both DCA and DPU, shifted from cultivators of communities in the early 2000s to promoters of urban redevelopment, which actually do more harm than good in terms of sustaining community mobilization. The actions of the private sector, including property owners and developers, also change drastically when the housing market is rocketing. While it is clear that public awareness remains determined by the property regime and development ideology, the case of Qing-Tien demonstrated that bottom-up actions and top-down actions could simultaneously influence one another in their interactions. Alternative values such as culture and history require commitment from both sides. In the future, more needs to be done to create room for 'community' to overcome the divide between private and public.

Case 3
Dancing in the Ruins –
Locating a Space of Insurgent Planning
in the Shadow of the Colonial State

Written by Shu-Mei Huang

This case study explores community activism as it has taken shape in opposition to a redevelopment proposal for the area of Huaguang, the former location of a colonial prison. The activists in this case wavered between progressive planning and the conservative politics of historic preservation, and in so doing approached new possibilities of 'insurgent planning' (Miraftab & Wills, 2005; Miraftab, 2009) in the shadow of the colonial state.[1] 'The colonial state' can be understood in two senses: it was the Japanese government that ruled Taiwan between 1895-1945, but it can also refer to the (neo)colonial state hidden within the ideology of modernist city planning, which privileges the abstract conceptualization of development as the only public interest. The case illuminates the persistence of the colonial state and how people deal with its domination over the city.

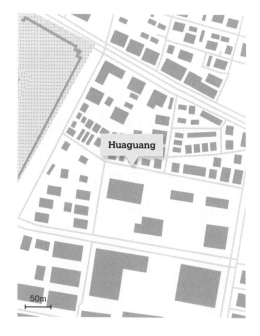

Huaguang

50m

Top
Dance performance in the ruins

Bottom
Huaguang Neighborhood

Previous spread (left)
The plum tree

Previous spread (right)
During a community tour near
the prison wall, visitors heard
an ex-prison guard telling stories
about working in the jail

1 The Taipei Prison Settlement Heritage Alliance and the
  Huaguang Student Group are two important actors in
  this activism movement.

2 Jeremy Bentham explained the concept of the
  Panopticon in The Rationale of Punishment (1830).

3 Those who resided in the dormitories were not sued.
  They moved out under the government's orders, with
  some cash compensation, at the end of 2012.

This case study begins with brief explanation of
the historic prison settlement, and moves on to the
relevant postwar urbanization processes of Taipei and
the recent displacement of squatters. Later sections
investigate how the communities established a
space of insurgent planning through transformative
and performative actions of urban preservation. The
conclusions present a reflection on the dynamics
between the state, the citizen and the city and how
community may approach a more inclusive and
equitable future.

The Colonial City and the Taihoku Prison
Before the 20th century, the area where the Chiang
Kai-shek Memorial Hall and Huaguang stand was not
part of Taipei City. It was not urbanized until Japanese
colonizers arrived, renamed Taipei as Taihoku, and
marked the regime's power by constructing a grand,
modern prison like the British did in Hong Kong to
realize the European idea of punishment by detention
instead of harsh torture. Construction of prisons, as
geographer Ruth Gilmore notes, is a 'project of state
building' (Gilmore, 2002, 16), and through this action
Japan aimed to qualify itself as a modern country.
Among the thirteen prisons, the Taihoku prison was
the most important (Botsman, 2005, 209). Even the
Japanese at home were amazed by the sheer size
and architectural design of the building: in 1904, the
900-meter-long old city wall was broken down and
became the 4-meter-high wall around the prison. Its
radial floor plan and cells for solitary confinement
exemplified the idea of the Panopticon.[2] Prisoners
were made to work in factories and farms and it
was believed that 'the labour by which the convict
contributes to his own needs turns the thief into a
docile worker' (Foucault, 1979, 243). In the Taihoku
Prison, prisoners were divided into groups to grow
vegetables, work in the print shop and wood shop, etc.
In effect, prisoners were cheap labor to make profits
used for operating the prison. The Taihoku prison
was a self-contained settlement comprising the grand
penitentiary, hundreds of dormitories to accommodate
the prison guards, wells, baths, farms and a graveyard
in the surroundings.

Displacement and Punishment
After World War II, when the Japanese left and the
KMT government fled to Taiwan, Taipei became
the capital city of a nation in exile. The government
decided to relocate the prison to make room for rapid
urbanization, and so the prison was demolished and

the land was sold to Chinese Telecom and the Chinese
Post Office. Yet the area continued to accommodate
the existing prison dormitories and migrants from the
Mainland even built shacks between these Japanese
buildings. The former prison settlement became a
hybrid, informal neighborhood inhabited by at least
3,000 people as of 2007.

Soon after, redevelopment plans for this area were
made[3] and those who lived in the dormitory buildings
were asked to leave while the roughly 200 squatter
families found themselves sued by the government,
charged with unjust enrichment and illegal
occupation. They were asked to vacate the lands
and to pay a considerable fine. No resettlement was
offered, and no reference was made to the colonial
history of the early 20th century. More importantly,
the redevelopment proposal, which is loosely
based on the high-end, mixed-use Roppongi Hills
development in Tokyo, has never gone through public
consultation, despite Taiwan's great strides towards
democratization and community planning during
the 1990s. The lessons learned from the community
building (machizukuri) movement in Japan (Evans,
2002) and the promotion of 'community-making' at
all levels of governance were totally ignored in this
case. Because this land was owned by the state,
it was considered to be the state's exclusive asset
– a position that excludes 'community' from the
outset. The charge of unjust enrichment somehow
resonates in this place and its forgotten prison,
where the colonial state exhibited its power over the
colonized through incarceration as a civilized form
of punishment. The charges and the burden of fines
following the lawsuits, in a sense, operated as an
invisible prison to punish the modern squatters.

Turning the tables:
locating a space of insurgent planning
The community undertook a range of actions against
displacement[4], but here we will focus on how the
communities engaged with the idea of historic
preservation. In March 2013, some concerned citizens
formed an alliance and submitted an application to
designate the historic settlement a heritage district.
The application received considerable attention, and
the authority in charge of urban preservation agreed
to convene the cultural heritage committee for a
comprehensive review of the prison settlement. In this
way heritage activism temporarily stopped demolition,
and the community bought more time for advocating

an alternative vision of the future. Before, only a small part of the prison wall had been designated as heritage in 1998[5], but with the alliance's effort to link the prison with colonial urbanism and postwar history, the significance of the prison was rediscovered in 2013. The remains of the prison walls and twenty-two Japanese-style houses near the south wall were designated as historical buildings; forty-nine trees were listed as protected trees in addition.

The fact that only a fraction of the whole settlement was recognized seems to suggest that the government still wants to keep the site for development as much as possible. Still, the designation is remarkable because it successfully changed the way the place is imagined. With the listing, the government has to revise its plan. Moreover, it became a point of departure causing citizens to question the whole project. They began to consider the prison remains as an example of 'negative heritage', a site that can open up a discursive space for reflecting on negative memories and envisioning the future (Meskell, 2002). Indeed, heritage must be about the present as well as the past (Ashworth, 2009).

It is also important to note that the contested space of heritage can lead to conservative politics dominated by the middle class and elites if community-based ways of remembering are absent (Hayden, 1995). Meanwhile, the state tends to manage heritage as a tool to institutionalize a sense of place (Ashworth, Graham & Tunbridge, 2007, 63). The alliance is aware of these issues and is working hard to ensure the inclusiveness of the politics of heritage through more bottom-up actions.

Making claims to the city through mobilizing place memories

Among many other spontaneous, bottom-up practices of insurgent planning at this location, three stories stand out: a moonlight party to preserve a plum tree, a dance in the ruins, and the Huaguang Envisioning Workshop.

One of the most inspiring stories revolves around a plum tree planted by a Mr. Chen at the front of his house. For two decades, the plum tree bloomed in a beautiful signal of winter's end. Many passers-by would stop by and take photos of the tree. Later in every year, Mr. Chen would harvest the plums and make plum wine for his friends and visitors. The

tree became meaningful as a social space where the neighbors met. As redevelopment plans brewed, rumors circulated that the plum tree was going to be stolen by gangsters and sold. Mr. Ho, a long-time activist concerned with civic culture and urban greenery, decided to physically guard the tree until the government adopted a more active measure to protect it. The crisis was solved creatively: for more than two weeks, people spontaneously threw nighttime parties in order to guard the plum tree. Every evening, people gathered around the tree after 10 pm, bringing snacks and beer and expecting Mr. Ho to come. Most of them could not stay throughout the night but wanted to at least keep him company. The waiting process became a party, during which people exchanged information about how displaced people could try to continue their everyday lives. Activists from other groups stopped by to share greetings and support. Eventually, the press coverage of the plum tree parties attracted the authorities' attention and official protection was expedited. In this simple act of caring for a tree, people instinctively grouped together regardless of any conflicting opinions about the site's future. In a way, this also testified to the social significance of the plum tree, which had an impact far beyond any physical measure of the tree's age or height, the quantitative standards that qualify a tree for official protection. It also demonstrated the power of place, even though the place was just a corner defined by one single tree.

Despite the fact that half of the Huaguang neighborhood had been turned into ruins by September 2013, as redevelopment went forward, young students and artists continued to express their feelings of loss and resentment through performance art. In the 2013 Taipei Fringe Festival, a piece titled 'Chen Yu-Lan' was presented with help from displaced residents and student activists. A fictional story was developed to capture the social network among the neighbors across class and ethnicity and to expose the kind of 'root shock' (Fullilove, 2004) that threatens people's emotional ecosystems. The social network intertwined with place contributes to the continuity of self-identity over space and time (Giddens, 1991).

Zhihan Xiao, a dancer and previously a reporter, launched 'A Land Project' in mid-November 2013. The dancer recruited a group of lay people to document and represent the stories embedded in the ruins through their bodies. Through a month-long ethnographic study of Huaguang, they orchestrated

Next spread
Plum tree in blossom at Huaguang

the dance on the site, turning the setting into a temporary theater (Yeo, 2003). Through their moves, grounds covered by relics became a stage; abandoned rooms filled with messy left-behind furniture became living spaces again.[6] The bright colors of the dancers' dress and their powerful moves were transient but transformative. The artistic, wordless interpretation of land grabbing and displacement connected complicated cases across geographies, enabling the public to question the speculative mechanism covered by the empty promise of development.

Emily, a woman in the audience, described how deeply she felt the wounds of the site when she heard the sound of broken glass under the bricks. 'Stepping on the relics I feel like being the dancer, the displacee ... I cannot but look back and apologize to the scene of devastation again and again', she said.[7] From her comment it is easy to see how people were moved by this storytelling through art, which is one of the best ways of communication and persuasion. Another attendee, Orchid, noted that the dance was the most powerful 'protest' she had ever seen. As Edward Soja (2003) suggests, storytelling is a form of communicative action, 'the very act of plan making and plotting'. People don't care about issues when they cannot make sense of them, when they are complex and distant from their lives. Joe Barthel succinctly notes that, 'What's the story here? If we can begin to answer that satisfactorily, ... [we] can make decisions out of compassion rather than fear' (2003, 227-228). The power of storytelling through art can invoke hope in the midst of ruins.

A new phase started in early September 2013 when the government claimed that all squatters were gone and the land would be ready for bidding by June 2014. The revised plan divided the site into nine parcels, including three parcels kept for historic preservation and six parcels marked for redevelopment. Again, the new plan was delivered without any consultation. Its strong focus on tourism and creative industries looks to 'the creative quarter' as a panacea (Evans, 2009). It serves the goals of a specific set of stakeholders – 'the creative city regime' (Huang, forthcoming) that keeps an eye on the real estate market.

In partnership with the Daan Community College and the Organization of Urban Re-s (OURs), activists launched three thematic workshops during October and November 2013. Each workshop was a half-day-long event attended by thirty to forty participants, including neighbors and a mix of concerned citizens. Their outreach extended to middle-class residents living in the nearby areas. In a way, concerned citizens have not left but instead grown into a more extensive community. The three themes of the workshops – resourceful city, historical city, and sustainable city – encouraged participants to rethink urban redevelopment from multiple viewpoints. They were given a thematic tour and then split into discussion groups. They examined the histories and geographies of the Prison Settlement and from there they came up with ideas in response to their daily experiences, needs, and desires. Their conversation prioritized use values over exchange values, appreciation of the social network and social memories, and urban ecology much more than abstract economic growth.

These events, like a collective learning process, brought together individuals and enabled them to understand the city they collectively inhabit. The whole process engaged citizens in making models, maps, and displays to close the gap between the 'representational space' of the inhabitants and the 'space of representations' dominated by architects and planners (Lefebvre, 1991). Nearly one hundred model trees were made by a group of senior residents, who were at first hesitant to participate in urban politics because they held negative memories of the political oppression of earlier years. The participants' multiple voices restored the lost human touch to modernist planning; the stories they shared even explored 'the magical properties of city lives' (Raban, 1974, 156) that were crucial for urban dwellers to survive isolation and impoverishment. Moreover, separate individuals become fellow citizens by collectively exercising their right to plan. Eventually, the workshops led to an exhibition and public forums, urging political recognition of this community in place and its changing, expanding nature.

The workshops were at times contested spaces where conflicting ideas met. For example, the displaced communities and their neighbors have varied expectations for (re) housing. Imaginations are limited by the home ownership scheme offered to the privileged few during the 1970s and 80s. This kind of distributive rehousing is exclusive and exploitative, leading to a stereotyping of squatters as greedy 'nail households'. Facilitated conversations allowed participants to reconsider housing as not

limited to exclusive commodities. This epistemological transformation is key to bringing about more inclusive actions and citizenship. In January 2014, the alliance organized a forum to present alternative proposals based on the ideas collected from the workshops. In response to these community actions, the Taipei City Government's attitude has been changing from disengagement to actively negotiating with the central government for ensuring an outcome that is in the public interest. It is likely that the Taipei City Government will advocate for developing some public housing at Huaguang, yet no definite results are available at the time of writing.

Lessons: towards a more imaginative and insurgent planning

In the shadow of the colonial state, communities re-territorialize the city. Powerless people move beyond the ideological framework dictated by the state to 're-own' the city, in other words, to repossess their 'right to the city' (Lefebvre, 1996; Harvey, 2008). The exercise of power, as Bruno Latour argues (1986), is an effect rather than a cause. Power can be thought of as 'a topological arrangement — as a relational effect of social interaction' (Allen, 2004).

In the face of massive displacement, the communities created a transformative effect of power from below through place-making, art, and storytelling to arrange imaginative, insurgent social relations around the plum tree and the abandoned houses. Instead of worrying about crime, safety and hygiene — all the stigmatized ideas about the to-be-demolished settlement – the ones who participated thus liberated themselves from the invisible prison of 'poor-crime panic'.[8]

In Huaguang, citizens have regained power through their spatial practices. It is a city inhabited by active, insurgent citizens; it is a postcolonial city reinterpreted by memories and imagination. The category of community is performatively extended. Their actions remind the state that the city is, indeed, owned by active citizens who refuse to become passive voters. This insurgent planning holds citizens together to confront 'the failure of nation states' (Holston & Appadurai, 1999). After all, the birth of cities predates the rise of the modern system of nation-states.

There are two lessons we can learn from this case. First, it is important to reconnect citizens with city

space to counter the ownership-based property regime, which allows 'the state' to exclusively act upon the land regardless of what the urban communities really need. Thus, the city should insist on itself as a meaningful place of lived memories rather than an empty administrative category. Cities are important sites where the imaginary and creative breakdown of civility and nationality can carry on. Secondly, memory is about how we live with one another – a 'shared authority' (Frisch, 2004). For enlightening memories, it is important for the local authorities to work with the concerned communities through initiatives beyond conversation at the meeting table to encourage individuals to tell stories about themselves, others, and the city. Insurgent citizens emerge with a refusal of the anonymity of the urban. Through sharing memories and stories they become WE – insurgent and creative citizens who own the city.

4 There have been many protests against the forced eviction over the past four years. For examples, see recent reports in Jake Chung (March 20, 2013) Protesters, police clash in Taipei, Taipei Times.

5 The designation was especially dedicated to the execution of fourteen American airmen held at Taipei Prison during WW II. In June 2005, the Taiwan Prisoners of War Society held a memorial service to commemorate the 60th anniversary of the execution at Taihoku Prison. The brother of one of the executed airmen and his two sons were invited from the US to attend the event.

6 A video of the performance is available online at https://www.youtube.com/watch?v=cPQjj_6wHOc

7 Nov. 18, 2013, comment posted on the Facebook page of the performance: https://www.facebook.com/pages//1409909692571817

8 Drawing inspiration from the 'sex-crime panic' discussed by Chauncey (1993) and Lancaster (2011), the term 'poor-crime panic' has been coined to refer to the emergent resentment toward the poor and a conflation of the poor and the criminal in Taiwanese society.

Case 4
Green Life Roosevelt – An Alternative to the Greenwash of Urban Renewal Underneath Taipei Beautiful

Written by Jia-He Lin

Event-led urban regeneration
Around the turn of the 20th century, an urban reform philosophy called 'City Beautiful' was advocated by idealistic architects, urban designers and policy makers in the United States with intent to refine the cities. Enforcing orderly planning and comprehensive urban design, it was thought, would make the cities better looking and better run (Bogart, 1994). Today, the movement is still frequently referred to in policy papers around the world, including in Taipei, where a policy scheme called 'Taipei Beautiful' (台北好好看) was initiated by the Taipei City Government (hereafter TCG) in 2009. Despite the imitative's name, the policy is focused more on accelerating regeneration than on creating a utopian urban future. In reality, Taipei Beautiful seeks to channel the city into a neoliberal mode of urban renewal: it is designed to encourage

Green Life Roosevelt

50m

small-scale and stand-alone 'building renewal' projects that are mostly initiated or executed by private developers without much comprehensive consideration of the collective good. It is essentially pro-market and profit-driven, in favor of speculative real-estate development (Weber, 2002; Peck, Theodore & Brenner, 2009).

Taipei Beautiful was at first proposed as a complement to the mega event that was the 2010 Taipei International Flora Exposition (hereafter Flora Expo). Official publications stated that Taipei Beautiful was designed to 'revitalize the [city's] shabby appearance' and to transform Taipei into a 'beautiful international city' (TCG, 2011). Such event-led urban development has been trendy around the world lately and in many cases has brought about 'staged cities'. Advocates celebrate how mega events, such as the Olympic Games, can regenerate their host cities (Chalkley & Essex, 1999) while critics point out that displacement is the inevitable social cost (Olds, 1998; Greene, 2003). This case study will explore the Taipei Beautiful policy to demonstrate how a seemingly progressive urban vocabulary such as 'community mobilization', 'street greening' or 'open space sharing' may be

used to generate problematic real-estate profits. Civil society has responded to this rhetoric by launching an alternative space-making initiative called 'Green Life Roosevelt' in a noteworthy effort to contest the original policy logic.

Controversy: greenwash or good policy?
Taipei Beautiful consisted of a number of programs; Series II, which was launched in March 2009, generated dozens of temporary green spaces around the city. It was widely criticized as 'greenwashing' or masking problematic real-estate development with 'environmentalism', In a city where green space has not been allocated evenly, the idea of turning potential sites of urban renewal into green spaces is appealing. The proposal was simple: it required the property-owner to demolish deteriorated or abandoned building structures on a given site and turn the lot into a public green space (which by law means a lot with a green coverage of 70% or above). As long as the space was properly maintained as 'green' and 'open' for at least 18 months, up to 10% extra Floor Area Ratio (FAR) could be given to future building projects on the site as a reward. Such incentive zoning intends to encourage the private sector to invest in the grand

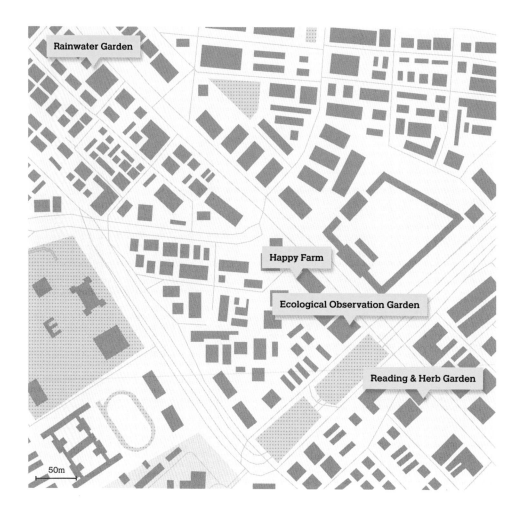

Rainwater Garden

Happy Farm

Ecological Observation Garden

Reading & Herb Garden

50m

mission of urban renewal but in the end, the green space would still be wiped out and yield to real-estate commodities. According to the government, a total of 74 applications were approved within two years. The Urban Regeneration Office (hereafter URO) of TCG claimed that through this program they had created roughly 37 acres (15 hectares) of green spaces for the citizens (even only for a temporary period) and had reduced carbon emissions equal to fifty times of the carbon absorption of the Daan Forest Park, the biggest urban park in the city center (Hsu, 2010). With these numbers, TCG proudly considered the Series II a success.

As a matter of fact, the citizens soon felt the benefits of the policy in everyday life. Quite a few places throughout the city, including the landmark old United Daily News headquarters located in the hub area of eastern Taipei, were demolished. Tidy lawns with bushes, flowers and even recreational facilities filled

those once derelict lots. These visually appealing and accessible spaces meant that Series II was enthusiastically welcomed at first. Yet the high-profile marketing of the program also attracted the attention of some professionals and activist groups. Their review of the program pointed out that the cost of maintaining such spaces was negligible compared to the benefits given to the developers – the costs could be as little as tens of thousands of dollars a year, but the money generated from the sale of additional property units could add up to hundreds of millions.

The review disputed the legitimacy of the whole concept of trading development rights in return for ephemeral green spaces. Opponents of Taipei Beautiful criticized that by launching this program TCG's only intention was to privilege controversial urban renewal projects, sheltering them by 'greenwashing' them. They considered these spaces created under Series II 'fake parks' since TCG failed

Previous spread
The urban farm contrasts with
a highrise under construction

228 | 229

to deliver a genuinely green and sustainable future
to its fellow citizens (Chen, 2013).

Green Life Roosevelt

Becoming aware of the dissenting voices, the URO
sought to resolve some of the obvious flaws of the
Series II. URO tried to involve some professionals to
help demonstrate better models of how to integrate
greening and community participation in the
designated lots. Making use of the resources provided
by the government, non-governmental units were
brought onboard to help improve these projects.

Among all of these, the Roosevelt Road Green Life
Axis (hereafter Green Life Roosevelt) was by far the
most successful case. This project was designed
by Classic Landscape Design and Environmental
Planning (hereafter Classic Design) to create several
green spots along the Roosevelt Road – a main
avenue stretching through the south of the city center.
Classic Design has a good reputation for working
closely with local communities and NGOs, and TCG
hoped that professionals such as Classic Design
could transform the Series II projects to better engage
communities. Classic Design also considered it a great
opportunity to intervene in the problematic program.
Chen-Yu Lien, a senior planner with Classic Design,
explained that by preventing the construction of
more 'fake parks', Classic Design sought to mitigate
the negative impacts Taipei Beautiful might bring
to the city, and, at the same time, create some real,
experimental public spaces in an experimental way
that would encourage further dialogues and even
policy debates (Lien, 2013).

In order to encourage ideas about sustainability
and heterogeneity, the professionals of Classic
Design tried their best to involve the neighboring
communities as well as various non-governmental
institutions in each project. On November 28, 2009,
a successful event kicked off the experimental Green
Life Roosevelt. Hundreds of citizens were mobilized
to save the roof tiles from an abandoned Japanese-
style house that was waiting to be torn down. In the
following months, Classic Design hosted a number
of community activities and planning workshops to
stimulate collective imaginations and come up with
feasible action plans (Lien, Chang & Shih, 2010). As a
result, during the year 2010, four unique spaces were
created:

Rainwater Garden

Based on a plan resulting from collaboration between
Green Citizens' Action Alliance and residents from
the neighborhood, the Rainwater Garden integrates
ecological design and community participation. It is a
pocket park equipped with various kinds of facilities
to create a recycling system to collect, save and make
use of rainwater to ensure a self-contained cycle.
The construction of the garden followed the principle
of minimizing the waste: it reused a lot of materials,
including tiles, timbers and concrete fragments, taken
from demolished buildings. Ever since the garden was
completed in 2010, the local community has been in
charge of maintenance. Now the garden is a popular
spot for outdoor education for nearby schools.

Ecological Observation Garden

The Ecological Observation Garden was located on
the prominent site of an urban renewal project that
had been under negotiation for years. Classic Design
reached an agreement with the landowners to make
use of the lot before construction started, and brought
in the Taiwan Permaculture Association of Sustainable
Development (TPASD) to introduce 'permaculture' to
the neighbors. New design was carefully orchestrated
to work with the preserved original vegetation. The
highlight was an unplugged and fully functioning
mobile baking oven, completely made of natural
materials such as dry sliver grass, clay, timber and
rocks. It was built by the community members with
the help of TPASD designers. There were lively baking
activities and community gatherings in the garden
until the site was returned to the owners for building
construction in early 2012.

Happy Farm

Happy Farm, the largest site of all selected by Green
Life Roosevelt, is located right next to the Ecological
Observation Garden. It is named after the most
popular online game on Facebook at that time and
was designed specifically as a space to promote
urban agriculture. Classic Design also hosted quite
a few agricultural forums there to disseminate
knowledge and techniques of organic farming as
well as to discuss issues around food security and
sustainable living. The farm has become a gathering
space in the neighborhood as every resident in the
neighborhood may register to have free access.
A number of residents, especially the elderly, stop
by the place almost every day to share produce
and farming experiences, and chat with one another.

Reading & Herb Garden

The Reading & Herb Garden is perhaps the most famous case of Green Life Roosevelt, for it is connected to a far more diverse social network than others. The site is located in a neighborhood next to the campus of National Taiwan University, where there are many independent bookstores, live music houses and stylish cafes. The property is owned by Sun-Ten Pharmaceutical Company, which is dedicated to promoting herbal medicines. Because of this complex context, for this project Classic Design partnered with the Willow Den Independent Consortium, a coalition of local shop owners, to remake the space for promoting 'reading in a herb garden'. The detailed and thoughtful design of the garden is very impressive.

More importantly, ever since the garden was completed in mid-2010, the member shops of the consortium have taken turns hosting a series of 'salons' to make this space a free public forum. Exchanges have gone far beyond literature and herb gardening to include social campaigns and debates on gender, immigration, labor, LGBT rights, and urban development. Here, people read, listen, and share thoughts and ideas day and night.

Because of these successful space-making initiatives, Green Life Roosevelt has gained wide recognition from the TCG. Later on, in 2011, Classic Design and URO continued their cooperation to launch a series of workshops called 'Who is Coming to the Picnic?' on the Series II green spots. The series brought together

TCG officials and general citizens to learn about other creative green initiatives around the world. Since then, more and more community-based projects for promoting 'green life' have been developed by the partnership between Classic Design and the URO (Chen, 2012).

Not quite a people's victory

Green Life Roosevelt successfully transformed the government's idea of a beautiful environment from meaningless calculations of visual greenery to substantial realizations of green living in general citizens' daily lives. However, suspicious critics have also wondered whether it is just a facelift. Is Green Life Roosevelt merely a more sophisticated version of the greenwash of urban renewal?

This is not to say that the participants and supporters of Green Life Roosevelt are all naive. But there are both theoretical and practical issues in need of critical discussion. As time has passed, campaigns and social networking have withdrawn from these private-owned public spaces, though they were once imagined as important bases for insurgent activism. As these public resources have run out, the continuity of the social momentum generated by community participation is in question.

It is worth noting that activism in the name of socially, economically and environmentally sustainable urban development has never been absent in Taipei. Among others, there are groups such as the Taipei

Metropolitan Development Research Center (hereafter TMD), a group of young planners and activists that is constantly monitoring the urban policies, and Gorilla Guerrilla for People (hereafter GGP), a group of students dedicated to promoting 'guerrilla gardening'. Both spoke out throughout the Flora Expo frenzy.

TMD coined the 'fake park' label by launching a Facebook page with a countdown calendar of the temporary green spaces. They also initiated several street campaigns to address the importance of FAR regulations to prevent the city from overdevelopment or real-estate bubbles. For their part, GGP did various creative flash-mob actions to question Taipei Beautiful and persistently called for the release of state-owned vacant lots for public use (Gorilla Guerrilla for People, 2013). Moreover, they formed an alliance to urge the government to be more accountable to the public. As 'fake park' became a popular concept, some people came to realize the tricks underlying Taipei Beautiful.

These campaigns did raise the public's awareness immediately. However, there has not been enough momentum to make effective structural changes to counter speculative urbanism. In contrast to the grassroots efforts mentioned above, TCG still largely prioritized encouraging private investment in urban renewal in the Taipei Beautiful Series. In August 2010, TCG launched another disastrous incentive program, which gave extra FAR of up to 100% to projects that redeveloped those buildings aged over thirty years and were four or five stories high. In addition, TCG planned to amend the Taipei City Autonomous Ordinance on Urban Renewal to make the short-term 'fake park' game a regular legal tool even though the Control Yuan (the highest investigatory agency of the central government) had addressed a serious concern about its legitimacy in 2012.

These arbitrary policies have turned the city into a battlefield of unruly redevelopment speculation. As Chang (2012) insightfully comments, the ways in which TCG treats 'citizenship as entrepreneurship' and 'citizens as developers' have largely extinguished the possibilities of community-based urban redevelopment. Instead, they only reduce the diversity of urban experiences to a single-minded mechanism of property trading. Eventually, it may result in all-around gentrification of the neighborhoods in central city, as Neil Smith (2002) has been warning for decades.

Beyond everyday green life

While the consequences resulting from Taipei Beautiful may seem discouraging, there are lessons to be learned here. It is undeniable that creative initiatives like Green Life Roosevelt still have the potential to generate significant social momentum to involve general citizens in public affairs. Meanwhile, the juxtaposition of the well-received Green Life Roosevelt with the activists struggling against suspicious development reveals the multifaceted and tangled nature of contemporary urban problems. The refreshing Green Life Roosevelt undertaking had a really important value in terms of enhancing people's know-how about effectively intervening in a suspicious policy. But within the given policy framework, there is no room for such interventions to make permanent improvements to the general livability of the city. It is obvious that the gap between personal experiences and structural problems demands more creative, critical actions.

In sum, we cannot assume that social mobilization through interesting green space practices could spontaneously give rise to a radical force against problematic urban governance. Living out a green life at the personal, familial or even communal level is meaningful. But we also need to bring such enthusiasm beyond the everyday life of individuals to enable more substantial policy changes for all. It is the only way for general citizens to win permanent and decent public spaces for themselves. People do own the city, but only in certain conditions. To remove the conditionality is the challenge.

Conclusions
City as Network

Written by Shu-Mei Huang

In these four case studies, we have drawn attention to the development of participatory planning in the city of Taipei over the past two decades. Each case represents a unique moment of planning breakthrough that counters not only the relics of non-democratic past but also emerging neoliberal urbanism in the city. Yet the momentum won't last unless there is continuous effort to keep community participation a lively part of the conversation.

Each case illustrates urban planning as an unfolding struggle, in which citizens, community workers, planners, developers, and governmental authorities all play a part. Other than human agencies, ideology about how a city should develop, and sense of ownership that connects citizens with the city, also heavily shape processes of urban design and planning. These stories suggest that this city is indeed a dense network of existing urban fabric, social relationships (of common interests and conflicts), and memories of colonialism and oppression. Moreover, it is not a network occupied exclusively by human beings – urban citizens are just learning to realize how important urban ecology is to our well-being and moreover, to democracy (Hester, 2006). When the city imposes programs to improve the built environment for 'the public', citizens learn to engage history, culture, and urban ecology to challenge the abstract conceptualization of 'public' and 'public interest'.

Accordingly, city planning from above that prioritizes improving the built environment without regard to the existing network of communities is by default detrimental to democratic society, which is critical to a relatively young democratic citizenry. With each case we examined the various top-down urban strategies carried out by the authorities and their impacts including: demolition of habitat and everyday life around historic buildings, formalization of urban informality (Roy & AlSayyad, 2004), privatization of public assets, etc. All of these give rise to the neoliberalization of the city, or nurture existing neoliberalism (Brenner & Theodore, 2002). Communities do resist.

They formulate actions and alternative narratives to counter, challenge, and sometimes cooperate with institutions to regain their ownership in these processes of urban transformation. What they are fighting, nevertheless, is beyond the modernistic ideology of development. What's at play, as Neil Smith (2002) reminds us, is that real estate development has become the central piece of urban economy, 'an end in itself'. It generalizes gentrification and displacement; it could empty political and ecological meanings from communities, parks, and historic sites. There are moments when the struggle against the destructive creation driven by gentrification leads to planning experiment.

Moments of city remaking
These four cases in Taipei bring to light specific moments, planning challenges that may often be ignored in a static analysis of urban design and planning. There are three moments emerging from the four cases:

Moment of hope
The Qing-Tien neighborhood, with those beautiful Japanese Wooden houses and historical trees, was once a place where something magical happened: for a brief

moment, the community was willing to support a downzoning project at the cost of their own land profitability. Their enthusiasm for culture and nature at that juncture challenged the stereotype of the indifferent, self-interested middle class in Taipei. Nevertheless, Wei-Hsiu Chang's long-term study documented the transformation of the community in a neoliberalizing Taipei City where profit-driven urban renewal gradually takes the lead. The perception of the downzoning dramatically changed from 'good environmental steward to 'urban renewal profit killer', which sadly reflects the transformation of the community. There was a moment of hope, as Chang concluded, when these residents almost owned the city. Nevertheless, the overwhelming power of property rights came to dominate over social relations and urban politics, leaving little room for utopian thinking. This serves as a reminder that planners and community workers have to deal with how the exclusive exercise of property rights would shape urban communities in a neoliberal city.

Moment of festive celebration
While a moment of hope is transient, a moment of festive celebration is more than necessary in the city of Taipei today. Jia-He Lin's review of the Taipei Beautiful urban regeneration program illustrates the ways in which event-led urban regeneration actually encourages speculative urbanism rather than accommodates 'everyday urbanism' (Chase, Crawford & Kaliski, 2008). The celebration of temporary urban green space – 'fake parks', as Lin calls them – only greenwashes the controversial promotion of urban renewal. The dozens of temporary green spaces that resulted from Taipei Beautiful, in line with the 2010

Taipei International Flora Exposition, were temporary events or eventful space. Rather than conceiving a utopian urban future, what's underneath the rhetoric of Taipei Beautiful is relentless urban redevelopment.

Lin's examination of Green Life Roosevelt also points out that engaging community in those short-lived spaces cannot challenge the profit-driven logic of urban regeneration but it can contribute to the festivity of urban events. The real task lies in finding ways to bring forth community movement beyond enjoying these events. Otherwise, people only own the city in moments of festive celebration. The eventful making of community, however, cannot be sustained once the owners shut down the space.

Moment of creativity in urban informality
The stories of Treasure Hill and Huaguang draw attention to the urban informality that can give rise to creative practices. Moments of creativity, as presented in the Treasure Hill case study, occur when diverse activities and communities are connected rather than divided. Moreover, these encounters can bring new life to existing urban settlements, turning a marginalized landscape into a lively space of encounters and alternative culture, which can be much more socially and ecologically creative than a regular park.

The same is true in Huaguang. Communities representing various interests came together to make claims to this space and in so doing they developed a more diverse project. The historical informality of both settlements has inspired the creation of art, performance, literature, cinema, and more. Planners and policy makers should learn to appreciate the rich heritage embedded in existing urban landscape and moreover, to recognize their social and ecological significance.

Ying Tzu Lin's presentation of the Treasure Hill case also demonstrates that current departmental management of the city fails to accommodate the complexity of urbanism. The organization of housing is integral to community development; the arrangement of resources and spaces is critical to art, culture, and community. Largely, it is the government rather than the built environment that demands serious reform to accommodate creative initiatives from below. Urban informality, far from being a problem, actually sheds light on the limits of modern bureaucracies. As Shu-Mei Huang reports, it is hard to predict whether or not community efforts in Huaguang will successfully intervene with the top-down project. We hope that at least the significance of urban informality will reach a wider audience.

Lessons learned for designers, planners, and community workers

In a city where civil society is in flux and burdened by concerns about economic stagnation, people are largely disconnected from urban politics. In comparison with the early 1990s, it is now less likely for people in Taipei to feel the need to participate in the public sphere since many people now are overwhelmed by job hunting and the skyrocketing cost of living. When asking 'Do We Own the City?' we should be aware of the diminishing commons in the city. We cannot be satisfied by the transient staging of community in short-lived public spaces. Then, in restating 'We Own the City!' we insist on this idea to confront the binary construct of public and private, which is largely serving the ownership-based property regime. With lessons learned from the four cases, it should be clear that the public is comprised of both interest-based and place-based communities, which cannot be exclusively defined by property ownership. When memories and histories are taken into consideration, the sense of ownership can extend outward. There are three useful tips in practice:

To understand the dynamics and transience of communities and cities through heritage: Urban heritage is crucial to understanding communities and cities, because it encourages us to rethink both past and future as dynamic processes connected with the present. In contextualizing urban issues in history, we can better see the hidden threads that actually connect different classes, needs, and tastes.

To create possibilities to bring together different communities: To diversify rather than homogenize conversations, we should embrace rather than avoid conflicts when discussing issues of class, gender, and ethnicities so that we may resist rather than reinforce the actually existing neoliberalism.

To diversify forms and sites of participation: It is important to reach out to marginalized citizens, especially those who are left behind by the ongoing transformation of the city. While the government tends to diminish urban informality, planners and community workers should attend to the energy of informal space and community, where the most underprivileged often come up with creative initiatives that can never be planned ahead of time.

Suggestions for authorities

Pay attention to the changing margin: It is important that the city government engage the communities early when framing agendas and objectives, so that

1 Press release. (Nov. 18, 2013). The City of Taipei announced as World Design Capital 2016. http://www.icsid.org/news/year/2013_news/articles1784.htm

the conversation about designing the city does not degenerate into tribalist polemics. Communities may transform and expand in the process; they are in various ways interconnected. Therefore, communities should never be exclusively dominated by a small group of homeowners and their boundaries should not be taken for granted. Failing to capture the dynamism of communities would reify rather than mitigate existing inequality. Urban planners and policy makers must pay attention to the constantly changing margins of projects and communities, where creative and progressive initiatives are more likely to take place.

Everyday urbanism rather than speculative urbanism:
Local authorities should live up to their responsibility to ensure that the city is a lively space where citizens can thrive, rather than an economic space for capitalists to harvest land rent. It is important that local authorities work with civic groups that represent multiple interests, especially underprivileged people such as tenants and the working class, to retain non-capitalist socio-economics intertwined with everyday urbanism rather than superficial events deployed by speculative urbanism. In many cases, it is the authorities that need to creatively reorganize themselves to accommodate urban informality. Only then can a city become lively and challenge the discourse of state-led development and the abstract formation of the 'public interest' dominated by the capitalist state.

Moments of festive celebration can be exciting and inspiring temporarily, but what we need is space and time to allow bottom-up efforts to sustain moments of hope and creativity through urban informality. It is through these processes that we can see unorganized citizens become connected across existing social and political boundaries. A city is supposed to host such dynamic processes of continuous community building and disintegration, through which networking can shape urban landscapes and urban citizenship. In view of Taipei's becoming the 2016 World Capital of Design[1] we look forward to seeing the city realizing its campaign slogan of 'adaptive city' by acknowledging citizens' ownership in shaping space and society.

Bibliography

Allen, J. (2004) 'The Whereabouts of Power: Politics, Government And Space'. Geogr. Ann. 86 B (1). pp. 19-32.

Ashworth, G.J. (2009) 'Paradigms and Paradoxes in Heritage as Development', paper presented at the International IAPS-CSBE & HOUSING Network 2009 on Requalifying Old Places for New Uses, Istanbul, 12-16 October

Ashworth, G.J., Graham, B.J. & Tunbridge, J.E. (2007) Pluralising Pasts: Heritage, Identity and Place in Multicultural Societies. London: Pluto Press.

Barthel, J. (2003) 'The Meanest Streets'. In: Eckstein, B.J. & Throgmorton, J.A. (eds.) Story and Sustainability: Planning, Practice, and Possibility for American Cities. pp. 227-242. Cambridge, Mass: MIT Press.

Bogart, M.H. (1994) Public Sculpture and the Civic Ideal in New York City, 1890-1930. Chicago: University of Chicago Press.

Botsman, D. (2005) Punishment and Power in the Making of Modern Japan. Princeton: Princeton University Press.

Brenner, N. & Theodore, N. (2002) 'Cities and the Geographies of 'Actually Existing Neoliberalism''. Antipode. 34. pp. 349-379.

Casagrande, M. (2010) 'Urban Acupuncture'. Retrieved February, 29, 2012. from Urban Acupuncture: http://helsinkiacupuncture.blogspot.com/

Castells, M. (1997) The Information Age: Economy, Society and Culture. Volume II: The Power of Identity. New York: Blackwell.

Chalkley, B. & Essex, S. (1999) 'Urban Development through Hosting International Events: A History of the Olympic Games'. Planning Perspectives, 14: 369-394.

Chang, L.P. (2005) 'Production of Space, Urban Social Movements and Cultural Strategies: The Boa-tzang-yan Anti-Relocation Struggle'. Taipei. (Master dissertation, Shih Hsin University Institute for Social Transformation Studies)

Chang, W.H. & Huang, H.H. (2006) 'Selling Country: A preliminary observation toward privatization of public lands in Taiwan'. Paper presented at the Modernization & Regionalism - Re-inventing the Urban Identity -, International Forum on Urbanism (IFoU), Beijing

Chang, W.H. (2012) 'The rise and transformation of urban renewal regime'. Unpublished doctoral dissertation, National Taiwan University. [in Chinese only]

Chang, W.H. (2012) 'Urban Renewal Did Not Take Place: Policy Analysis of Urban Gentrification in Taipei'. Journal of Building and Planning, National Taiwan University, 20: 63-92 [in Chinese only].

Chase, J., Crawford, M. & Kaliski, J. (2008) Everyday Urbanism. New York: Monacelli Press.

Chauncey, G. Jr., (1993) 'The Postwar Sex Crime Panic'. In: William Graebner (ed.) True Stories from the American Past. New York: McGraw Hill.

Chen, Y.H. (2012) 'A Greenwashing City: Exploring the Social Construction of City Nature through the 'Taipei Beautiful' Programs in Taipei'. Master Thesis of the Graduate Institute of Geography, National Taiwan University [Unpublished, in Chinese only, English abstract available].

Chu, T.X. (2002) The Ancient City. Taipei: INK Publishing.

Evans, G. (2009) 'Creative Cities, Creative Spaces and Urban Policy'. Urban Studies. 46. pp. 1003-1040.

Evans, N. (2002) 'Machi-zukuri as a New Paradigm in Japanese Urban Planning: Reality or Myth?'. Japan Forum. 14 (3). pp. 443-464.

Fainstein, S.S. (2010) The Just City. Cornell University Press.

Foucault, M., (1979) Discipline and Punish: The Birth of the Prison. New York: Vintage Books.

Friedmann, J. (2002) The Prospect of Cities. Minneapolis: University of Minnesota Press.

Frisch, M. (1990) A Shared Authority: Essays on the Craft and Meaning of Oral and Public History. Albany, NY: State University of New York Press.

Fullilove, M.T. (2004) Root Shock: How Tearing Up City Neighborhoods Hurts America, and What We Can Do About It. New York: One World/Ballantine Books.

Giddens, A. (1991) Modernity and Self-Identity: Self and Society in the Late Modern Age. Stanford, CA: Stanford University Press.

Gilmore, R.W. (2002) 'Fatal Couplings of Power and Difference: Notes on Racism and Geography'. The Professional Geographer. 54. pp. 15-24

Gold, T. (1985) State and Society in the Taiwan Miracle, Armonk. NY: M.E. Sharpe.

Gorilla Guerrilla for People (2013) 'Yes! It Only Takes a Person to Change the City'. In: Hou, J. (ed.) City Remaking. pp. 194-211. Taipei: Rive Gauche Publishing House [in Chinese only].

Greene, S.J. (2003) 'Staged Cities: Mega-events, Slum Clearance, and Global Capital'. Yale Human Rights and Development Law Journal. 6. pp. 161-187.

Harvey, D. (2008) 'The Right to the City'. New Left Review. 53. pp. 23-40.

Harvey, D. (2012) Rebel Cities: From the Right to the City to the Urban Revolution. Verso Books.

Hayden, D. (1995) The Power of Place: Urban Landscapes as Public History. Cambridge, Mass: MIT Press.

Hester, R.T. (2006) Design for Ecological Democracy. Cambridge, Mass.: the MIT Press.

Holston, J. & Appadurai, A. (1999) 'Introduction: Cities and Citizenship'. In: Holston, J. (ed.) (1999) Cities and Citizenship. Durham, NY: Duke University Press.

Hsia, C.J. (2007) 'Thinking Communities and Cities as Social Dynamics: Theorizing Community Empowerment in Globalization'. Taiwan: A Radical Quarterly in Social Studies. 65. pp. 227-248 [in Chinese only]

Hsiao, H., Michael, H. & Liu H.J. (2002) 'Collective Action Toward a Sustainable City: Citizen's Movements and Environmental Politics in Taipei'. In: Peter E. (ed.) Livable Cities? The Politics of Urban Livelihood and Sustainability. Berkeley, CA: University of California Press, pp. 67-94.

Hsu, J.Y. & Chang, W.H. (2013) 'From State-Led to Developer-Led? The Dynamics of Urban Regeneration Policies in Taiwan'. In: Companion to Urban Regeneration by Leary, M. & McCarthy, J. (eds). London: Rutledge.

Hsu, Y. H. (2010) (ed.) The Agency of Greenness: A Review of Taipei Beautiful Series II 2010. Taipei: Taipei City Urban Regeneration Office [in Chinese only].

Huang, J.J. (2011) 'A Delicious Food Has Been Circulated From Site To Site – The Transformation of Taiwanese Hakka Ground Tea'. ChungLi (Master dissertation, National Central University Graduate Institute of Hakka Social and Cultural Studies)

Huang, L.L. (2003) 'Community Participation in Taipei's Urban Planning in the 1990s: The Impacts of the Globalization Process, Local Politics and Neighborhood Response'. Journal of Geographical Science. 34. pp. 61-78. [in Chinese only]

Huang, S.Q. (2012) Green Bulldozer: The Squatters, Parks, Nature Estate and Institutionalized Landscape in 90s Taipei. Taiepi: Pots Publication. [in Chinese only]

Huang, S. [forthcoming] 'The Japanese Houses in Taiwan: the Inhabitants of Colonial Sensibilities and the Creative City Regime'.

Kang, M.J. (2005) 'Confronting the Edge of Modern Urbanity–GAPP (Global Activists Participation Project) at Treasure Hill, Taipei'. Asian Culture Symposium.

Kang, M.J. (2013) 'The Dissidents' Territory of a Rhizome City: The Poetics and Politics of the Willow Den Independent Consortium'. In: Hou, J. (ed.) City Remaking. pp. 152-173. Taipei: Rive Gauche Publishing House [in Chinese only].

Kuo, B.S., (2007) 'Straddling Between Attachment and Disembeddedness: A Research on Place-Identity in Bao-Tzang-Yen Village (Treasure Hill), Taipei'. (Master dissertation, National Taiwan University Department of Building and Planning)

LaFond, M. (2008) 'Berlin Taipei Round Trip: eXperimentcity Meets Treasure Hill'. Umelec. 1. pp. 51-53.

Lancaster, R.N. (2011) Sex Panic and the Punitive State. Berkeley, CA: University of California Press.

Latour, B. (1986) 'The Powers of Association'. In: Law, J. (ed.) Power, Action and Belief. A New Sociology of Knowledge? London: Routledge & Kegan Paul.

Latour, B. (1987) Science in Action: How To Follow Scientists and Engineers Through Society. Harvard university press.

Latour, B. (2005) Reassembling the Social - An Introduction to Actor-Network-Theory. p. 316. Oxford University Press.

Lefebvre, H. (1991) The Production of Space. Oxford, UK: Blackwell.

Lefebvre, H., Kofman, E. & Lebas, E. (1996) Writings on Cities. Cambridge, MA: Blackwell Publishers.

Lien, Chen-Yu (2013) 'Seams of Possibilities: Community Building and the Making of Public Space'. In: Hou, J. (ed.) City Remaking. pp. 174-193. Taipei: Rive Gauche Publishing House [in Chinese only].

Lien, Chen-Yu, Chia-Chi Chang, and Pei-Yin Shih (2010) Walking with Reused Tiles: The Roosevelt Road Green Life Axis. Taipei: Taipei City Urban Regeneration Office. eBook, available: http://issuu.com/harleys.pan/docs/greenaxis_landscape_taipei (retrieved on November 30th, 2013) [in Chinese only].

Lin, C.F. (2013) 'Rethinking the Practice of Artist Village as Cultural Heritage Preservation - A Case Study of Treasure Hill Artist Village, Taipei' (Master dissertation, National Taipei University of Art Institute of Art Administration and Management)

Meskell, L. (2002) 'Negative Heritage and Past Mastering in Archaeology'. Anthropological Quarterly. 75 (3). pp. 557-574.

Miraftab, F. (2009) 'Insurgent Planning: Situating Radical Planning in The Global South.' Planning Theory. 8 (1). pp. 32-50.

Miraftab, F. & Wills, S. (2005) 'Insurgency and Spaces of Active Citizenship - The Story of Western Cape Anti-eviction Campaign in South Africa'. Journal of Planning Education and Research. 25 (2). pp. 200-217.

Olds, K. (1998) 'Urban Mega-Events, Evictions and Housing Rights: The Canadian Case'. Current Issues in Tourism. 1 (1). pp. 2-46.

OURs (Organization of Urban Re-s) (2004) The Treasure Hill Co-living Artsville Planning Report, commissioned by the Bureau of Cultural Affairs, Taipei City Government.

Peck, J., Theodore, N. & Brenner, N. (2009) 'Neoliberal Urbanism: Models, Moments, Mutations'. The SAIS Review of International Affairs. 29 (1). pp. 49-66.

Pow, C.-P. (2009) 'Neoliberalism and the Aestheticization of New Middle-Class Landscapes'. Antipode. 41 (2). pp. 371-390.

Qing-Tien rezoning plan (2013) Qing-Tien rezoning plan, Taipei: Department of urban planning. [in Chinese only]

Raban, J. (1974) Soft City. New York: E.P. Dutton.

Roy, A. & AlSayyad, N. (2004) Urban Informality: Transnational Perspectives from the Middle East, Latin America, and South Asia. Lanham, MD: Lexington Books.

Shen, S.T. & Huang, C.L. (2012) 'The Preservation and Adaptive Re-use of the Treasure Hill Settlement'. International Conference on History and Society Development.

Smith, N. (2002) 'New Globalism, New Urbanism: Gentrification as Global Urban Strategy'. Antipode. 34 (3). pp. 427-450.

Soja, W.E. (2003) 'Tales of a Geographer-Planner'. In: Eckstein, B.J. & Throgmorton, J.A. (eds.) (2003) Story and Sustainability: Planning, Practice, and Possibility for American Cities. pp. 207-224. Cambridge, MA: MIT Press.

Taipei City Government (2010) Taipei Yearbook 2009. eBook, source: http://ebook.taipei.gov.tw/yearbook/2009/ (retrieved on November 30th, 2013)

Taipei City Government (2011) Taipei Yearbook 2010. eBook, source: http://ebook.taipei.gov.tw/yearbook/2010/ (retrieved on November 30th, 2013)

Tsai, H.P. (2002) Lung yin-tai officer, Taipei, Lian-Jing. [in Chinese only])

Tsai, M.J, (2012) 'Right to the City: An Urban Ethnographic Research on Huaguang Community in Taipei', Master's Thesis, National Taiwan University, Taipei.

Weber, Rachel (2002) 'Extracting Value from the City: Neoliberalism and Urban Redevelopment'. Antipode. 34 (3). pp. 519-540.

Yeo, W. (2003) 'City as Theatre'. In: Bishop, R., Phillips, J. & Yeo, W. (eds.) Postcolonial Urbanism: Southeast Asian Cities and Global Processes. pp. 245-262. New York/ London: Routledge,

Yu, S.K. (2002) Premier speech note at state assets management commission, Executive Yuan press release. [in Chinese only]

Zeng, X.Z. (1994) 'The Formation of Urban Consciousness and the Urban Process of Taipei City After the Second World War'. Doctoral dissertation of the Department of Civil Engineering, National Taiwan University [in Chinese only].

Zhao, B.Y. & Chang, J. (2011) 'Positive Role of Nongovernmental Organization's Participation in Policy Making Process in Public Conflict Resolution – Case Study of Dismantlement Conflict Resolution of Treasure Hill Settlement in Taipei'. Journal of Tianjin University of Commerce. 3. p. 010.

Interviews

Interviews with Practitioners

Conducted and written
by Mark Minkjan
(CITIES Amsterdam)

Emerging urban topographies, in which
citizens are no longer passive clients of
urban development but active producers of
their environment, call for new approaches
in planning and architecture.

This requires a new role for traditional top-
down institutions such as governments and
housing associations in city-making, but
also for architects, who are able to mediate
between both ends of what used to be a
hierarchical spectrum but has the potential
to be a more collaborative effort.

Architectural practices have developed
innovative approaches to incorporate the
co-creation of urban space in what has long
been a top-down routine. In four interviews
with prominent firms (OMA, MVRDV,
UNStudio and NEXT Architects), these new
ways of working are explored in order to gain
insight into how end users and communities
can be included in the design processes of
buildings and urban areas. These findings
provide clues about how large firms are
finding a balance between changing societal
demands, their own design ideas and the
demands of the client. They range from
the micro scale of direct interaction with
residents to the level of masterplans and
discuss the responsibility of architects,
governments and citizens. The interviews
suggest tools and methods that can help
institutions to enable citizens' production
of social and physical urban fabric.

Interview with David Gianotten, architect and partner in charge of OMA in Asia. Prior to that, he was managing director-architect at SeARCH.

Mark Minkjan: OMA uses a certain set of parameters that are usually taken into account in urban planning projects. Two of them are 'culture' and 'preservation'. For the masterplan for a new town in Hanoi, OMA was asked to erase existing villages and create an iconic new plan from scratch. OMA reimagined the commission and involved the villages' inhabitants in creating the new plan. Can you elaborate on that process and how the plan developed?

David Gianotten: The area where we are planning is quite outside of the city and it has a rich history, especially in agriculture. It is closely located to the Red River, which is a big river in Vietnam. One of the biggest issues that we came across is that the site is so unbelievably huge that when you would start planning it as a masterplan it would take years and years before it would ever be a real part of the city. To first erase everything that is there and outplace it and then not

make the best use of the plan for so long, but also to not use the power of the people that are already there to spark the development and create immediate life on the site, we thought was not a smart thing to do. On top of that, we did a lot of research for the masterplan and especially the program of the masterplan, including things that were to be planned such as health care, but also R&D facilities, et cetera. Many of the people that were there could already be part of the workforce for the new program and this would probably give them a better development perspective and a better life. When people would kind of program themselves inside of that, or find employment there, that would also mean that they would get more prosperity and more freedom, and they would start development of their urban environment themselves. We thought it would be very interesting to start part of the masterplan in a very planned way and then through the program it delivers and the transformation that would happen automatically because of it, to initiate the rest of the development around it. So while these people would start to develop their lives, they would also initiate the development of their villages, especially their houses. You can also envision that you would inject in these existing villages new civic

桂畔湖全景
Guipan Lake overall view

facilities such as public libraries or areas where people would be able to gather, such as restaurants, et cetera, and because of that, the village would transform itself. When we introduced that approach to the developers and the government, which was in this case a combination, they really liked that approach. Firstly, they wouldn't have to go through an unbelievable process of outplacement, which is not uncommon in socialist countries, but still is a difficult process. Secondly, you would instantly give the people that were already living there a better future through planning. Normally you offer these people nothing but a disrupted life. Because of that, they immediately went along with the idea. We worked it out in such a way that we made all kinds of scenarios of what could happen. Current computer techniques are very helpful in this. You can simulate things such as, 'If you start a development here, what would happen to the villages? And what would happen if you would start there?' And this was very convincing. When we started talking to the people living there, getting to know their needs, ambitions and aspirations for the future, we figured that our plan tied in pretty well to the program that we proposed. So we were able to more or less mobilize the local opinion for the plan. That is also why it was

selected and why we are now going into the detailed stage of that, and soon will start the development of the first part.

MM: What kind of variables do you use in these scenarios?

DG: The scenarios look at locations to start, the program that we inject in the existing villages, population graphs, how they would evolve over time, what the available workforce would be like, et cetera. By using many of these elements, we were able to simply simulate how a village would grow, how it could incubate and how it would respond to developments. It is a constantly developing tool that we also apply to other projects.

MM: During the We Own The City symposium in Hong Kong you mentioned that some of the inhabitants of the villages act as advisors. How does that work?

DG: They act as a sounding board. It is not a public engagement process as we would have it in the Netherlands, Australia or the US. It is more about trying to get ideas back from the people that are

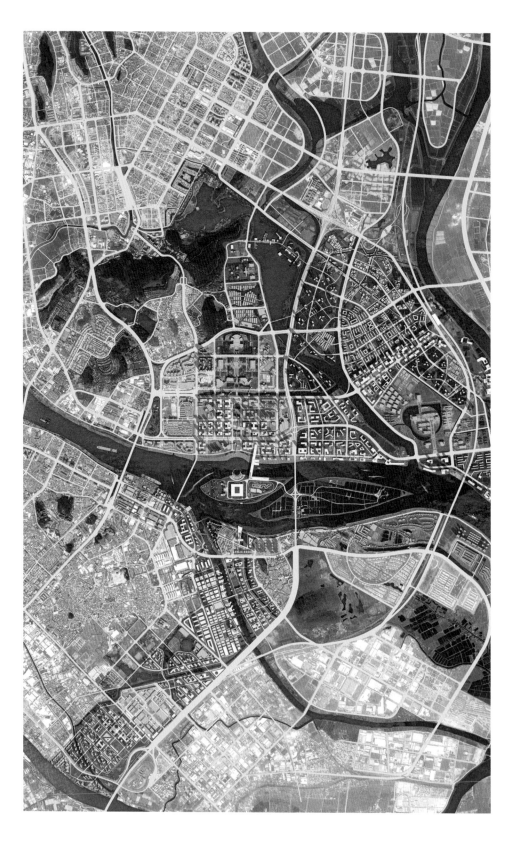

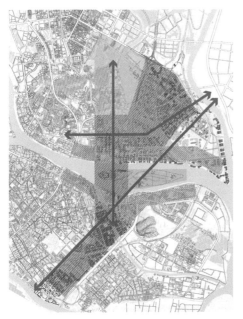 

there and involve them in a positive way in the development.

MM: In an interview with <u>Architizer</u> you stated that the public shouldn't consist of just passive consumers. The aim of We Own The City is similar: the project explores how clients (can) take ownership of their surroundings. In Western urban planning, there's already an increasing interest in fostering informal and spontaneous dynamics. Given the vigorous developments in China, do you think there is room for a similar discourse in Chinese urban planning?

DG: In Greater Chinese urban planning you see similar movements; however, it is still always government-initiated. It is never a real bottom-up approach where people start uniting themselves and then start participating in a positive way from their own point of view. It is really the government that gives people an opportunity, a platform. They orchestrate the platform and record the opinions and also really listen to these opinions. And this is a slightly different way of doing it. But yes, we're working in Shunde in the south of China on a very large masterplan where the government created a sounding board as well from the citizens and they were simply involved in how they saw the future of their city but also how they wanted to deal with sustainability issues from the perspective of the end user, instead of from the overall city plan that is usually mainly interested in numbers. But you can't consider citizens as numbers that add up, because it has to work for each number. That is

a very different approach. It is coming, but obviously the urbanization rate in China is about thirty times higher than the urbanization rate during the Industrial Revolution in Europe. So you cannot compare the current urbanization rate in Europe – which is so slow – to what is happening in China. Therefore the moments at which participation happens and the influence it really has is still quite limited, but it will become more over time, when the urbanization stabilizes. Personally I also hope that – when people start to realize that urbanization leaves something behind, namely the countryside and whatever is there, the original way of living of the Chinese society – they would start paying attention to the part that was left behind as well. Therefore the countryside is probably the best platform to really start establishing a form of participation because it is of a smaller scale, which makes it possible to address much more personal issues. Urbanization, and at such a rate, is not very personal. So yes, it is there on the larger scale, but I think you will soon see that also on a community scale, driven by necessity. It will be there in cities as well but it will be less visible because there are such unbelievable big questions that it is not easy for a normal society to deal with. You need knowledge and education to even understand it.

MM: The approach of the sounding board implementation in urban planning you referred to, is that really a thing that is coming up generally in Chinese urban development projects, or is it just where you are involved?

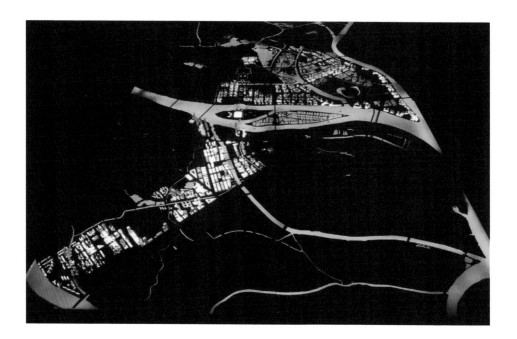

DG: I think it is a combination. We are involved because we have an ambition, but also because somebody else has an ambition. I cannot change somebody else's ambition, I can only add to it. In the end the government or the developers have to be interested in the participation of others and probably we are involved because we are known for that type of approach. And when we are involved, then of course we will make it stronger. I would not say it is because we are involved. It is rather because people who have a vision of developing their cities in our countryside in a different way than the tabula rasa approach are interested in working with us. And because we are on board, in the end it will become an ingredient that can't be omitted. It is definitely not because we are involved that this happens. It already started somewhere else. We only act as a catalyst.

MM: What kind of citizens, organizations or communities are involved in these 'sounding boards'?

DG: It varies a lot. It is people with an interest in urban planning. It could be groups of people of the elderly, the young guys, the farmers – when it is about transforming the agricultural land into a city – it is very diverse. It is always alongside the planning bureaus of China that are capable of giving people a basic understanding of what is happening. That of course is something I cannot do because my task is of a much larger scale. I cannot, on an individual level, explain to people what is happening and therefore what their contribution can be. That is something

another organization needs to do, so there is an intermediary.

MM: How do you consider your role in this (enabling community practice or organic dynamics within the rapid development in Asian cities), as a prominent architectural office, to address and apply participatory processes?

DG: I don't see it as a role. For me it comes naturally because I feel it is my obligation, so it is simply a natural approach of my colleagues and me. We cannot design for the people when we don't work with them. We can only work with people that we know. It is not only the client that needs to be known, but also the end user. I cannot work in a fata morgana situation where I don't know what is going to happen. So it is not a role, it is an obligation.

MM: Looking at your proposals for the West Kowloon Cultural District and Hong Kong's Central Market Building, and listening to what you have said in several interviews, you seem to be fascinated with the vibrancy of urban life. Markets, people mingling – essentially the spontaneous and everyday urban life. As an architect, to what extent do you plan or stimulate such organic and unpredictable interaction?

DG: That is a good observation. I think urban life is only urban life when it is vibrant. A CBD is not urban life, it is only there to facilitate business. Urban areas need to be alive 24/7, they need to be unpredictable

Previous spread (right)
Connected Identity Case –
Key diagrams of strategy
and zoning

This spread
Connected Identity Case –
Model

and they need to be fun. Only then people will want to live there or be there, in whatever culture or circumstance. I would not call it an obsession, but I am indeed fascinated by what creates urban culture. As an architect I cannot create urban culture, that is totally impossible because there are so many factors that create it together and they need to come together before it works. As an architect I am only a very small tool in that. However, if I start working on the right premises and stimulate the process in the right way at the right moment, then the impact of what I do can be much bigger than when I ignore it and just keep my fingers crossed and hope it works. So in that sense I am very consciously aware of the fact that urban vibrancy and urban culture are not things you can orchestrate or plan; it is something that needs to happen. For something to happen you should not plan it, you should spark it. When it is initiated, you need to work with it, alongside it, to facilitate it and to try to emphasize certain qualities of it. I think that is my task as an urban planner. I see the role of an urban planner not as someone who only envisions something on a drawing board and then delivers it for execution by other people. An urban planner's role does not end there. I think urban planning is a trajectory of years. In the Netherlands, Peter Kuenzli, Pi de Bruijn, me and others, were responsible for initiating the redevelopment of the Roombeek neighborhood in Enschede after the fireworks disaster in 2000. I'm still following the aftermath of that process now, and it has been more than ten years. I'm still very interested in the current dialogue and how people experience the end result of the rebuilding of the area. Urban planning is not something that is a technical matter, and that is also what is so nice about it. With urban planning you can never predict the outcome, with a building you can. With a building you can orchestrate how it is going to look like and how people are going to use it. With a part of a city you can never do the same; your ideas act as a framework only. That is what fascinates me.

MM: So it is an ongoing and perhaps even a personal process?

DG: I influence some of the parameters but I am not the creator. It is nice to be the creator but it is also a huge responsibility. I cannot handle that responsibility for a large group of people that inhabit a city, that is simply impossible. If you would say you were able to do so, people could easily start referring to the Bible.

I don't want to make a claim like that, and I think nobody should.

MM: Is it perhaps even a bit frightening that it is not in your hands as an architect?

DG: No, that is fun! I think it is frightening when things are completely in your hands, because the responsibility for it then becomes very, very big. When things are present that you can facilitate, you can really participate. That is a very different way. You really put yourself in it. When it is only in your hands, you need to be almost the salesman of it. If you are the facilitator, things happen automatically after you have done your work. That is a very different effect.

MM: So it is a participation from two ends, from the end users and from the architect or planner?

DG: Yes!

MM: If you would be in charge of an urban planning commission, how would you ideally include citizens' engagement – what would be your most effective tool?

DG: The easy way out is to say that I would never ever want to be in charge of an urban planning commission but I cannot say that because I have been. I would do it in a very similar way to how I want it as an urban planner, and in a very similar way to if I would live in a part of a city where something would happen – how I would want to be involved? Again, it is about obligation. When you are planning part of a city, which has such an impact on many lives of people, there is simply no way you can afford to forget that these people will live there in the end and therefore you must hear their opinion. I think there are many approaches that work, but for me the best approach is when all parties involved have an ambition to deliver to the maximum and to give their real intentions and ideas. Many public engagements and forums are actually a platform for complaints. That is usually not fruitful. When you, as a client, can initiate public engagement where ideas and real ambitions are actually shared, then it becomes extremely useful and extremely clear. So I would always create a platform that is free of complaint, except maybe that the coffee is bad. It should be an idea generator, so more of an incubator than anything else.

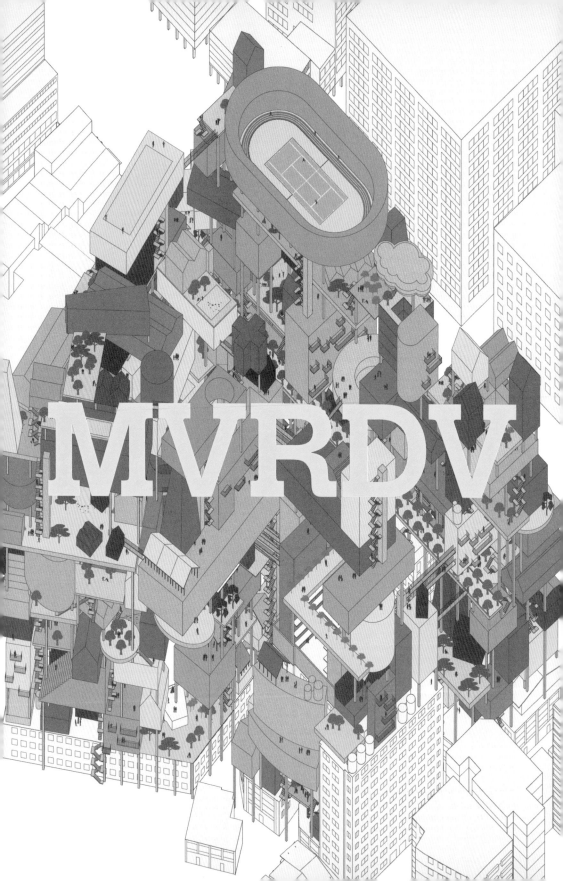

Interview with Winy Maas, architect, urbanist and co-founder of MVRDV. He is also a Professor and director of The Why Factory, a research institute he founded in 2008, which is connected to the Delft University of Technology.

Interview conducted on November 11, 2013 in Rotterdam.

Mark Minkjan: Super-Kampung, a project by The Why Factory – the think-tank and research institute run by MVRDV and Delft University of Technology – investigated urban villages ('kampungs') in Jakarta, which are characterized by informality and little top-down influence, but at the same time are subject to demolition, displacement and gentrification. Super-Kampung aims to find a way to create a mixed social composition and preserve the organically grown microeconomic fabric and informal developments, without letting the existing make-up drown in the wave of globalized urbanization. Urban design can be considered a way to arrange non-organized forms. In light of this view, how can design contribute to informality?

Winy Maas: In this case the suggestion – and the study – is about whether neighborhoods can specialize in their microeconomics. And whether this will lead to a demand that goes beyond the

initial specialization. For instance, if there is fishery, you also need a market. If you have a market, you also need storage. This increase seems to me very crucial to make that economy less vulnerable and more effective, and ultimately more sustainable and enduring. That is the first observation. What architecture can do then, is showing what that would look like, and how even then the fabric of that village could be preserved as such. It is an illustration of the mechanics and in this case of the economy, but trying to add maybe one or two parameters that are in the field of lifestyle or the way of living in that area.

MM: What would be the role of governments and inhabitants in a development that aims simultaneously at the freedom of informality but also seeks the outcome of a socioeconomically mixed population?

WM: In the case of the Super-Kampung, simple illustrations already help to emancipate them. Most of the Kampungs are strongly organized and governed; they have a very classical organizational structure. To suggest intensification – something that is not yet accepted – is what Super-Kampung is about. The university Kampung – the one subject to our study – is threatened by the idea that it will be bought out and replaced. There, it is easier to suggest the adaptation of the area rather than its erasure. The governance structure hopefully helps to establish acceptance or understanding of the considered fusion step that was suggested for this Kampung.

Previous spread
Freeland Oosterwold

Left
Freeland Mannheim

MM: What did you learn from this study?

WM: From an architect's point of view, to start with, that all kinds of possible fantasies of the intensification with this specialized approach can result in settlements that I didn't know yet and that were surprisingly beautiful. The second point would be that the idea of specialization within the city – which is nothing new, take for example the Red Light District in Amsterdam – could be applied to urban villages in Jakarta. It even makes much more sense there, because a planning process will take long. As an architect, I hope for things to go fast, but it implies more than only this kind of intensification. It doesn't touch on the infrastructure of the whole town or the issue of water management yet, things that are especially important in Indonesia. These things were not disappointing, because I knew this in advance. This project is part of an operation to believe that Jakarta can contain its status as the capital of Indonesia and needs to update itself in order to get a proper international status and continuity. Then this is only a part of that project, which is much bigger, and includes new ministries, more safety, more access and more sanitary objectives. But to have the habitat on the agenda now, already was the good thing to come out of this project.

MM: In order to preserve these habitats?

WM: I must say that these Kampungs are very Indonesian in the way they are organized. They have a very classic background. It is a quality that may become a cosmopolitan one later. That would be marvelous and I defend that. I am aware that currently some eighty percent of the Kampungs are associated with poverty. Some ten percent is subject to gentrification processes. We are in the middle of the discussion about whether that gentrification can be prolonged and if that can still incorporate some kind of social mixture. But that is very rare still. There are very beautiful examples of this internal gentrification and in general we know that it is needed – the people know it too. But the most difficult steps are the first steps. In eight years from now, after the first steps have been taken, then I think it will be already done.

MM: A project similar to Super-Kampung is the Vertical Village. It is one of the ways MVRDV sees future cities, specifically urban areas that experience rapid urbanization, such as Asian cities. The result

nowadays is a relatively monotonous landscape of giant residential towers that hardly leave room for individual expression and informality. What you envision is a vertical village consisting of a wide variety of typologies built atop of each other, ranging from residential functions to education, business and amenities. The result should be a socially and programmatically diverse vertical neighborhood. What shape would participation of citizens take in this development?

WM: With the global growth of the middle class, the possibilities and desire to speak out become bigger. These projects are the kind of vehicle to make that possible in different places. The vertical is a very radical component on the one hand. This 'dream village' that is painted in our book and that our client wants to build is one that is on the higher end of the middle class, to be honest, because it is quite expensive to have it built in such a way. There are recent proposals for two tower blocks in Taipei which should also serve the lower parts of the middle class. They are more or less based on the experiences in the Super-Kampung, but translated to the Taiwanese potential. It is a very nice project that will be realized, with an easier way of doing it, compared to the perfect Vertical Village, which basically wanted to beat Vitra design in its aesthetics, but in an urbanistic way. Finally, to illustrate the range on offer from the higher end to the lower end, we also do a project in Taipei to imagine a classical block much more individualized. In this case we shrink the slab, make a stable main structure and hang boxes per house, in different sizes that are to be chosen by individuals and are added to the volume. That is one of many translations of the Vertical Village – to make part of the building fixed and then add things. In this case it becomes more spectacular because you have all these boxes hanging out. So it is also about getting attention. Having said that – because this is say lower-middle class – do they accept hanging boxes in China? No, stability and Feng Shui and other cultural rites have other demands. So there it is also under negotiation how much of it will be realized. It is part of the momentum.

MM: Relating to both Super-Kampung and Vertical Village: MVRDV is currently very active in exploring the notion of Freeland – urban development by private individuals without government dictates. Both in the AnarCity Studio at TU Delft and the Berlage Institute,

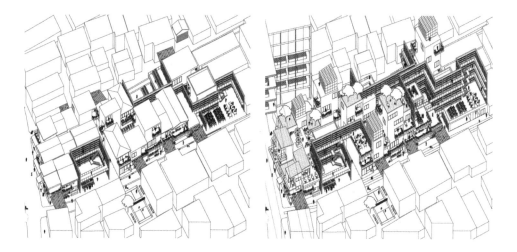

and in concrete practice, in the form of a development strategy for a 43 km area as an expansion of Almere. Within this Almere Oosterwold project, individuals will collectively determine the outcome of the masterplan from 2013 onwards. This entails enormous freedom, but also the responsibility for the entire framework, including local infrastructure, water cycles, food and energy supply, etc. If cities are considered a social product – a result of 'the practice of everyday life' – how can we incorporate the 'collective intelligence' of citizens into a sound and functioning urban fabric whose design is often in the hands of a small group of professionals?

WM: Freeland already describes part of that possible knowledge. In Freeland you are allowed to do whatever you want, but you cannot harm your neighbor and you have to do everything yourself. When merged, these three simple notions have an incredible effect on the intelligence of the in-between. For instance, if you would live in such a development, the neighbor always has to pass your lot in order to get to the next lot. Given current circumstances and laws, you basically have to have a setback of 7 meters on which you can't build to provide for movement. This is interesting, because you never know how your street will grow. So classic urbanism is out at that moment, because urbanism then has to follow individuals. So that is already a notion of how collective intelligence is emerging in accepting that simple first rule. It also goes with make-it-yourself – you have to make a water drainage system that doesn't harm your neighbor. So this is also an intelligence that can emerge easier in a middle-class society than in a very poor part of a city. So it is not directly a slum that we are proposing – although it looks slum-like – but it uses slightly raised economies. We have to be honest in that, because in that economy there is also a collective intelligence,

from a cultural intelligence – behave nicely to your neighbor – to technical collective intelligence: the knowledge of generating electricity or having sewage on the plot. There is also a collective intelligence and an economic strategy already behind it – it is also in the land price – this whole package of land price history of, in this case, the Netherlands and the state of technology at the moment make it possible to do that.

MM: How important is collaboration? Or will these all be small individual systems?

WM: Collaboration is a possibility for me. It should not be forced, to start with. It does not mean that the aim of such an environment is to be completely autarchic, but it can be. Then I will quickly need my neighbors because I simply don't have the time to produce chickens and bananas. So the issue is that you need your neighbor and that is why negotiation, and therefore specialization is occurring. Collaboration will be always there from my point of view. It helps a little bit to explain the range of the project. Freeland does some parts but I cannot do everything yet. The belief is also not there yet at this time and in this specific zone in the Netherlands to make it possible. But I am already happy to get these kind of mini-pieces tested, because I think it makes sense to learn from them. Moreover, there is a big group of people who want it. It has to do with of self-expression and maximization of your own thoughts, up to a certain price.

MM: Until what stage should you as an architect be involved?

WM: In this case we act as eye-openers, to show what the possible advantages are. We have a role as facilitator, to show for example 'for a certain price you can build this house'. We can convey this message

Left
SuperKampung –
Rawajati Herbal Kampung –
After 5 and 20 years

Top left and bottom
Vertical Village Exhibition

Top right
ZhongShan Vertical Village

to the authorities, or the bigger service providers, the energy providers, convincing them that instead of constructing a pipeline to your house they give you a package. That's already a move that an architect can help with. Ultimately I think there's also a role in the monitoring of such a test zone. That would be about the software that comes out of that, the updates, seeing if it works, et cetera. There is also an urbanistic role in the relationship between qualities and price of the land, which needs to be illustrated. So there are different roles that architects for the moment still have in this enterprise.

MM: So you will not be able to step away from this anytime soon?

WM: Not in this case, no. We do this project in both Almere and Mannheim. German society is completely different from Dutch society, funnily, except for Berlin of course. But Mannheim is more bourgeois, so that takes a while. In Almere, the landowner also has certain responsibilities and economic goals. That restricts, or frames, the enterprise. That is why it is not Siberia; it is in the middle of a metropolitan area. That helps. This type of product can be realized in our metro zones but not in the middle of nowhere. It is an economic issue and there is already a cultural situation there.

MM: Highly unregulated planning often leads to speculative developments. How can this be prevented?

WM: For Almere, the good thing is that there is less speculation there due to the crisis in the Netherlands, so it connects to the zeitgeist. It doesn't mean that people are not going to speculate. We have some rules for the sake of the experimentation, for instance that we maximize the size of the plot and the time in which you have to build on it, and other parts of the test. Ultimately you don't want that, but there's the risk that one owner will buy everything and do with it whatever he likes in his own manner. In a way that is okay, maybe, because that is what our society is like. But then we cannot learn from that wide range and mixture that we would like to find in this operation. So it is not complete anarchy. Speculation is one risk, but there are others. As you can see in Caracas, wars can also occur in this kind of unregulated zones. In Almere and in Mannheim that is not the desire of the society,

so that also limits the anarchy or the freedom. The existing cultural institutions already frame it.

MM: You have done projects in a wide variety of countries and cultures – do you see differences in the active engagement of citizens in design projects between cultural projects?

WM: For example, the hanging boxes in Taipei I just referred to, that doesn't immediately fit Feng Shui and other cultural rites. The Freeland project started in Shenzhen. So the first time that we somehow went in that direction, was with the design of the northern new town in Shenzhen to explore this process. That was not accepted in China. And then it went back – it came to the Netherlands. We were too early. They wanted to have a more regulated town. They weren't up for that idea yet.

MM: So the current momentum in the Netherlands is a better match?

WM: Yes. At this moment in the Netherlands there is a desire by a big middle class to get out of these kind of existing predictability, to surprise more and do more yourself. But it also has to do with the fact that there is more knowledge and trust in it. And there is also the financial crisis, which most people won't see as a good thing, but there is a desire for a new kind of economy and that can be tested in Freeland. So the momentum to do it in the Netherlands is partly there. Mainland China will inevitably do that in a while because of other developments – when the middle class also has grown. It also explains why Taipei wants to do it now. They believe in it more than the Chinese. This immediately makes it political, but also economical, because the economy of Taiwan has changed and the aspirations of Taiwan are to survive and to show itself, to be Western.

UNStudio

Interview with Caroline Bos, art historian and urban planner, co-founder of UNStudio and professor at Princeton University, the Academy of Fine Arts in Vienna, Austria and the Berlage Institute in Rotterdam, the Netherlands. In 2012 she started an Honorary Professorship at the University of Melbourne.

Interview conducted on December 4, 2013
in Amsterdam.

Mark Minkjan: The projects by UNStudio are very outspoken, with distinct shapes and details. Over the past years, there has been an increasing interest in re-using and adapting existing architecture. To what extent should your projects be adaptable after realization?

Caroline Bos: Reuse, adaptation, and flexibility are important pillars of sustainability, which comes to the fore in two ways. On the one hand there is a plethora of existing stock in need of costly transformation. This is a crucial societal issue that needs to be fundamentally addressed by investors and politicians before architects can realistically progress. On the other hand, architects can and must learn to anticipate and accept anything from minor adjustments to complete revisions of their built work. This entails quite an interesting ideological shift; just a short while ago adaptation of an existing project would be anathema to many architects – and maybe to many it still is. How do we see this playing out; is any notion of artistic integrity now irrelevant? Can architects still claim a moral right to control their vision? Or is that just an illusion, sacrificed on the altar of pragmatism and bigger powers? Compared to these big questions, I don't think that the issue of distinct shapes or details or design is in contradiction to adaptability. Some 15 years ago, when we wrote MOVE, UNStudio's manifesto, we already said a blob or a box don't matter. Flexibility is more about performance .We are now at a time in which we don't identify one form as being more flexible or more functional than another. From the point of view of the architect the measure of adaptability of a project after realization therefore is a question of mentality – to what extent and even more challengingly, <u>how</u> do you conceptualize control of your artistic vision? Secondly, but related to the first question; how do you balance different, and

sometimes conflicting needs? For instance, in the UNStudio Tower on Amsterdam's Zuidas the possible future transformation from office into apartments in the design hinges on the balance between cost effectiveness versus larger, more flexible spaces.

MM: So form should be about facilitation, not dictation?

CB: In our architecture, movement is very much the central theme.. People don't use architecture just statically. For this reason, over the last ten years or so, we have worked within UNStudio on a short oeuvre of temporary installations, collectively known as 'the pavilions' that address issues that can be thought of as building stones of architecture and/or urbanism but are speculative, 'vague', and difficult to define in a rational or quantitative manner. They evade, perhaps even oppose, the values that are thought of as positive and compulsory in the common understanding of the architectural essentials, such as functionality, clarity, and fitness for purpose. Instead, the pavilions explore ephemeral qualities and notions that are actually complex composites rather than singular parameters; for instance light-orientation-vision Holiday Home), or day-evening-color-social activity (Burnham Pavilion).

MM: On a different scale, this relates to your concept of 'deep planning', a concept coined by UNStudio. One of its starting points is to map and project all kinds of relations and flows, from the political and the communal to the managerial, because as you state 'no program is thinkable without people, no value can exist without users'. An important focus of We Own The City is how to incorporate the 'practice of everyday life' – which to a large extent is informal and dynamic on a small scale – into urban planning and architecture. How are people included in the process of deep planning?

CB: This question broaches the sociopolitical aspect of planning and architecture. It is problematic for architects, who need to align themselves with powerful actors in order to realize their work, to accept the contested nature of space. The temptation to identify with one party or another is perhaps even unavoidable. And yet it is even more problematic if we don't acknowledge that in most situations ground and space are fought over and are subject to many contrasting claims. When UNStudio first became involved in Arnhem Central, the masterplan for

the station area of Arnhem, we chose to go back to basics and investigate what was happening on the location in terms of people dynamics. We found that the railway station could more justly be defined as a mixed-use transfer area involving eight or so modes of public and individual transportation. The whole plan was subsequently based on the movement of pedestrians, as the binding factor. Clearly, this is an ever-shifting population whose wishes and needs are diverse to begin with, and will also fluctuate over time. Therefore, in this case, but also in my view in general, we must strive for a more complex understanding of the concept of involving people, which goes beyond the here and now, and beyond the logistics of the everyday, to incorporate future as well as present users. Since future users cannot be addressed directly, it follows that we also need to find new ways to understand the concept of participation. In the example of the Arnhem project we don't include people in the sense of inviting them to express their view in a meeting, but we arrive at the user as the central element in the process of the design through a more abstract analysis of stakeholders and flows.

MM: How is this movement or presence of the pedestrian analyzed or taken into account?

CB: The pedestrian analysis took a quite technical form, using public transport timetables and traffic engineers' calculations of movements on the site in its projected situation. I think that sometimes using the professional tools that we have today can be more effective than just inviting people to have their say. In these kinds of participation processes, at least in my experience, you generally only reach a very select group, unfortunately, which results in very exclusive and biased views.

MM: Are instruments such as public hearings in participation processes too limited?

CB: It is not enough to second-guess, form focus panels, invite people to give their opinions, give them a say, or even a stake. Because these people will only be able to react to what they are presented with. Farther-reaching change is only possible when architecture and urbanism will take up a more pro-active stance and begin to experiment with built forms designed specifically and directly to approach the art of living. It could well be that what the community, in the extended sense, mostly wants and needs is

not involvement in some half-hearted, bureaucratic process, but real, concrete and substantial evidence that architects and urban planners are doing pertinent work – that they are engaged, and are capable of both sincerely and adequately representing the general good when they design. Just a few years ago, a statement like this would be so naive as to be offensive to the profession at large. But today, questions pertaining to the art of living are central to all the most vital discourses; art, science and philosophy have assumed a new directness in relation to addressing the art of living and architecture and urbanism are still reluctant to take this on. Instead, the mainstream clings to an internal logic of rationalizing arguments about efficiency, utility and economy, while alternative practices seek a rationalization in anthropologically inspired analyses of non-western, non-capitalist forms of building. But both avoid the simple, direct question at the heart of the matter: how does this change life for the better?

MM: Do you have ideas about how these participatory processes can be taken to the next level in order to be productive?

CB: While in no way conclusive, the ongoing series of pavilions can be seen as a form of community practice in practice, beyond the restrictive boundaries of just the present-day. These temporary installations do not ask people for their verbal responses regarding specific wishes related to their domestic or urban environment, but provide situations in which a whole range of actions and behaviors can be triggered, and different, transient communities be formed. Made up of essential building stones and honing in on the simple essences of the art of living, these temporary installations allow us to study the interaction between more 'vague', speculative, combinatorial architectural parameters and those time-based, urban communities. This in turn has led us, as architects, to apply some of what we learn from the spontaneous community reactions to the pavilions in other, more lasting and larger-scale projects, thereby shifting the borders of our own profession.

MM: About these temporary installations. UNStudio designed a variety of pavilions, often temporary and often located in (semi-)public spaces. During the We Own The City symposium in Hong Kong you presented the pavilions as experimental installations

to engage with urban communities. Can you tell us more about how this works?

CB: In the pavilions we can test out how new media (light, projections) can provide diversified environments within one structure over the course of a day and evening, and how different communities react to this. They also seem to generate behaviors that are outside the normal categories of user functions, which prioritize efficiency; in the pavilions we see, for instance, a lot of posing – a way of spending time that is expressive of a certain appreciation, which might be indicative of a potential to keep people on site that might be made productive, but which is not a recognized quality. These pavilions thus are test case structures that are put up to invite or enable a public use that is largely not predefined. With these installations we have seen all sorts of individuals as well as temporal communities forming and occupying the space in different ways. This interaction has been instigated by the objects themselves, rather than by ancillary processes that have no intrinsic relation to the content or the design of the proposal. The first pavilion was called Holiday Home. It was a vivid pink on the inside. We tested the effect of light and different facets on that color and what sort of experience it generates for people. As the name suggested, we were exploring it as a place of well-being, leisure, pleasure and being outside the normal sphere of life. Some time later we applied the same color to the foyer of a theatre in Lelystad, the Netherlands. The color would probably not have been proposed for that situation, had we not been able to explore the visual, spatial, atmospheric and social effects first on the smaller, temporary scale.

MM: If it's about testing how to attract people and to make them feel good, it calls for sociological or even psychological analyses. How can you measure the success of these experiments?

CB: We can measure the effects phenomenologically, rather than scientifically. Clearly, these are not controlled experiments taking place in laboratory-like conditions, but life-sized design models transiently occupied by shifting populations. Development and progress on the basis of these pavilions is perhaps an instance of experiential learning, design-thinking, or trained judgment. We have no instruments or methodologies in place to measure the success or failure of these parameters quantitatively, but that is not to say that the effects we monitor through our

own presence and feedback from the client and users are not real or valuable, or translatable to different situations.

MM: Recently, UNStudio set out on an ambitious endeavor – it relaunched as an open-source architecture studio, in which knowledge-sharing through your online platform is key. Ben van Berkel stated that 'we all live in the iPhone 5 phase, while architecture is still in the Walkman phase'. What does this entail?

CB: Architecture thrives on newness. Without continuous material, cultural and ideological innovations the profession loses its specificity and becomes simply a bland part of a generic building industry. With UNStudio we have long realized this, which is why we have pushed ourselves in many different directions, continuously addressing new challenges and questions. But at the same time this experimental attitude has led us to consciously seek to build as much as we could. Disengagement from the dangers of the building industry within the globalized economy has never been our preferred option. As a result, we have amassed a huge amount of experience and practice-related knowledge. It is this wealth of knowledge and experience that constitutes our design capital. How do we utilize it? How do we preserve, maintain, share and expand our knowledge? This is knowledge, it should be emphasized, that has been laboriously gained by working through numerous design phases on hundreds of projects of all scales and typologies in all parts of the world –
it is completely unique, design-related architectural knowledge, not something you just come across everywhere on the internet. Presently, UNStudio foresees two strategies to handle and propagate its design capital. Whilst the primary objective of our project teams is to deliver the 'result' of architectural thinking (buildings, plans, designs), the objective of the Knowledge Platforms is to distill knowledge from within the practice of architecture in order to propel design thinking and innovation. In April 2013 we launched an open-source knowledge network, after having worked for three years internally on the development of four knowledge platforms.

MM: Is this going open-source mostly about output, about sharing your knowledge and experiences or can it also be about input from outsiders?

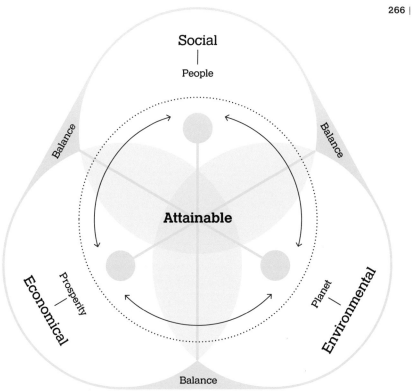

Social
|
People

Balance

Balance

Attainable

Economical

Prosperity

Planet

Environmental

Balance

CB: Yes, that's what we want. We organized the knowledge platforms in such a way that everyone can assemble their own specific platform, and we want to make it interesting for people to contribute.

MM: You said that it is not just about connecting professionals. Could the project also be a way to relate to citizens?

CB: Absolutely! At the moment many of the posts are highly technical, so currently the UNStudio knowledge platforms are probably most attractive to people who are interested in those things. But this is a deliberate choice on our part, as we feel that technology is underappreciated in architecture. Ben's Iphone quote can be read in that sense too; before you obtain something this popular and user-friendly, there is a lot of invisible technology to work through. We want to encourage that this becomes a real part of architecture again, instead of seeing 'design' and technology as two independent entities. That said, the Platforms are essentially open to all and in fact are inspired by bottom-up, citizens-driven community initiatives and by the open source movement. I have been involved in projects aimed towards expanding

the role of the community in urban and architectural design and found that this is far from straightforward. It is very questionable whether we are currently practicing in ways that really promote this goal in a meaningful way. Opening up and sharing the internal mechanisms of our practice can be seen as an equalizing tool, designed to enable crosslinks with all communities; not just power nodes in the professional network, but all possible strands in the meshwork.

MM: You are a prominent architectural office. Do you think you have a leading role in going open-source?

CB: Since the founding of the practice, UNStudio has been developing knowledge as a result of combining the design and building of projects with an active participation in architectural theory. Following on a continued interest in geometry, digital production, material effects and attainable design solutions, this communal knowledge led to the introduction of Knowledge Platforms. Economic issues, climate concerns and an increase in production speeds made it necessary to rethink the role of the architect and therefore the organization of the practice of architecture. This is a long-standing interest. When

I studied art history, my thesis was on Le Corbusier and his concept of the architect. How architects see themselves in relation to culture, society and technology is still very fascinating to us. In those relationships the responsibility of the architect and the relevance of architecture to our world are revealed.

MM: Is there a project that you are working on that you would like to highlight for the project of We Own The City

CB: One project that immediately comes to mind is Rachel's Forest; a competition we did at the end of 2013 for the city of Osaka, together with the Japanese architectural firm Yamasita Sekkei. It is an urban regeneration proposal for a site consisting of left-over railway tracks. As the surrounding area has already been overdeveloped, resulting in vacant offices, we are proposing a strategy of exponential value growth based on the model of biodiversity. The title of the project is a tribute to Rachel Carson, who with her book Silent Spring was one of the founders of the ecological movement in the 1960s. Our proposal consists of a scenario which leads urban citizens, young and old, into a new direction. Redeveloping a new garden for the city is taken as an opportunity of creating awareness for the community and become a smarter city, transitioning from fossil fuel-based local economies to sustainable economies connected to a smart grid of low energy sources. To create a sustainable urban environment we have to engage its community and its city's policy, they all become part of the smart grid.

MM: If you would be in charge of an urban planning committee, how would you ideally include citizens' engagement – what would be your most effective tool?

CB: That is an unexpected and difficult question.... It may not always be the best if the actors are very closely involved. I don't know if the citizens have to be the literal citizens of that particular area.

MM: So you would take into account a hypothetical citizen?

CB: Yes, but then a very conscious and aware citizen. If citizens form a very homogeneous group, the resulting project can be a bit inward-looking. I would like to explore planning processes and techniques that encourage citizens to think of themselves as a very diverse group, which transcends a particular time and place and includes future users and citizens.

MM: Would that mean that it is important for planners to steer on mixed populations?

CB: Yes. But I think we still have a very limited and static idea of what a mixed population is and we need to learn to see urban populations as more sophisticated, transient and complex. The globalized condition of transnationality describes so many people. I am often asked how we deal with local conditions, because UNStudio has been fortunate enough to be able to work in different cultures. My intuitive answer would be that I think that the bonds we have with our cultural past are very thin for each and every one of us. We are, generally speaking, not that culturally embedded. This means that we need to respect the remaining links all the more, because they are so fragile, but at the same time we shouldn't be too protective of them in a way that completely shatters the very thing that was real and authentic.

MM: So planners should respect culture but not fall into cultural determinism?

CB: Exactly. When you understand of the ambiguity of connection with your own roots, it is easier to put yourself in the place of others who are living in rapidly transitioning situations.

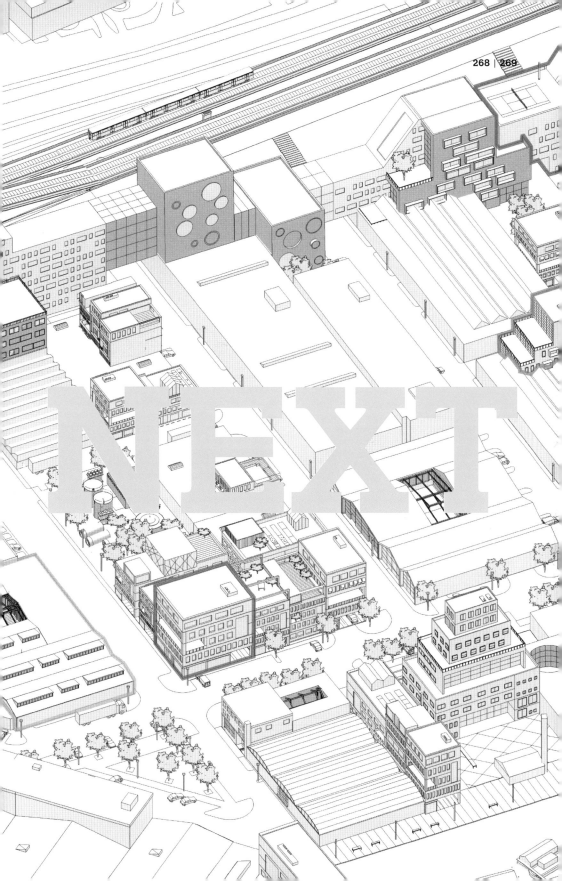

Interview with Bart Reuser, architect and
co-founder of NEXT architects. He has
worked as a researcher and taught at the
Delft University of Architecture, and also
lived and worked in Seoul as a visiting
professor at the University of Seoul.

Interview conducted on November 20, 2013
in Amsterdam.

Mark Minkjan: You contributed to 'Sense of Place:
Atlas of the Cultural Ecology of Rotterdam'. One of
its conclusions was that spontaneous and informal
developments contribute to a sense of place, and
that cities are ever-changing organisms, a fact that
planners, policy makers, architects and developers
should be aware of. The publication interprets the
city as a cultural product. How can we channel the
local collective intelligence of citizens into urban
planning, which is often in the hands of a small group
of professionals?

Bart Reuser: We were already very much involved
in analyzing the city and thinking of new ways
of ordering or setting out the planning strategies
before this Atlas. The way everybody was making
maps was still pretty limited. In projects before that
we already tried to combine the factors of time and
transport into map design and analysis. For the Atlas,
the municipality of Rotterdam delivered a lot of data,
which gave us a good way to think about the city by
combining data and maps. So we could start a new
story about how urban patterns work and how the
city is connected. This is different from overlaying
the city with a large plan, which is always very one-
directional. In that sense the Atlas was a good setup,
a framework within which the city would be easier
to read for end users or developers, to get a grip on
a larger scale beyond their own plot. There's always
this big gap between on the one hand trying to make
an entire city or neighborhood and on the other
initiatives that are mostly interested in making their
own environment. This has always been done through
telling people what to do, by making plans. This Atlas
was a different way to feed them and create a new
framework and see if they could come up with their
own ideas.

MM: You also collaborated with urban sociologist
Arnold Reijndorp there, who is an expert on the
everyday use of urban space. It is interesting that
you combined his expertise with Rotterdam's data
and translated that into a larger scale to go beyond
the more traditional way of mapping and interpreting
the city. How do you think that can be translated into
urban planning?

BR: The Atlas was mostly analysis, but later on
we have set up other schemes in which it came to
the fore. One important scheme was a project in
Eindhoven's Woensel West neighborhood. We were
asked by the municipality and one of the largest
housing owners in the area, a housing association,
to work on this deprived area. The conventional
strategy to bring these areas to a higher level used
to be to tear down some houses and try to get the
weak spots out of it, attract new populations. They
didn't want this anymore and tried to look at a more
participatory trajectory and see if there were also
smaller, more sensible things that could be done to
have a big impact. We set up a framework in which
we gave people a voice. We did this by making a tool
kit from which they could make choices – which
they could either carry out themselves, ask other
people to do, or ask help from the municipality. This
included a wide range of interventions, from putting
up a fence or taking a fence down and opening up
an area, to setting up schools and taking ownership
of empty corners. There were a lot of these empty
plots that didn't contribute to the overall reputation
or livability of the area. By taking ownership of it, the
public domain would change from no-man's-land
to places that people could relate to. We created a
game in which local residents could choose the most
important things we had to work on. That resulted
in 'Top-3s' or 'Top-5s' which we discussed with
the local government to figure out which things we
could do immediately and which should be part of
a development strategy. This became the basis of a
plan called Smaken Verschillen, or Everybody Has
A Different Taste. The whole idea should be about
different tastes and how people relate to their taste
within a neighborhood. This is very contradictory to
what usually is done, when the taste of the architect
or the choice of the housing association dictates what
people should like.

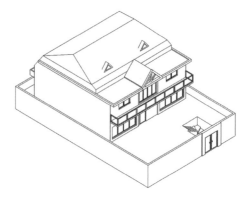

MM: How did this game work?

BR: We made cards. The first thing was 'choose your tools'. We had different tools on different levels – the level of the neighborhood, of the city, of the plot. Some were about open space, some about the physical makeup, some about social amenities such as a meeting place, health care services or education. So people had to choose from these tools. Then, together with us, they would sketch on the area, discussing how to use those tools and where to use them, and which were the best steps to take. So together we made this plan. A lot of important things came out. On the level of education it became clear that they needed a good local school, so that's where the architect could take over together with the municipality and actually realize something. Along the area's main axis, one of the tools, called 'cornerstones', was used very effectively to enrich the area with mixed program and landmark buildings. The main housing association organized a competition for young architects to design a small corner house, a couple of which are currently being developed. That was more of an acupunctural way of urbanism through interventions which can have a larger impact.Another important feature of this process is that we evaluated every step. So there was not an end plan, there was this stepped plan. It has been going on for a few years now and it is still ongoing as an alliance between the architect, the housing association, which played a big role, social groups, and the local government. So the planning is continuous and adaptable, constantly evaluating its previous steps and coming up with incremental improvements.

MM: Did you encounter any difficulties in this process?

BR: Of course we did. Not everyone wants to participate. Your own credibility as an architect is important, you have to show people that they are part of something, have influence and that they will get something out of it for themselves. But for a lot of people it often takes too long, because it is an urban process. It might take two years to get something done. That will always be a problem with every initiative – both if they initiate it themselves or if you invite them. Participants have to understand that the payoff doesn't come within a few weeks and that it is a long-term investment. Investors are used to this, but people who are not in this professionally just have to do with promises, which can be difficult. So there's 'owning of the city' in a very literal way – do they own a part of the process? Do they have a contract?

MM: And perhaps this is especially the case in stigmatized areas where people's ambition is often to leave the neighborhood?

BR: Yes, a lot of residents said, 'Just tear it down and give me a new house somewhere else because I want to leave'. That is something else you have to work on, to deliver the message that you don't want to tear it down and say 'no, our intention is to keep you here'. So generating a trusting relationship is something you have to invest in because they feel that they are living in the city's worst area – and how long are they willing to wait for the area to improve? It is also the ownership issue again. These people didn't own it, they were all tenants. It is different when people own houses, because then they immediately know that they will have a change in value and every effort they will put in might contribute to the value of their property. So that is important in these processes, so you can take the title of this book very literally: 'Who actually owns the city?'

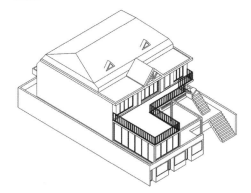

MM: You lived in Seoul for a year after being invited to work as a professor at the University of Seoul. Your book Seoulutions is a result of investigating Seoul's planning system. What's so unique about that system?

BR: Seoul is in a completely different situation than what we know from the Western context. For us the Seoul system feels almost like a next step, not planning too much in terms of urban thinking. For Seoul, accommodating the wishes of people is normal. That is something we also used to do before we arrived at such a rigid planning system in the 20th century. We work with a lot of ideas about the ideal city, which I think are very old-fashioned because the ideal city doesn't exist. The only ideal city is the one that can change, to accommodate the change of society. We should be careful with a too-restricted idea about what this ideal should be. In Seoul the city looked much more chaotic than most Western urban areas. But at the same time you see a lot of things happening, and happening very fast. Initiatives that were taken by either entrepreneurs or residents could go very fast, changing entire typologies within a year or so. This results in very vibrant areas with a lot of interesting qualities. We have the tendency to look at citizens as being consumers in urban space. In Seoul, citizens have the tendency to see themselves as producers of urban fabric.

MM: What was the focus of your research?

BR: I asked myself how it was possible that an area such as Hongdae changed so fast and became so vibrant, who influenced it, who invested in it and how the government responded to this. On the one hand the government tries to keep it within limits of regulations. But the growth of Seoul wasn't going fast enough so they had to do something. They abolished

some of the rules and changed the boundaries, from small regulations changes like the allowance to use underground space and not pay tax for it, to parking regulations – if you would park on your private lot or within your building volume, you were allowed to make your building a bit higher.

MM: Seoul's new District Plan includes these 'bonus regulations' which should seduce land owners to do more than is strictly required, such as creating public functions, eco-friendly architecture, mixed-use buildings, etc. In return, they can create more building volume. Does the Seoul government also value the qualities of Hongdae the way you value them, or is it more of a pragmatic decision to create these incentives instead of restrictions?

BR: It is more pragmatic. It wasn't so much a wanted dialogue between private owners and the government, but they needed each other. The government needed people to develop the area, also because ownership rights are very strong in Korea. And the required investments are then smaller. If they want to do something on a larger scale, there's a lot of potential – or need – for collective ownership. And that also happens in larger plans, co-ops are set up for that. But the scale remains a problem, requiring more control and shared responsibility over a lot of things. That's what didn't happen in the older areas with smaller-scale ownership. So scale is very important. This incentive planning system is used to improve the quality of life in these neighborhoods after finding out that a restrictions-only system is not the best way to go if you want to achieve quality. This bonus regulations system is thinking the other way around.

MM: How did your stay/research in Seoul influence your way of looking at the Dutch planning system?

Top
Old city:
Static rules and process

Bottom
New city:
Dynamic rules and process

BR: One of the things that you see in the Netherlands is that the entire planning system is too much based on long-term visions. But it takes an incredibly long time to realize them. It feels like we have gone a bit too far. One of the first things that urban planners should see is that we shouldn't work with a single system. We also shouldn't throw the system that we have overboard, but diversifying by area is an important first step. Certain areas will still need regulations – for instance, our heavily used inner cities – but for other areas we can let go of a lot of regulations. We are so used to zoning plans. There are a lot of areas that have the potential to transform, but the zoning plans are in the way. If you want to change small things you have to go through all these procedures that are actually too big for the change you want. That's what we studied in the Netherlands: what's in the way of these possibilities of transformation and what should the different actors do to get things going? We started analyzing different ways of working and the steps you could take. You have the city as we know it, which is more static. There is a vision, you start to build it and then you control it. Our idea about this city is that the city should be dynamic. It should be a continuous process in which you add a new layer every time and you constantly reevaluate. So these three steps become one, become continuous and happen at the same time. Also, actors should be able to act simultaneously. It is about finding out which roles everybody is playing and how to get people together to communicate. Especially the municipality is usually a bit slower than the individual because they work in larger systems. But how to act on that? They should think about their new role. To improve the quality of an area, we created a four-step plan. First inventory, then evaluate, then transform by adding quality, and finally stimulate. So in the diagram you see who are the actors that actually should participate in the separate steps. There is a big role for the government to accommodate this, do the communication and make it credible. They are the ones who can hold on to it for a long time and make people believe that it is going to work. That's what is currently the most in the way – the credibility and the promises. It is difficult to see what instruments the government has to work with. So we created another diagram in the form of an audio mixer. There are all kinds of handles that can either lock an area or make it dynamic. We made an inventory of what all these little things are and how they play a part. Sometimes the government says that they have a vision that is very dynamic. Great, but if

you simultaneously develop a masterplan which is very restricted – which very often happens – or you make an open masterplan but create a lot of small restrictions on materials, volumes, et cetera, then it still doesn't work. So you have to create a symphony in which these things and actors work together. But that means that the government can never do it on its own. There are a few legal instruments which they can influence, but these are all within the sphere of public law. They are still dependent on private law, that is simply how the legal system works. But some of those things are very important, because that is exactly what gives owners security. Of course, it works best if everybody is working on the same level and thinking about the same things. Often, you see that within the municipality. In the old, static and divided system – the first image in the diagram – everybody understood their role. But if you want to do it differently, someone for example handling legal work might not understand, doesn't want to take the risk or thinks it is too much work, and they will still do it the old way. This compartmentalization is a problem, also within the government. I have talked to people at the legal department who are writing the zoning plans next to the map of it created by the architect, but the architect never looks at the legal translations of it. So the outcome may be different. But there is no interest in this legal stuff. And that is why in the end we might not change much. So our analysis looked beyond what is within the realm of the architect or the planner, because such an understanding is crucial in bringing about actual change and get things going. Bonus regulations, for example, are not really allowed in the Netherlands. Our legal system works in such a way that everybody is the same, so we cannot privilege one over the other. Still, to get things going, you have to differentiate between areas. This is something that really has to be developed in order to create certain dynamics. Special Economic Zones are examples of such differentiation. Basically you should be able to have special spatial zones in which different rules are possible. And I would advocate not for less rules, but better rules, stimulating rules instead of restricting rules.

MM: You are also working out the idea of the dynamic city in the area where your office is located (Overamstel, Amsterdam). How does that work?

BR: We don't have any ownership in the area, so our role here is to influence people by constructing our

Vision

Execution

Conservation

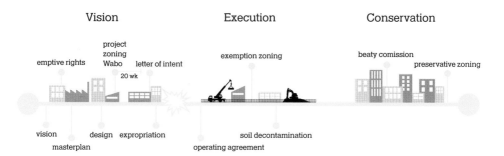

emptive rights

project
zoning
Wabo

letter of intent

20 wk

exemption zoning

beaty comission

preservative zoning

vision

masterplan

design expropriation

operating agreement

soil decontamination

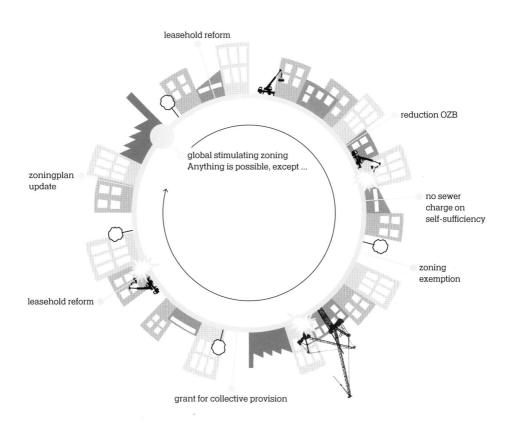

leasehold reform

reduction OZB

zoningplan
update

global stimulating zoning
Anything is possible, except ...

no sewer
charge on
self-sufficiency

zoning
exemption

leasehold reform

grant for collective provision

story and talk to a lot of people. We talk to the main planners, and they actually say, 'you are right, that's what we should do with the area'. But the problem is that the economy is currently down so there aren't many buildings being built. We have to wait until the market goes up again. But then we will have the problem that it doesn't go fast enough, also because the government isn't able to play this new role yet – this enabling role. In a way it is happening, but I'm afraid that it is very much related to the economic crisis, their opening up to new ideas. On the other hand, some of them are up for it. Like what we did in Eindhoven's Woensel West. But that was more related to large-scale ownership of associations, of course, which made it possible. The ownership was already there, we didn't have to influence everyone. For this area, we don't have an assignment, but we feel like we have to be pioneers. It is about being part of the initiative. We don't want to wait for others to develop a plan and then react on it, but act proactively. We try to take some of the possibilities in our own hand and try to influence people. From our side, it needs a lot of communication and effort to really get it done. We have to find the right actors, the right people, set up a communications plan.

MM: Are you positive about the idea of the dynamic city catching on and becoming culturally and institutionally accepted?

BR: I'm not sure, because nobody is really interested in the more difficult part of it. And that is exactly what is needed. We got very deep into it, but most people are talking more about the fast results – like creating community gardens. These are great examples of first steps, but nobody wants to look at actually realizing this on a larger scale and how we can really make something out of it. Then you have to dive to a much deeper level. That is the role that architects should play, if we actually want the world to develop in this direction, because you cannot expect the initiators to think too far beyond what they are already realizing. And that is what we are doing at NEXT: influence the government, because they are thinking about it and can understand it if they make a little bit of time to listen. There are definitely things happening.

MM: Much of it is temporary, and then it is easier to get things done, but how can we translate this into a more long-term plan?

BR: I think you see the larger scale coming up in certain places. There are possibilities, of course, also for developers, to find new ways of investment. The banks don't work the way they used to anymore – putting any kind of money into any area, so you were always able to get money for development. Now that the banks have limited this way of funding we have to go through other ways of funding, such as crowdfunding. That will also have a strong influence on the way we organize our urban systems. Maybe those influences will eventually accomplish more than local initiatives.

MM: If you would be a mayor, how would you regulate citizens' engagement – what would be your most effective tool?

BR: I don't want to say, 'we have to talk to the people', because we already know that. One of the bigger obstacles is that you need a different kind of civil servant, one who is proactive. So as a mayor I would find some proactive actors coming out of the real estate development world, or initiators, and see if you can play this enabling and stimulating role and rethink the current system. You have to ask what your main purpose with it is. It used to be to protect and control what is there. I think a new system, especially the legal system, that would be adapted to creating possibilities, opening up things instead of closing them off. But it is not just that. If you do not find ways to have the market participating in it, it will never become large-scale and it will be limited to small instances. Currently there are many citizens' initiatives, and there always have been. But a lot of them will never be more than local initiatives. If actors on a different scale step in we might get something more substantial done in the end. If you look at initiatives that take energy production into their own hands by simply adjusting the network and some regulations – I wish we could have some of these systemic changes also in the physical sphere.

Critical Analysis:
From Superdutch
to Sensible Dutch?

If we dichotomize between bottom-up and top-down city making, architects are often considered to be related more to the latter. But they can also operate closer to the ground level of the spectrum, and have the ideal position to be a potential bridge between the two ends in order to meet the needs of communities and simultaneously deliver what they are contracted for.

Four architects – OMA partner in charge of Asia David Gianotten, MVRDV co-founder Winy Maas, UNStudio co-founder Caroline Bos and NEXT architects co-founder Bart Reuser – helped us explore how prominent architectural offices are adapting to changing realities and rising bottom-up movements, and what tools can be deployed for the participation of citizens in city making.

NEXT architects is a relatively young firm, gaining international recognition for their work over the past decade. MVRDV, OMA and UNStudio are among the world's best-known offices. These three are often mentioned when the denomination 'Superdutch' is used, which is associated with architecture that can be defined by terms such as 'breathtaking', 'conceptual' and 'edgy'. Superdutch refers to spectacular designs by the internationally acclaimed Dutch firms that rode the wave of the 1990s, pushed by a great enthusiasm founded on market-thinking, globalization, speculation, branding and a desire for iconic designs, with less attention to the civic and public role of architecture. But times have changed. In many countries, public acceptance of expensive and extravagant architecture has dropped. Moreover, in times of austerity, governments increasingly retreat from the public sphere, leaving room for citizens to

take ownership of their surroundings, but also creating the danger of individuals being left behind. Hence, modes of influencing the development of the urban environment have to be rethought, and there is an increasing demand and potential for socially relevant design. In non-Western contexts this is often different. There is, however, a (sometimes slowly) growing interest in the civic consequences of architecture. Urban planning begins to pave the way for sensible interventions instead of displacement and tabula rasa mega developments. These interviews revealed that all four offices are involved in engaging people and/or community practice in urban planning and architecture, albeit on different scales and from various perspectives.

Of course, all four are still realizing 'fancy' architecture for corporate clients and the happy few that have little to do with involving community practice as described in this book. But that is how they were trained to make a living. However, beside this the firms have also developed innovative and ambitious ways to bring citizens into architecture and urban planning processes. Some more inclusive than others.

OMA and MVRDV are the two offices most involved in large urban planning schemes. Both do substantial research into urban dynamics (through their respective research branches AMO and The Why Factory), and incorporate the findings in real-life projects. For both, the focus is on preserving, strengthening and incorporating existing (informal) cultural and economic structures and citizens in masterplans. The two firms try to be initiators of urban transformation rather than dictators of it. For example, for a new town near Hanoi, OMA proposed that their masterplan could incorporate existing villages rather than displacing them (as was initially requested by the client). The intention was for the new town to benefit from the already-present culture and workforce, and for the local residents to get a piece of the development pie.

MVRDV proposed similar trajectories for the densification of urban villages (kampungs) within the fabric of Jakarta. Their Freeland project – currently carried out in the Dutch city of Almere and in Mannheim in Germany – is another ambitious masterplan, in which citizens take ownership of their environment by collectively determining the outcome of the plan, with hardly any preconditions. The freedom of the individuals to create their living surroundings also entails the responsibility of developing the infrastructure of water cycles, roads, food production, energy supply, et cetera. This undertaking can provide radically new strategies for city-making, putting it largely into the hands of citizens. However, the inclusiveness of this development is not complete yet, since it initially requires a significant investment and also knowledge and progressive aspirations. Therefore it is mostly aimed at end users with considerable financial and cultural capital. The same goes for MVRDV's Vertical Village proposal, which takes on the challenge of densifying Asian cities by building a variety of typologies on top of each other, from residential units and businesses to urban amenities. It is presented as an alternative to the 'block attack' – monotonous tower blocks that provide comfortable apartments, but lack social coherence. Though the concept is presented as a 'bottom-up residential development', Winy Maas admits

that in reality, because of financial reasons the materialization of the Vertical Village is attainable mainly for the upper-middle class.

UNStudio prefers to keep citizens at arm's length. Caroline Bos explicitly said she doesn't believe in direct public engagement. UNStudio counts on the knowledge and techniques of the architect to compensate for this. Their most direct way of public engagement is the realization of pavilions and (semi-)public experimental installations, in order to test the interaction between the design and the public. For their urban planning projects they don't directly involve individual end users but look at the aggregate of (potential) users on a more abstract level, using professional tools and scenario planning. Here we see an interesting contrast with David Gianotten of OMA, who says that 'you can't consider citizens numbers that add up and then a plan is finished, because it has to work for all the numbers. For urban planning you can never predict the outcome. Urban culture isn't something you can orchestrate, you can only spark it. After that, it is a trajectory of years. We cannot design for the people if we don't work with them'.

UNStudio's endeavor to relaunch as an open-source architectural firm is potentially revolutionary. Though the process is still in development, the office shared part of their research online – providing knowledge about materials, energy and sustainability, human behavior and societal issues for others to learn from. Next to that, outsiders can provide input on the platform. Opening up to the public is an ambitious step that has the potential to empower citizens to get involved and learn, and to share their experiences. Nevertheless, the content shared on the platform is still highly technical and full of jargon, making it hard to comprehend for most people and thereby relatively exclusive. Moreover, the articles are concise and abstract summaries, not in-depth specifics that could be used as how-to's for citizens to work with. In her interview, Caroline Bos acknowledged that the platform is still in an early stage. She also said she wishes a database would exist where socio-spatial research is shared. There is indeed a huge disconnect between social sciences and architecture. Perhaps UNStudio's open-source platform could be a good place to bridge the gap and include more knowledge about citizens' behavior in design processes.

NEXT architects as a firm didn't grow up in the heyday of Dutch architecture. Therefore, they didn't have to get acquainted with the bottom-up trend from a position of architectural stardom. Rather, they were part of the trend, both in research and in practice. Like Gianotten, Bart Reuser stresses the importance of being involved in an urban planning for a long period, as well as the need for planning processes to be dynamic. He argues that there shouldn't be an end plan; planning should rather be 'continuous and adaptable, constantly evaluating its previous steps and coming up with incremental improvements'. NEXT architects has now been involved in the redevelopment of a district in the city of Eindhoven for about ten years. With the main aim to preserve much of the neighborhoods, their contact with citizens of Eindhoven has been very direct, involving them in the ideas and sketching phases. Moreover, after researching Seoul's urban planning system, Bart Reuser calls for a system of rules that

are stimulating instead of restricting, in order to turn citizens from consumers of urban space into producers of urban fabric. NEXT architects also dives into the tough matter, finding out what rules, regulations and planning habits prevent this. This research feeds back into their practice. By proposing uncommissioned dynamic plans for the area in Amsterdam where they are located, NEXT architects tries to influence decision makers and shake up the rigid planning system.

Something all four architects seem to agree upon is that the old, passive way of public engagement doesn't work. At public hearings, only a few people show up and the meetings often result in complaining sessions. Part of the reason for this may be that citizens have become more cynical about participatory processes in urban planning, which they have come to associate with 'repressive tolerance': people can have their say, but in fact the outcome is already determined. NEXT, OMA and MVRDV specifically call for proactive engagement of the end users in urban planning. The plans should be more open-ended, responsive to urban dynamics and evaluated over time. The question is who will have the most impact. Will it be NEXT, an office that directly engages with end users on a smaller scale to fine-tune designs accordingly? Or will it be the big firms designing massive plans that are less able to take all bottom-up dynamics into account?

All of these firms have provided us with instruments that can be used by institutions to enable the production of urban space by citizens. UNStudio experiments with human interaction through temporary structures and stresses the importance of analyzing movements and flows of people, goods and information. OMA demonstrates how developing a plan from the existing socioeconomic fabric strengthens new structures and promotes the social mobility of locals. Similar strategies are suggested by MVRDV: helping neighborhoods to specialize in their microeconomics brings about positive cluster effects and encourages the empowerment of individuals and communities. They even suggest a far more radical way to empower end users: by giving them almost complete freedom of action in unregulated planning schemes. The central message of NEXT architects is to differentiate according to scale and location, and that plans should be open-ended and flexible instead of rigid. Specific areas can develop better, and with more input from engaged citizens, if a masterplan contains fewer restrictions and more incentives for individuals and communities to shape their own environment. NEXT advocates a 4-step plan for dynamic planning, which goes from inventory, valuation, and transformation to stimulation. Governments should embrace this and communicate it, in order to give it credibility. On the smaller scale, NEXT architects developed card games to involve local people in the planning process.

Clearly, the architectural profession is changing. On the one hand because of economic crises, changing societies and a call for socially relevant design, on the other because architects see the value of incorporating community practice in order to establish an optimally functioning urban fabric. Traditionally, architects have to balance between their own beliefs, societal demands and the wishes of the client, but they are increasingly finding ways to combine community interests with pleasing clients. The next decade or so will show whether incorporating the bottom-up trend on a higher level was merely a response to economically precarious times, or whether it will become the new norm for top-down actors.

Conclusion

Concluding Remarks
How to Enable Community Practice in Architecture and Urban Planning

Written by Francesca Miazzo
(CITIES Amsterdam)

It is with great satisfaction that we arrive at the epilogue of this global journey, where we have traced the contemporary development of a global urban phenomenon: the rise of community planning. We are not alone in taking on small-scale, tactical urbanism; the issue has been studied in an abundance of publications. None of these, however, has so far dared to address the opposing constituent of this rising movement: the traditional players, the 'top-downers' who usually engage in conventional urban development processes.

This publication illuminates the sometimes unconventional ways in which they are increasingly choosing to enable more comprehensive, inclusive urban practices. Our reasons for engaging in this research and analysis are quite simple and pertinent: we can no longer accept urban development processes (not just projects) that do not involve, or consider the needs, ambitions, potential and problems of local people living, working or recreating in a given area.

In this project, we address a specific selection of cities: cities that have a strong tradition of top-down urban management due to the established planning discipline, political regime or market forces. In the contexts under analysis here, communities are organizing themselves to respond, or more accurately, react to a certain degree of dissatisfaction concerning current urban development conditions. Although these cities are significantly different, they have in common extremely high land values and a professionalized planning and development sector, as well as an emerging current of bottom-up, citizen activism, outlined below.

In the Netherlands, where land must be created by effort of will, the public sector has shaped the country's form. Now, in the Netherlands as well as elsewhere, the economic crisis has led citizens and professionals to reimagine their ability to affect their cities – and their responsibility to do so. Amsterdam's case studies draw a picture of how different types of citizens are engaging in making changes to their neighborhoods, ranging from temporary low-budget functions to multimillion-dollar projects; from semi-institutional or government-requested projects to those with a loose, unstructured organization; and from highly conceptual to down-to-earth, practical community contributions. In Hong Kong, we have shown how traditionally bureaucratic, 'top-down' organizations – such as architectural firms and government agencies – are recognizing the benefits of integrating grassroots processes into their projects. In New York, a city that experienced a Golden Age of real estate development in the commercial and residential realms, collaboration between several layers of urban agencies is helping to develop an interwoven and comprehensive array of projects: from the redevelopment of an urban square, to a garden for a low income community, to collaboratively building a neighborhood cultural center, to the inclusion of new manufacturing processes. In Moscow and Taipei, where political and nationalistic regimes have greatly influenced urban development, we discover a broader vision of the general necessity to include citizens and give them a voice on a stage or platform. Muscovites in particular are starting to engage in a process of public space occupancy; they are reclaiming the streets, squares and infrastructure with the

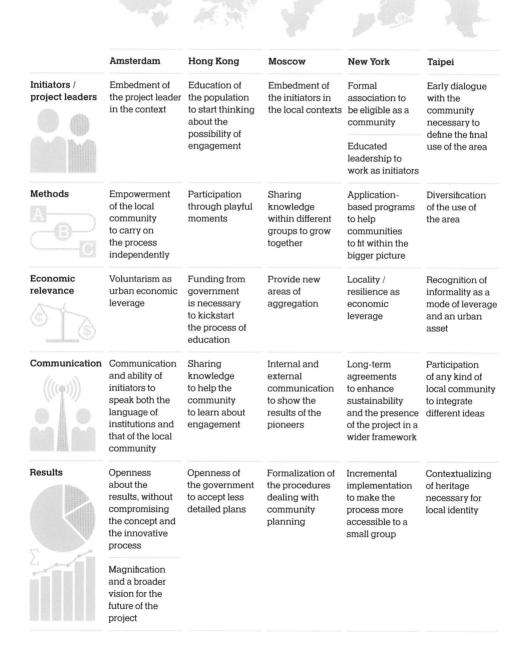

	Amsterdam	Hong Kong	Moscow	New York	Taipei
Initiators / project leaders	Embedment of the project leader in the context	Education of the population to start thinking about the possibility of engagement	Embedment of the initiators in the local contexts	Formal association to be eligible as a community	Early dialogue with the community necessary to define the final use of the area
				Educated leadership to work as initiators	
Methods	Empowerment of the local community to carry on the process independently	Participation through playful moments	Sharing knowledge within different groups to grow together	Application-based programs to help communities to fit within the bigger picture	Diversification of the use of the area
Economic relevance	Voluntarism as urban economic leverage	Funding from government is necessary to kickstart the process of education	Provide new areas of aggregation	Locality / resilience as economic leverage	Recognition of informality as a mode of leverage and an urban asset
Communication	Communication and ability of initiators to speak both the language of institutions and that of the local community	Sharing knowledge to help the community to learn about engagement	Internal and external communication to show the results of the pioneers	Long-term agreements to enhance sustainability and the presence of the project in a wider framework	Participation of any kind of local community to integrate different ideas
Results	Openness about the results, without compromising the concept and the innovative process	Openness of the government to accept less detailed plans	Formalization of the procedures dealing with community planning	Incremental implementation to make the process more accessible to a small group	Contextualizing of heritage necessary for local identity
	Magnification and a broader vision for the future of the project				

help of groups of highly involved, committed, and internationally educated people. In Taipei we see how citizens are engaging in communal spaces, practices and activities to reclaim a cultural heritage that is under continuous threat. The research has also revealed preservation processes where the local community has managed to stand against demolition and raise awareness about the global homogenization of the urban landscape imposed by what has been called neoliberal urbanism.

After studying these international case studies, it is possible to provide a simple overview of the tools that traditional top-down players are employing to enable and support community practices in architecture and planning. The table on the previous page organizes the information gleaned from the five cities under analysis, pointing out the role of initiators, the methods used to develop concepts, the economic implications, and the importance of communication and evaluation.

Through detailed descriptions of five urban development processes, where citizens are involved or even play a pivotal role, we have pinpointed one specific issue above all others. In each featured city, and more importantly in every case study, there is a moment when institutions employ unusual, progressive methods that help the local community to take (conceptual) ownership of the progress, and sometimes of the final results. This analysis shows that within a selection of five different cities, there is a common denominator, an aspect of community planning that cuts through socioeconomic variations, economic contrasts and landscape dissimilarities.

It seems that we can argue in favor of the emergence of a generational shift in traditional planning practices. A significant number of progressive top-down players are prototyping innovative methods to enable citizens' engagement in the act of city-making. This publication does not address directly the reasons why this is happening, but it does demonstrate that this trend is emerging, and perhaps even becoming mainstream in several urban realms. Since we have been engaging in a deeper understanding of the practices used to embrace, support and enable this trend, we consider this issue the connecting thread of the publication, and the most important point of argumentation in favor of a more established, international and institutionalized debate around issues of community planning. This issue is also approached and developed by architectural firms that have a global scope. In order to generate a more profound and comprehensive overview, we decided to ask established architectural practitioners to explain their views on how to give more power and authorship to the end users of their architectural designs. Through a series of in-depth interviews, we portrayed a generation of designers facing a turning point, highlighting how architects are implementing new methods and planning strategies in order to channel bottom-up energy, human interaction, decision-making processes and participation in a proactive way. This contribution to the book confirms the growing attention given by traditional players to a more community-centered approach.

In fact, this book not only portrays the emergence of a process of city-making where citizens play a greater role than ever before, but especially focuses on the reaction of the institutions or bigger players. The international comparisons illustrate this trend's global reach, varieties of scale and results. In the following section, we attempt to provide an overview and critical understanding of how traditional top-down players are re-thinking their implementation processes in order to enable the involvement of civil society or the local community.

In the process of analyzing the rise of community planning, the authors realized that it was important not only to pinpoint institutional organizations and governments as the actors who could help the bottom-up movement become more established, but also that they were themselves looking for patterns, similarities and differences in order to set new institutional standards that could accommodate participatory approaches. This new openness on the part of traditional top-downers represents a generational shift in the urban planning discipline, but how does that work out in practical terms? Local governments, housing associations, real-estate developers, architectural firms and other types of traditional top-down players encounter plenty of difficulties when trying to accommodate community practices. After all, their working processes are usually based on rigid bureaucratic procedures that are geared toward providing high levels of control and accountability. It goes without saying that compiling a list of recommendations to be generally applied (without taking into consideration each context under analysis) is hazardous. The introductory section of each chapter demonstrates how each city under analysis presents a unique set of circumstances, generating context-specific

bottom-up initiatives. Comparative analysis is superfluous in the sense that this book does not seek to understand every aspect characterizing bottom-up development, but simply to generate some ideas on how institutions can incorporate innovative urban processes and begin to standardize such practices. For this reason, each chapter presents a list of recommendations, learning points and inspirational suggestions in the concluding remarks, derived from local experience. The additional chapter dedicated to interviews with practitioners provides a further set of ideas about which tools to use to engage bottom-up development from the point of view of prominent architects. Each local researcher (or research team) has pinpointed specific issues to address in order to enable community planning in architecture and urban design. We can generalize a series of urban contexts or situations, springboards from which to start contemplating new trajectories for more comprehensive, less traditional urban development practices:

If the city in case is in the process of supporting campaigns and programs to enable an emerging range of bottom-up initiatives (e.g., Amsterdam), we advise starting by talking with representatives of the local community. The ideal representatives would be embedded in the local context and be able to speak the language of the people they represent as well as that of institutions. There should not be a concrete final 'deliverable' for the area, but the focus should be on the process of discovering local issues with the citizens and empowering them to take ownership of this process in the future. Support should be provided to compensate for volunteer work with social, environmental or material benefits, while a wider goal should be producing the capacity to replicate or magnify beneficial processes.

If the city in case is in need of developing a general social consciousness among citizens regarding the possibility to engage in urban development practices, there is a general understanding that both sides want to work together, and participatory planning has become mainstream (e.g., Hong Kong), institutions should develop a campaign where participation is encouraged through a wider program of educational activities from elementary schools to vocational training. The end results of this campaign should be left in the hands of citizens, who should have a platform where studies and previous findings are easily accessible and understandable. Together with funding, this knowledge will be channeled into prototypes and further examples of citizens' engagement processes.

If the city under consideration presents sporadic signals that top-down players cannot forge ahead by mimicking development trajectories of the past (e.g., Moscow), we advise giving as much visibility as possible to activities that are already making a difference. Also, taking the work of inspirational professionals and making it public (e.g., through media support) in order to enhance additional engagement and ultimately education among citizens. The final aim is to formalize this process into new development trajectories sanctioned by top-down players.

If the city in focus already has a wide-spread program of support and institutionalized recognition of bottom-up development's potential (e.g., New York), efforts should focus on enhancing the creation of formal associations among citizens to benefit from this situation. Specific programs can address the needs of the community by focusing on making long-term agreements for incrementally implemented activities. Important aspects are resiliency and the development of an educated leadership that can bring this process to higher levels of government and real estate development.

If the city in case has a densely networked existing urban fabric, social relationships (of common interests and conflicts), and a history of colonialism (e.g., Taipei), it seems the most important aspect to consider is the need to provide historical and social identity to a specific area, valuing heritage preservation. In addition, due to varied social composition, supporting the intermingling of different communities, enhancing diversification through the involvement of citizens in an early stage of redevelopment, and recognizing the positive added value of informality, are considered crucial decisions to make when enabling community practices in architecture and planning.

The above-mentioned points are the results of a short but deep global probing into bottom-up urbanism and its relationship with the act of implementing urban initiatives, focusing on the role of top-down players. We analyzed cities that are quite different, but that nonetheless share a long tradition of top-down urbanism. In this context the challenge for traditional top-down players is to enable more bottom-up urbanism. It seems that it is time to employ a new method to think about urban development, where the focus is not on the final result but on the process of developing that urban product.

Indeed, the act of city-making is always a process, and truly innovative practices can be generated at every step. For an institution, changing the whole process of urban development can be an impossible task, eased only by generations of committed 'change makers'. However, while analyzing different processes of community practices in architecture and planning, we learned that the focus should move from the final product (being a park, a square, a housing estate, neighborhood laboratory or cultural center, for example) to innovative process-related moments. Variations on the steps or actions undertaken to reach a particular goal are the most important aspects to develop innovation while enabling community practices in architecture and planning. As a consequence, we can allow ourselves to speculate in favor of the argument that when approaching urban development as a quest towards the perfect form, a partial approach to city-making is deployed. At the other end, and complementary to this approach, there is the phase of implementing micro variations to the process and the methods by reorganizing, categorizing and analyzing different moments. The method we used to analyze the cases in this book is a simple journey through the narrative of a bottom-up urban development process and can be widely employed to depict those aspects.

In practice, while researching our cases, by extracting the actions of a specific actor, or group of actors, we pinpointed the innovative micro-interventions implemented in the process of city-making. The table previously presented in this section is an example of how to reorganize progressive institutional behaviors by contextualizing them. Simple investigations like the ones carried out in this book suffice to bring up questions as to the operational context and the best course of progressive future action. It goes without saying that, when analyzed in detail, each neighborhood presents a unique mixture of typologies calling for additional conversation in order to define tailored local strategies. In order to define institutional change, a more detailed analysis of the actual process of city-making should be performed. However, with the insights provided here, we hope to facilitate the realization of the positive values

that one specific case study presents, in order to trigger curiosity about further actions and possibilities.

In conclusion, in the course of developing this publication we gained a certain degree of understanding as to how to lift the bottom-up movement up to the institutional arena. Designing, analyzing and arranging processes for communities is what the team of We Own The City will continue to engage in. Due to our particular approach to the operationalization of city-making (giving most of the attention to the process of urban development in terms of the operations used to determine it), we would define our work as an act of community process design. It is our aim to prototype and sanction a contemporary, process-based urbanism that binds together top-down and bottom-up in order to form and create professional figures that are able to act as mediators of urban development, understanding the local circumstances and enabling community practices in architecture and urban design.

The Book in Numbers

The charts show how many times a specific word has been mentioned in the book, focusing on the concepts in the title. The result shows that this book is mostly about urban community, while planning holds more relevance that architecture.

When we compare how many times 'people or groups' have been mentioned, as opposed to 'institutions', the numbers are close but people are given more space in the book.The same is confirmed by the comparison between 'top-down' and 'bottom-up': 'bottom-up' is mentioned more often in the text.

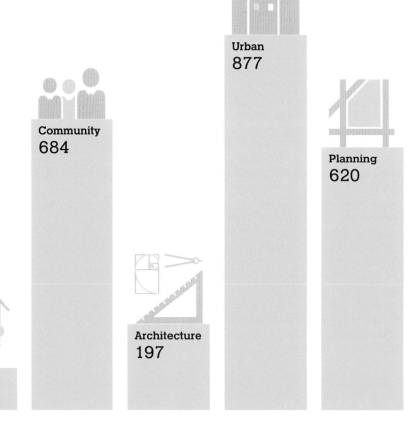

Urban
877

Community
684

Planning
620

Architecture
197

Enable
74

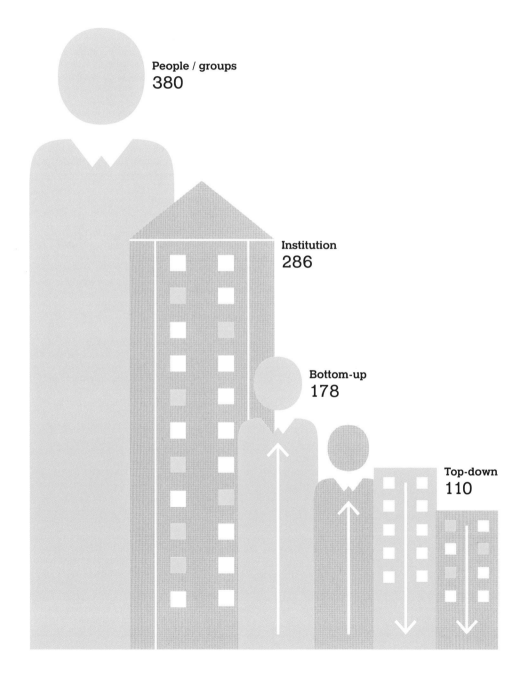

People / groups
380

Institution
286

Bottom-up
178

Top-down
110

Information on the authors

Beatriz Pineda Revilla
During her studies as an architect and urban planner, Beatriz Pineda discovered a passion for urban issues. Since then, she has been working as an urban planner and urban designer in the Netherlands, Spain and the Dominican Republic. Her interest in the social sciences and eagerness to combine research and practice motivated her to go back to university and pursue a Research Master in Urban Studies at the University of Amsterdam. Currently she is studying at Fordham University in New York while working on a master's thesis on urban agriculture and resilience in Amsterdam and New York.

Bob Knoester
Bob Knoester is an urban geographer from Amsterdam, working as a researcher for CITIES Amsterdam and a consultant for Jonge Honden. He specializes in urban development topics such as active citizenship, collective commissioning projects, the future of social housing and neighborhood livability. For this book he covered the research on the Amsterdam cases.

Chris Webster
Professor Chris Webster is the Dean and Chair Professor in the Faculty of Architecture The University of Hong Kong. Professor Webster has degrees in urban planning, computer science, economics and economic geography and is a leading urban theorist and spatial economic modeller. Chris has published over 150 scholarly papers on the idea of spontaneous urban order and received over US$20M grants for research and teaching and learning projects. Chris was co-editor of Environment and Planning B for ten years. Books include: Webster and Lai (2003) Property Rights, Planning and Markets, Cheltenham, Edward Elgar; Glasze, Webster and Frantz (2006) Private Cities, London, Routledge; Wu, Webster, He and Liu, (2010) Urban Poverty in China, Cheltenham: Edward Elgar; and Wu and Webster (editors) Marginalisation in Urban China. London: Palgrave McMillan; and Sarkar, Webster and Gallacher (March 2014) Healthy Cities: Public Health Through Urban Planning. Cheltenham: Edward Elgar. Professor Webster has written five prize-winning academic papers on urban theory. His present professional mission is to change the way cities are planned in China and his current research agenda is to establish systematic evidence for the relationship between urban configuration and health.

Francesca Miazzo
Francesca Miazzo is the managing director and co-founder of CITIES Foundation. Francesca is Italian, but based in Amsterdam, the Netherlands, where she graduated in Research Masters in Metropolitan Studies. Francesca manages and coordinates several CITIES-led projects, initiatives, events and studies. She has been managing several global urban researches on industrial renewal, food and the city, polycentric development and urban waste upcycling. Besides studies and researches, she has been active in several local interventions related to the above-mentioned themes, designing various urban-related processes. Examples are the global platform and publication Farming the City, the workshop series Pop-Up Farm, the movie format CITOPIA, the Old City Food Tour, the sustainable transport concept Foodlogica and the laboratory for neighborhood plastic upcycling WASTED. At the moment, she is advising the city of Stavanger (Norway) on a food-based concept for waterfront redevelopment, and she is prototyping the development of a Food Council in Amsterdam, Francesca developed the original concept for this publication at hand, curated the local contents collection and set up the international research design and production.

Jessica Niles DeHoff
Jessica Niles DeHoff is a licensed architect, educator, and writer whose built work includes several adaptive reuse projects, the renovation of a 19th-century row house in Washington DC, and a new studio building for a painter in Wisconsin. She has written art and design criticism for many international publications and she does editorial work for major publishers. Jessica holds degrees from Harvard University and the Yale School of Architecture and has taught at universities in Hong Kong, the USA and Japan.

Jia-He Lin
Jia-He Lin is an observer of the city with a multidisciplinary background in journalism, spatial planning, international development and social studies in science and technology (STS). He used to be a magazine editor/writer in Taiwan and is seeking to start a career in in-depth urban journalism with a perspective among Asian cities. He currently studies the first-generation urbanists of postwar Taiwan as well as the social-technical history of quantitative measures and regulations in Asian urbanism.

Mark Minkjan
Mark Minkjan is an urban and architectural geographer with a special interest in the interaction between architecture and societal dynamics. He is a researcher and writer. Besides working for CITIES, he is part of Non-fiction, an interdisciplinary studio broadly focused on culture and the city. He is also Editor in Chief and researcher at Failed Architecture, which analyses architecture but not only from the perspective of the architectural discourse.

Mehdi Comeau
A sociological mindset integrated with potent curiosity in exploring and applying progressive thinking in urbanism keeps Mehdi motivated and always seeking newfound possibilities. As a dual French/American citizen, Mehdi is currently living in Amsterdam, where he is completing a mobilities-focused master's thesis in Urban Sociology at the University of Amsterdam and works as the Communications Coordinator at CITIES. In the past, he earned a degree in international environment and development focused on sustainable agriculture, food systems and community resilience in the U.S., including fieldwork with communities, organizations and governments in Africa and Europe.

Peter Cookson Smith
Dr Peter Cookson Smith is an architect, planner and urban designer. He has been a resident of Hong Kong since 1977, when he founded Urbis Limited, one of the first specialist planning, urban design, and landscape consultancies in Southeast Asia, which over the past 35 years has won more than a hundred local and international awards. He sits on the Advisory Council for the Department of Urban Planning and Design at the University of Hong Kong and is a member of Government's Harbourfront Commission, the Land Development Advisory Committee and the Commission on Strategic Development. He is the Immediate Past President of the Hong Kong Institute of Planners and Vice-President of the Institute of Urban Design. He is a Member of the Faculty for the Salzburg Global Seminar on Sustainability and the City.

Shriya Malhotra

Shriya Malhotra is an urbanist and artist from New Delhi, India. She is a member of the Partizaning collective in Moscow, Russia promoting art-based urban activism and participatory research through urban interventions in the city. Shriya has an MA in Cities and Urbanization and is interested in urban sustainability, DIY cultures, mobility and migration, and the role of art/artists in the city. She is currently a fellow at the Zentrum for Art and Urbanistik in Berlin, conducting a project in the neighborhood of Moabit.

Shu-Mei Huang

Shu-Mei Huang received her PhD in Built Environment at the University of Washington. She is currently teaching at the Department of Cultural and Creative Industries Management at the National Taipei University of Education. Her main interest lies in exploring the complexity of cities through working/walking with communities. She has been involved in activism and community-based design practices in Taipei, Hong Kong, India, and Seattle. She is currently preparing a manuscript for publication based on her dissertation titled 'Tracing Carescapes of Hong Kong: Two Systems, One City'.

Tris Kee

As the Director of the Community Project Workshop and an Assistant Professor at the Faculty of Architecture at the University of Hong Kong, Tris' interests encompass the fields of Architecture, Urban Planning, Professional Practice, Contemporary Building Construction and Community Engagement Processes. A graduate of the University of Waterloo with a Master of Architecture, Tris grew up in Canada and worked in Rome, Amsterdam, London and Vancouver before moving to Hong Kong. She has worked on a broad range of projects including urban revitalization schemes, district aspiration studies, waterfront planning research, sustainable development, heritage conservation and public engagements in the district of Kwun Tong. Tris advocates an active approach to engaging community participation in the practice in architecture anddesign. Tris' work received the Royal Architectural Institute of Canada Roll of Honor, the Ontario Association of Architects' Guild Medal, and an Outstanding Thesis Award in 2002. She is a recipient of the '40 under 40 Architectural Design Award' in 2012 and the Green Building Award 2012 from the Hong Kong Green Building Council.

Tris was a curator for the 2012 Hong Kong / Shenzhen Bi-City Biennale Exhibition for Urbanism and Architecture, an exhibitor for the 13th Venice Architectural Biennale, an invited speaker at the International Design Alliance Congress in Taiwan in 2011, Workshop Architettura Venezia 2012 and a keynote speaker at the Crossover Comprehensive Conference in the China Academy of Art 2012. Devoting her time to serve the architecture community, Tris is also the Chief Editor for the Hong Kong Institute of Architects Journal and an executive committee member in the Hong Kong Interior Design Association and Hong Kong Architecture Centre.

Wei-Hsiu Chang

Wei-Hsiu Chang obtained his PhD in Building and Planning at National Taiwan University. His main interests are urban regeneration and historical/cultural landscape preservation.

Wang Weijen

Wang Weijen, architect and professor in the Department of Architecture of Hong Kong University, received his MArch from UC Berkeley, and his MS from National Taiwan University. His projects have received AIA Design Awards, Far Eastern Architectural Award, HKIA Design Awards and a Merit Award from the Green Building Council; his works have been exhibited in the Taipei Museum of Modern Art, Beijing Architecture Biennale, 2005 Shenzhen Biennale of Architecture and Urbanism and Venice Architecture Biennale of 2008. He was also the curator of the 2007 Hong Kong Biennale of Architecture and Urbanism. His research focuses on Chinese architecture and cities, and his recent publications include the book Refabricating City: A Reflection (2010), as well as Study of Macao's Historical Urban Fabric (2011). Two monograph issues on his design works were published by TA in 2011, and the July 2011 issue of UED. He was a visiting associate professor in the Department of Architecture at MIT in 2008-2009.

Ying-Tzu Lin

Ying-Tzu Lin received her master's degree in Landscape Architecture and Planning at Wageningen University, the Netherlands. Having had various working experiences in Taiwan, Brazil and the Netherlands, she now develops her main interests in urban farming, community-based planning and democratic community empowerment. She is currently working as a planner in Taipei.

Information on the partners

This publication has been made possible thanks to the development of a wide network of local organizations that helped the researchers in selecting the most appropriate cases and to communicate to a wider public the contents and the message of We Own The City. The involved organizations are:

CITIES is a foundation based in the Netherlands that works on urban analysis, research, communication and community-based project development. CITIES catalyzes urban explorers with the will to drive innovation in city life, policy and practice. CITIES and its community connects and shares, in person and online, through research initiatives, events, workshops, exhibitions and publications. Samples of CITIES' work can be found in the three-year-long FARMING THE CITY project (www.farmingthecity.net), for which a global platform promoting sustainable and local consumption, production, transportation and processing of food has been developed. The project consists of a series of temporary interventions in the city of Amsterdam, from community pop-up gardens to mapping the old food trails of the city, to community workshops to grow mushrooms out of clean urban waste. Each of these interventions is evolving into an independent self-sustaining project, currently gaining international momentum, such as the Old City Food Tour, which is also being considered for Milan, Stockholm and Utrecht. At the moment, CITIES is advocating the implementation of a local food council in Amsterdam and working as urban food strategist advisors for the city of Stavanger (Norway). CITIES' research touches upon other urban development issues, such as waste upcycling. Communication work entails the production of online magazines, iPad publications, research reports, the documentary 'Foodlogica', traveling exhibitions and two books.

The Community Empowerment Network, Taipei (CENT), initiated by the Department of Urban Development, Taipei City Government, is a think tank and incubator of ideas and actions related to community empowerment in Taipei City. The CENT was officially opened in the former building of Ren-an Hospital, one of the few modern and westernized hospitals set up by the Taiwanese during Japanese colonization. The CENT develops training programs to teach people the skills to enable community empowerment, and builds a platform for groups and communities to make contacts and to share resources.

The Community Project Workshop (CPW) of the Faculty of Architecture at the University of Hong Kong provides design and consultancy services to government and non-governmental organizations, and undertakes other non-commercial projects requiring interdisciplinary expertise drawn from all disciplines of the faculty: Architecture, Landscape Architecture, Architectural Conservation, Real Estate and Construction, and Urban Planning and Design. CPW has developed consultant teams that critically evaluate, analyze, and synthesize problems in a 'real-life' project context. Teams are composed of academic staff members from the faculty, outside professionals, university students and community representatives. The community projects the CPW undertakes aim to address the pressing and changing needs of all sectors of society. CPW teams consider the rationale behind the current design and planning concepts of each project, generating sensitive and practical design solutions. In order to meet specific community aspirations, needs, and objectives, CPW adopts an interactive and participatory approach, leading to a continuous process of discussion and feedback.

The Design Trust for Public Space is a not-for-profit organization dedicated to the future of public space in New York City. Projects bring together city agencies, community groups, and private sector experts to make a lasting impact, through design, on how New Yorkers live, work, and play. The Design Trust was founded in 1995 to unlock the potential of NYC's shared spaces. Today, it is a nationally recognized incubator that transforms and evolves the city's landscape with city agencies and community collaborators. The Design Trust's work can be seen, felt, and experienced throughout all five boroughs – from parks and plazas to streets and public buildings.

The **Strelka Institute** from Moscow helped the Moscow researcher to select the case studies to analyze, and contributed to the organization of the book presentation in Moscow, working as communication partner.

Pakhuis de Zwijger is a cultural and creative center and a meeting place, a new source of creation and innovation in the city of Amsterdam. It opened its doors in September 2006, and since then has set a great example as a platform where creative people from the city, professional and amateur, can meet, get to know each other and exchange experiences. Mutual exchange between creative people, but also exchange between creative people and 'the market' are the core concepts guiding its full daily program of activities. Every day, many professionals find their way to Pakhuis de Zwijger for network meetings, lectures, drinks or workshops that have something to do with 'creation and innovation'.

trancity*valiz is a co-operation between two independent publishers that share a common understanding regarding the function of publications. Their books offer critical reflection and interdisciplinary inspiration, and establish a connection between cultural disciplines and socio-economic issues. Publications on the city, urban change and the public domain are at the core of the collaboration between Trancity and Valiz.

Credits of the images

Amsterdam
All images by Marten van Wijk

Hong Kong
Case study 1:
Energizing Kowloon East Office

Case study 2:
CPW, Hong Kong University,
Museum of West Kowloon
Cultural District

Case study 3:
Hong Kong Housing Authority

Case study 4:
Wang Weijen Architecture

Moscow
Case study 1:
Fedor Lavrentiev, Anton Polsky,
Archives of Let's bike it! project

Case study 2:
Shriya Malhotra for Partizaning,
Kristina Ukhina, Alex Melnikov,
Tony Kolobakhen

Case study 3:
Anton Polsky, Oleg Misyak

Case study 4:
Co-working Nagatino

New York
Case study 1:
Beatriz Pineda Revilla, The Myrtle
Avenue Revitalization Project

Case study 2:
Beatriz Pineda Revilla,
NYC Department of Cultural Affairs,
Downtown Brooklyn Partnership

Case study 3:
Beatriz Pineda Revilla,
Downtown Brooklyn Partnership

Case study 4:
Beatriz Pineda Revilla

Taipei
Case study 1:
Ying-Tzu Lin, Fang-Cheng Lin

Case study 2;
Wei-Hsiu Chang

Case study 3:
Citizen Visual Documentation
database, Chun-Horn Cheng,
Shu-Mei Huang, Sham Chi,
Eason Lee

Case study 4:
Pei-Yin Shih, Jia-He Lin

Interviews
OMA:
OMA

MVRDV:
MVRDV, Katharina Wildt

UNStudio:
Michael Moran Photography,
Ronald Tilleman, UNStudio,
Jan Maarten Lieverdink

NEXT Architects:
NEXT Architects and daum.net

Colophon

This publication was made possible through the generous support of the **Creative Industries Fund NL**

creative industries fund NL

and **The University of Hong Kong**

THE UNIVERSITY OF HONG KONG 香港大學
faculty of architecture 建築學院

Chief Editors:
Francesca Miazzo
(CITIES Amsterdam),
Tris Kee
(Department of Architecture,
The University of Hong Kong)

Content Editors:
Jessica Niles DeHoff,
Mehdi Comeau

Co-curators and communication partners:
CITIES and Pakhuis de Zwijger (Amsterdam), Community Project Workshop (Hong Kong), Design Trust for Public Space (New York), Strelka Institute (Moscow), and Community Empowerment Network (Taipei).

Contributors:
Beatriz Pineda Revilla, Bob Knoester, Mark Minkjan, Peter Cookson Smith, Shriya Malhotra, Shu-Mei Huang, Tris Kee, Wei-Hsiu Chang, Wang Weijen Architecture, Ying-Tzu Lin, Jia-He Lin.

Preface:
Chris Webster, Dean, Faculty of Architecture, The University of Hong Kong

The text of this publication was evaluated through a peer review process by Arie Graafland, Antoni van Leeuwenhoek Professor TU Delft and Visiting Research Professor at Hong Kong University and Lia Karsten, Associate Professor in Urban Geographies at the University of Amsterdam/AISSR.

With text and images contributed by the Hong Kong Housing Authority and the Energizing Kowloon East Office.

Book design: Chris Knox (CITIES)

Proof editing: Leo Reijnen

Prepress: Colorset, Amsterdam

Printing: Wilco, Amersfoort

Publishers:
Simon Franke –
Trancity, info@trancity.nl,
www.trancity.nl /
Astrid Vorstermans –
Valiz, info@valiz.nl,
www.valiz.nl

ISBN 978-90-78088-91-2
NUR 758

Distribution
BE/NL/LU: Coen Sligting
www.coensligtingbookimport.nl;
Centraal Boekhuis
www.centraal.boekhuis.nl
GB/IE: Anagram
www.anagrambooks.com
Europe/Asia: Idea Books
www.ideabooks.nl
USA: D.A.P. www.artbook.com

Individual orders:
www.trancity.nl,
www.valiz.nl